TENSION TURNAROUND

The 30-Day Program
for Inner Calm, Confidence and Control

by Sharon Faelten, David Diamond
and the Editors of *PREVENTION* Magazine

Rodale Press, Emmaus, Pennsylvania

NOTICE: The information and ideas in this book are meant to supplement the care and guidance of your physician, not to replace them. The editor cautions you not to attempt diagnosis or embark upon self-treatment of serious illness without competent professional assistance. We encourage anyone who is experiencing distress beyond the scope of this book to seek competent professional advice. Also, if you are under professional care or taking medication, we suggest discussing any changes in diet or lifestyle with your doctor.

Cover design by Lisa Farkas
Book design by Anita G. Patterson

If you have any questions or comments concerning this book, please write:
Rodale Press
Book Reader Service
33 East Minor Street
Emmaus, PA 18098

Library of Congress Cataloging-in-Publication Data

Faelten, Sharon.
    Tension turnaround : the 30-day program for inner calm, confidence, and control / by Sharon Faelten, David Diamond, and the editors of Prevention magazine.
       p.   cm.
    ISBN 0-87857-885-4
    1. Stress management. 2. Life change events – Psychological aspects. 3. Health.
    4. Prevention (Emmaus, Pa.) I. Diamond, David, 1952-   II. Title.
    RA785.F34 1990
    155.9'042 – dc20   89-24342
                                                        CIP

Distributed in the book trade by St. Martin's Press

2 4 6 8 10 9 7 5 3 1   paperback

CONTENTS

TENSION RELIEF, THE BIBLIOTHERAPY WAY

People are just beginning to realize that reading the right how-to book may provide the therapy to counter the tension they feel when depressed, tired, lonely — just plain down in the dumps. A study conducted by psychologists at the University of Alabama, published in the *Journal of Consulting and Clinical Psychology,* concluded that for some problems, reading a self-help book — "bibliotherapy" — is as useful as consulting a psychotherapist.

In fact, for many common problems, reading the right book may be *better* than visiting a counselor. When you think about it, the kinds of situations that most often create tension — arguing with your spouse about where to spend this year's vacation, being criticized by a co-worker or depending on a car that's always in the shop for repairs — rarely require professional analysis. Yet strung together, these niggling annoyances and upsets can leave you tense and distraught.

Add a major stressor — starting a new job, moving into a new house, or getting divorced — to the so-called minor stresses of life, and you can find yourself desperate, anxious and unhappy. Worse still, your *physical* health is apt to suffer. Studies show that three out of four people visiting a doctor's office are seeking help for stress-related complaints like headaches, fatigue, back pain and colitis. Others suffer silently with insomnia, anxiety or other tension-fueled ailments.

A surplus of tension can also wear down your immune system, leaving you vulnerable to colds, sore throats — even serious diseases like cancer. And evidence indicates that poor coping skills can contribute to the development of heart disease, ulcers and other major medical problems.

Enter self-help: What you really need are practical tips to help you cope with stress, either by eliminating the sources of tension or by staying calm under trying circumstances. Counselors themselves often give this kind of advice. If you have this kind of information in book form, available day or night, you can turn to it for help, mull over the information, refer to it again and again or apply what you learn to new situations as they arise. (And the fact is, *change* – in the form of new situations – is the number one source of stress in life.)

Tension Turnaround provides a systematic plan to beat stress. You'll find 60 entries on topics like anger, back pain, competition, disappointments, frustration and other everyday hassles. These entries are arranged in such a way as to actually constitute a program – one used daily to gain the knowledge you need to manage stress.

The program is based on modular learning methods, a highly effective way to master new information and skills. The program is set up so you can read just two entries a day. This two-a-day plan makes it easy for even the busiest people to fit this program into their hectic schedules. As you read, you'll notice that a common theme runs through the program. Each day's lesson teaches specific, practical skills for easing tension – how to remain calm in the face of a crisis, how to feel confident about meeting deadlines, and how to control difficult situations at work, at home and on vacation.

We suggest that for the first 30 days of implementing this tension-reducing program, you read two entries a day until you finish the entire book. Then, when a specific problem arises – a family quarrel or a financial crunch, for example – you can review the appropriate section to refresh your coping skills.

The best thing about this innovative program is that you won't have to wait 30 days to see results! Right from the start, you'll feel tension evaporate, so you'll be able to think more clearly, sleep better and get more done. In teaching you how to master stress, this book will change your life dramatically.

One last note: Knowing when to send up a distress flare is an essential part of self-help. If you're experiencing distress that's beyond the scope of this book, you should seek competent professional advice from a trained mental health profes-sional who can help you design a plan of action tailored to your individual needs.

Chapter 1

ALCOHOL
AND SUBSTANCE ABUSE

Of all the reasons people drink alcohol, "unwinding" often tops the list.

"Shifting gears from the responsibilities and high energy level of the day to a slower and easier evening mood is a very common purpose of drinking," state Roger E. Vogler, Ph.D., and Wayne R. Bartz, Ph.D., in their book *The Better Way to Drink.*

Yet the brief and vivid sense of relaxation produced by alcohol is quite temporary. Over the long haul, alcohol abuse *escalates* stress. Drink too much too often, and your body produces an excess of hydrocortisone and other stress-related hormones. But even a moderate intake of alcohol has a curious effect on a bluish area of neurons in a part of the brain called the locus coeruleus. Apparently, inhibiting these locus coeruleus neurons sets off a chain reaction that activates other brain cells, increasing arousal. After hitting a blood alcohol level of about 0.05 – half the usual legal standard for intoxication – relief from stress usually ends and anxiety generated by additional alcohol begins.

For many people, drinking tends to increase whenever the overall level of stress increases. Divorce, unemployment and other losses generate severe stress and the need for relief. (Among problem drinkers, women are more likely to date the onset of their drinking to a particularly stressful event, such as divorce, whereas men date the onset to job-related or legal problems.)

"Your health, your job, your financial and marital situations may all get worse . . . from an overreliance on alcohol to relax," say Dr. Vogler and Dr. Bartz.

Are You Abusing Alcohol?

Dr. Vogler offers the following guidelines to determine if you are abusing alcohol as a means of stress relief.

Do you drink every day? Occasional use of alcohol to enhance a good time is okay; relying on alcohol is a bad habit.

Do you drink enough to push your blood alcohol levels higher than 0.05? On those occasions when you drink alcohol, do you consume less than one drink an hour? Regardless of weight, your rate of alcohol consumption should not be greater, because the body cannot metabolize alcohol any faster. Keep in mind that a "drink" is defined as 12 ounces of beer, 4 ounces of table wine or 1¼ ounces of liquor.

"If you drink more than that or drink every day, you will grow tolerant to alcohol and need more and more to achieve the calming effect usually experienced after a glass or so," says Dr. Vogler.

Does drinking alcohol trigger negative behavior? Do you become abusive —

Substance Abuse: Overdosing on Stress

Cocaine. Many users start out looking for relief from tedium or tension (or both). Eventually, though, they end up as stress personified: nervous, irritable, angry, paranoid, anxious and depressed.

Cocaine's instant, euphoric high is replaced by less pleasant feelings, which seem to last longer and longer over time. But people keep chasing the once-certain high, all in a frenetic search for more relief, more fun, until they are financially and emotionally bankrupt, according to Joanne Baum, Ph.D., author of *One Step over the Line: A No-Nonsense Guide to Recognizing and Treating Cocaine Dependency.*

"When they do come for help, they are once again looking for relief," says Dr. Baum, who practices in the San Francisco Bay Area and specializes in the treatment of chemical dependency.

At the very least, your self-respect — a precious commodity in stress resistance — evaporates.

If any stress-reducing chemical — be it cocaine, alcohol, marijuana or tranquilizers — plays too significant a role in your life, you may need professional help to regain control. Consult the blue pages of your local telephone directory for the location of Narcotics Anonymous or other drug dependency treatment centers in your area, or call the National Clearinghouse on Drug Abuse, located in Maryland, at (301) 443-6500. This group will refer you to organizations in your residential area at no charge.

verbally or physically — no matter how little or how infrequently you drink? Do you unleash hostility behind the wheel of your car? Do you neglect your kids or tune out your spouse?

Do you also abuse other substances (tranquilizers, sedatives or amphetamines) to relieve, for example, anxiety and depression? Alcohol abuse is often only one of various poor coping techniques.

If you've answered yes to any of these questions, it may be time to stop and evaluate the role alcohol plays in your life.

How to Step out of the Alcohol Rut

"As tranquilizers go, alcohol is legal (for adults), relatively inexpensive, widely available and works fast," says Dr. Vogler. But drinking for relief from tension or stress is the use of alcohol for self-medication, not for enjoyment.

"We tend to get into comfortable ruts and then deviate very little from our routine, which quite often results in an overreliance on alcohol." Here are some suggestions to limit stress-induced drinking.

For a few weeks, keep a written record of your drinking habits. "Describe the settings and circumstances," says Dr. Vogler. "Think about your feelings. If you can identify the people, places and moods that provoke excessive drinking, you can get a pretty good handle on how much you drink, how often, and why. By recognizing these situations, you can learn which you need to control and which you may have to avoid," he says.

If you're a woman of reproductive age, note whether or not you tend to drink more often during your menstrual period. In one study, nonalcoholic women reported significantly more bad moods, more frequent drinking to relieve tension or depression and more frequent solitary drinking during menstruation.

Take concrete steps to resolve conflicts or worries. "Stresses will always exist," say Dr. Vogler and Dr. Bartz. "And being tuned out by alcohol may mean that you avoid dealing with the stress-producing situation. In the long run, that can only mean more stress and more need to escape — a vicious circle."

Substitute nonalcoholic beverages for your customary drinks. "The alcohol in the evening cocktail does not alone account for the shift in mood," explain Dr. Vogler and Dr. Bartz. "Just sitting comfortably away from a stressful environment, sprawled in an easy chair and forgetting about work, leads to relief of stress."

"Stock your fridge with other fun beverages such as imported mineral water or guava juice," says Dr. Vogler. "Near beer and dealcoholized wine are fine, too. Then make your first drink nonalcoholic and sip it while you get out of your work clothes or whatever. That 15-minute decompression period buys you time, helping you to shrug off a layer or two of tension. After 15 minutes, you may find you need only one beer instead of several to finish unwinding. Or you may not want any alcohol at all."

Find alternative ways to dissipate stress. Walking, tennis, swimming, reading, drawing, listening to or playing music, gardening and meditation are just a few of the many satisfying ways to deflect stress. Dr. Vogler and Dr. Bartz suggest people make their own lists, based on individual preferences and abilities.

If you try these tactics but still find yourself overusing alcohol when stress looms, do yourself a big favor and consider professional help.

"Counseling can provide the direction you need to make changes that will minimize or help you handle stress better," says Dr. Vogler. Also, self-help groups such as Alcoholics Anonymous and Women for Sobriety can provide opportunities to meet people who have learned to deal with stress without relying on alcohol or other drugs.

Chapter 2

ANGER

In Japan, an individual who feels angry is not likely to lash out at the object of his anger with a torrent of furious words. Instead, he will show it by excessive politeness and a neutral expression.

Among the Mbuti hunter-gatherers of northeast Zaire, humor is routinely used to dissipate quarrels. Individual disputes turn into full-scale tribal laugh fests.

The Utku Eskimos are likely to ostracize anyone among them who loses his or her temper, regardless of the reason.

Welcome to the fascinating world of anger. Virtually every culture has its own rules that spell out the socially acceptable causes and the permissible methods of expressing the emotion. In our culture, the way we think about anger – and how best to handle it – is changing.

For years the popular wisdom was to vent all anger. Those who suppressed anger, it was argued, risked everything from ulcers to heart attacks to overeating hinges, not to mention disastrous relationships. Now experts suspect that such a universal link between anger and physical ills may be overstated, and that people who express their anger without hesitation or reflection may want to consider the potentially devastating social consequences of their actions. Sometimes the "let-it-out" philosophy is counterproductive.

Let's start with the link between suppressed anger and illness. In the controversial book, *Anger: the Misunderstood Emotion,* social psychologist Carol Tavris, Ph.D., drew on a great number of research references to write that "the popular belief that suppressed anger can wreak havoc on the body and bloodstream had been inflated out of realistic proportions. It does not, in any predictable or consistent way, make us depressed, produce ulcers or hypertension, set us off on food binges, or give us heart attacks."

She wrote that ulcers, traditionally considered the ultimate symptom of suppressed emotion, "turn up among people who express anger readily and among those who don't." It may partly have something to do with your genes. "If you have a particular kind of genetic capacity and are socialized in a certain way, chances are you might [get an ulcer]. We still don't know," says Ernest Harburg, Ph.D., a University of Michigan senior research scientist.

Just as some individuals may be genetically predisposed to heart disease, some seem to be genetically predisposed to having a greater capacity for anger. However, the way people *express* their anger will vary with the social and psychological environment.

Dr. Harburg studied how the anger responses of 2,300 individuals in Detroit impacted on their blood pressure. Whose was lower – those who kept anger in (Anger-In) or those who freely expressed anger (Anger-Out)? Neither. Significant numbers of both groups experienced high levels of blood pressure arousal. And other research by Dr. Harburg linked unexpressed anger with early mortality. But while he cautions that it's only a hypothesis that suppressed anger is a risk factor that can lead you to an early grave, he adds: "If you play the percentages, you'd find a better way to deal with anger." Fortunately, there's a third method of handling anger: reflective coping.

Reflective Coping

Both Anger-In and Anger-Out are reflexive responses. They just *happen,* like when the doctor tests your reflexes by hitting your knee. When you're angry, you don't necessarily *think* about what you're doing. And you certainly don't think constructively – for example, considering ways of getting to the root of it. That's why many psychologists now recommend reflective coping as a way of dealing with anger. You don't lash out at someone. You don't sit and stew. Instead, you think about the source of your anger, about the consequences of your response. "People who respond with reflective handling of anger seem to have lower blood pressure, on average," says Dr. Harburg.

Keep two things in mind. First, as we understand from the Eskimos and others, the way we express our anger is something we learn how to do. It doesn't come naturally. So you can learn to cope in new ways – whether it's a matter of keeping a diary of your anger so you can track its ebbs and flows and your responses, or whether it's a matter of learning relaxation techniques as a way of responding to what in the past would have sent you flying off the handle.

The second thing to keep in mind is that reflective coping techniques don't mean that you can never tell a boss or a loved one precisely how you feel. You can. The difference is that you do it in a constructive manner.

Dr. Harburg gives this simple example. The boss flings open his door, emerges and yells at the near-top of his voice: "Where's that report you owe me? Haven't you finished it yet?" If this is, in fact, a wrong accusation – if you already put the report on the boss's desk but he hasn't discovered it – you can simply stand up, look him in the eye and say, "I already put it on your desk. And I don't like it when you yell at me like that."

Finding What's Good for You

There are two reasons for expressing anger, according to Dr. Tavris – to make the other guy feel as bad as you do, and to draw the other person's attention to the fact that something is wrong that you want fixed. Sometimes losing your temper is the only way to let a person know how serious the issue is, which is why our culture permits it. Dr. Tavris believes anger should be expressed only in circumstances that satisfy three conditions: when it represents a legitimate plea for justice; when it is directed at someone who is the cause of the anger; and when it would correct the situation or not cause retaliation.

But suppose you find yourself constantly yelling at your kids and getting temporary relief, yet later feeling remorse over your own behavior. It could be time to look for a strategy that works better for you – a strategy in which the object of your anger is open to your message and a strategy that you feel comfortable with over the long run.

Many psychologists agree that a rational method for handling your anger is often the best approach. But some people just seem to blow their top, despite lots of promises that they'll never do it again. If you think you have no choices and control over how you respond, you might try this "thought system." In his book *Anger: How to Live with and without It,* Albert Ellis, Ph.D., offers a step-by-step method to change and undercut irrational responses to anger. You may never throw another tantrum.

Foremost, he says, "Acknowledge that it's *you* who creates the anger." Someone may displease or frustrate you, but they don't create the anger. Second, he suggests you rate people's behavior instead of evaluating them as a whole. "Acknowledge that there are people who do badly, not rotten, bad people," he says.

"That diminishes the anger, but you still have the displeasure of the act, and you have to decide whether to assert yourself or not. If it's a friend or family member you're angry with, you can feel free to tell them. Your diminished anger will enable you to be assertive, but without the aggression that is likely to either intensify your anger or alienate your friend. If it's your boss you're angry with, you may not be as free to assert yourself without consequences," he says. What many therapists suggest is that you tell friends about the anger if you can't tell the boss.

"Try to understand the circumstances that are provoking the anger in the first place, whether they are stored memories from the past or from the current predicament," says Charles D. Spielberger, Ph.D., director of the Center for Research in Behavioral Medicine and Health Psychology at the University of South Florida. "If you know what provokes the anger, you have lots of choices. You may be able to avoid the circumstances of people who make you angry. And if you can't avoid them, you may be able to anticipate that they're likely to make you angry. So you can develop alternative ways of coping." Try taking a deep breath, for example, and slowly counting to ten.

Chapter 3

ANXIETY AND PANIC ATTACKS

It's as if the symptoms jump you from behind without warning. Your heart begins to beat wildly, your forehead is suddenly wet with perspiration, your hands tremble, your throat dries and swallowing is almost impossible. Your mind races to grab control of your body, but even as you tell yourself, "stay calm," it happens. You look for the nearest door, any door, so you can run away, far away, because that's the only thing that seems to help.

If this scene sounds familiar, then you know what it's like to be gripped by a panic attack. It's estimated that anywhere from 1 to 6 percent of the U.S. population suffers from panic attacks or other anxiety disorders. Panic attacks are far more severe than phobias, general anxiety or butterflies in the stomach. The attacks often start in early adulthood and, although the condition can be debilitating, it is not usually life-threatening.

It's now felt by many that panic attacks have a biological basis. They can be triggered by a number of things. People with diagnosed physical problems, such as asthma, hypertension or a heart condition, can suddenly fall victim to a panic attack when they believe they are about to experience another round of their physical illness. The fear of the future and the feeling of being unable to handle the pressures of responsibilities also can trigger an attack. In other cases, panic episodes can be an offshoot of a psychological disorder, such as depression, alcoholism or agoraphobia.

To gain control of panic when it arises, you'll find the support of others — family, friends and perhaps professionals — makes it easier. You'll also need some basic tools, the main one being breathing. "By changing your breathing pattern during an anxious episode, you can reverse your body's panic-provoking symptoms," writes psychologist R. Reid Wilson, Ph.D., in his book *Don't Panic: Taking Control of Anxiety Attacks.*

When faced with a stressful situation, your upper chest lifts upward and outward, and you take breaths that are shallow and rapid. By consciously changing to diaphragmatic breathing, you fill the lower part of your lungs with air so that with each breath, your stomach seems to be expanding and contracting. This slow, deep breathing will help you relax and become more calm.

When you notice the first signs of panic, Dr. Wilson advises that to calm yourself you take a long, deep breath and then exhale slowly while silently saying the word *relax.* Take ten natural, easy breaths, counting each exhale silently, starting with ten. Notice any tensions, perhaps in your jaw, forehead or stomach, and imagine them loosening. When you've counted back to one, slowly return to whatever you were doing when you felt the panic coming on.

If you suddenly find yourself in the grip of a panic attack, use the deep-breathing technique to disrupt the negative, self-critical, hopeless thoughts. Then, if possible, find some neutral or pleasant task to occupy your mind. "As you gain control of your breathing and thoughts, reinforce your will to overcome the panic by repeating some supportive statements, such as 'I can be anxious and still perform this task,' 'I can manage these symptoms,' 'I can take all the time I need to feel safe and comfortable,' 'I've survived this before and I'll survive this time, too,' " suggests Dr. Wilson in his book.

If you're prone to panic attacks, stay away from caffeine. Research at the Yale University School of Medicine, New Haven, Connecticut, has shown that when people with anxiety disorders were given caffeine, there were significant increases in anxiety, nervousness, fear, nausea, palpitations, restlessness and tremors. The researchers found that people who suffer from panic attacks appeared to be more sensitive to the anxiety-causing effects of caffeine.

As for medication, several drugs have shown promise in research trials, but there's an ongoing debate within the medical community about side effects. "It's something each patient has to decide," says Redford B. Williams, M.D., professor of psychiatry at Duke University, Durham, North Carolina, and head of the university's Behavioral Medicine Research Center. "In severe cases, where a person's fear of having an attack is so paralyzing that he won't leave his house, the advantages of using medication and resuming a normal life may outweigh the chance of side effects."

Two other factors that may help are a proper diet and exercise, says clinical psychologist Sue Breton, a victim of panic attacks. "Research has shown that just as there is a definite connection between diet and physical illness, so there is between diet and mental illness."

The key, she says, is to improve your vitality by avoiding foods with added sugar, caffeine, alcohol, salt and artificial additives. Instead, eating more fresh fruit and vegetables, whole grain breads, and lean meat and fish will help you feel "more alive and energetic than you did before, and less susceptible to anxiety."

Being in good physical shape also enhances your ability to cope, she adds. Exercise "replaces the symptoms of stress and fear by providing a natural physical response. Physically fit people who take regular exercise will testify to feeling mentally invigorated afterward, yet at the same time having a sense of calm and well-being."

Chapter 4

ASSERTIVENESS TRAINING

Picture this: You bought a curling iron that fails to curl. You do one of three things.

1. You stay home and fume about the inferior quality of modern appliances.
2. You storm back to the store, demand to see the manager, scream and yell about how you're tired of getting ripped off. You insist on getting your money back and you march out of the store.
3. You return to the store, calmly ask to speak with the manager and, in a very earnest, straightforward manner, explain that your curling iron isn't working satisfactorily and that you would like either to have your money returned or the iron replaced.

Now which of these situations produces the most stress?

If you're the stay-at-home-and-fume type, you're probably too passive for your own good. If you're the screaming-demanding-storming type, you may be too aggressive for your own good. Option number three, of course, is to be assertive: to know your rights and to respect the rights of others, and to have polished skills in effectively communicating your message, without hostility.

Let's look at another situation: You're at a party where you know very few people. You want to mingle, so what do you do?

1. You hang around on the fringes of other folks' conversations, waiting for them to include you.

2. You burst into a group and dominate the conversation. One by one the members wander away, and when each one does, you shout, "Hey, you're missing a golden opportunity!"
3. You approach a group with an effective opening line, such as, "How do you know the host?" or "Are you enjoying the party?"

Again, which solution appears least stressful?

From a stress-reduction point of view, the assertive behavior wins hands-down over the passive or aggressive solution. The trouble is, too many folks have been programmed to respond in business, social or intimate relationships in a manner that makes most psychologists cringe. Girls are generally reared to be too passive. Boys sometimes are treated as if aggression is a birthright. On top of that, we haven't grown up learning from people who exhibit calm, clear assertive behavior all that much.

Without the benefit of either upbringing or role models, the only way to learn this behavior may be assertiveness training. It's a method of unlearning habits that professionals call an "anxiety response" to other people's behavior. With the help of assertiveness training, the passive or aggressive find themselves becoming assertive in a matter of weeks. They know what they want and learn how to go after it in a healthy manner. They become more open with themselves and with others. And they understand the consequences of their actions. As a result, relationships improve and life becomes generally less stressful.

Who Needs Assertiveness Training?

Most experts agree that assertiveness training is not for everyone. But if you've learned how *not* to stand up to others, if you're fearful of rejection and emotional situations, if you're helpless and depressed, you may be a prime candidate.

"If your general fear of what other people think inhibits your self-expression, you may be causing yourself a great deal of stress, and you should consider assertiveness training," says Joseph Wolpe, M.D., professor of psychiatry at Temple University School of Medicine in Philadelphia and a pioneer of assertiveness training. And Eileen Gambrill, Ph.D., a professor of social welfare at the University of California at Berkeley says this form of behavior therapy is for those who find themselves generally dissatisfied with the course of their relationships. "Just ask yourself: 'Am I satisfied with my social life?' 'Am I satisfied with my relationships?' "

Advises Jean Baer, author of *How to Be an Assertive (Not Aggressive)*

Woman, "Systematically survey the problems you face, the things that make you feel bad, the situations that make you frustrated, the things that you'd like to have different about yourself and your life situation. Do these relate to the area of assertiveness?"

Some of the telltale signs that professional assertiveness training may help are unwanted feelings – depression, frequent outbursts of anger, frequent feelings of helplessness and frustration and of being pushed around by others.

But you may have been plagued with these problems for so long that it may not be easy to recognize your lack of assertiveness, your unrecognized inhibitions, as the culprits behind all that stress. So here's Dr. Wolpe's profile of the assertiveness training candidate, a person who is inhibited from performing "normal" behavior because of fear. Do you recognize yourself?

"He may be unable to complain about poor service in a restaurant because he is afraid of hurting the waiter's feelings; unable to express differences of opinion to his friends because he fears that they will not like him; unable to get up and leave a social situation that has become boring because he is afraid to seem ungrateful; unable to ask for the repayment of a loan or to administer a legitimate reproof to a subordinate because he is afraid of losing his image as a 'nice guy'; or unable to express love, warmth, admiration or praise because he finds such expression embarrassing."

If this sounds like you, here's some advice: *You have a perfect right* to your opinions and feelings. *You have a perfect right* to express yourself honestly – without stepping on others' toes, without trying to hurt others.

Learning to be assertive can make these words, your personal bill of rights, come alive for you. You will also learn the varying degrees of assertiveness and the appropriate times to assert yourself. Sure you have a perfect right to feel your boss is a dimwit, but it won't improve matters to tell him so. Assertiveness training can help you gain good judgment.

It's all designed to increase the effectiveness of your social behavior so that you get more positive feedback and less critical, punishing responses from others. It is based on the idea that by changing your actions, you change your attitudes and feelings about yourself. The result will be a new feeling of self-esteem – in many ways, a brand-new you.

Your local mental health organization or the psychology department at a nearby university can put you in touch with assertiveness training professionals.

A first decision is whether to opt for a group therapy workshop setting or to go it alone. "A group lets a person realize that they're not the only shy one. It gives people a chance to see the way other people do things successfully. It offers a buddy system," says Dr. Gambrill. "You get to practice what you're learning," adds David C. Diffendale, Ph.D., a psychologist in Clearwater, Florida, who runs assertiveness training workshops.

On the other hand, you may prefer the individualized attention of one-to-one therapy. "This is particularly good for people who are not going to be aggressive enough to get what they need out of a group," says Dr. Diffendale.

Either way, you will first learn clearly the differences among assertive, passive and aggressive behavior. A therapist or group facilitator can provide endless examples of each type of response.

A second step may be to evaluate your own response to specific situations. Also, you determine which relationships you would like to single out first for improvement. "You want to find out which areas you're assertive in and which areas you are not. Some people are assertive at home and not at work, and vice versa," says Dr. Diffendale.

The lack of assertiveness at work is a major source of stress. Say your boss tells you he is dissatisfied with a major project you spent months completing. Many women in that situation would simply burst into tears, says Marion R. Frank, Ed.D., a psychologist who works with individuals and groups in assertiveness training. "They feel overwhelmed and put down and respond with tears. It's a passive response and it's totally inappropriate in the workplace." Turning on the waterworks won't get you what you want.

On the other hand, the employee may respond with expressions of anger, aggressively shouting back at the boss or lashing out at others. But you can be angry and behave assertively, not aggressively. "Instead of blowing up, you can say 'I'm having trouble with this,' " says Dr. Frank. "The proper assertive response is to ask for specifics of what your boss doesn't like about the project, without being defensive." You need to be calm and clear, have direct eye contact, good posture, and a well-modulated voice. Easier said than done, it's true. But everyone can learn with practice.

Working Up a Script

Once you've determined where your assertiveness skills need a boost, you may be asked to draw up sample scripts of assertiveness in action. How best to communicate the message that you don't want to visit your husband's parents every Sunday, without causing hard feelings. How best to communicate your displeasure when your husband comes home from work late and inebriated — without calling to warn you.

Then you'll be asked to complete tasks that set you on the road to assertiveness. If it's shyness you're overcoming, you may be instructed to strike up one conversation a day with a fellow passenger on the bus. For those who have trouble saying no, therapist Albert Ellis, Ph.D., suggests an assignment in his book *Anger:* "Risk saying no or refusing something yourself. Pick something that you don't usually want to do but that you do in order to please others – such as going out to eat, having sex in a certain way or carrying on a conversation for a long period of time – and deliberately take the risk of refusing to do this thing."

For those with trouble asking for things, Dr. Diffendale often assigns people to ask for something they want but don't ask for, such as asking the person next to you not to smoke or simply asking your spouse to get you a glass of water while in the kitchen.

A final step may be to examine how your nonverbal behavior communicates nonassertiveness, and to learn to change.

It's Not Just Your Words

Yes, your weak gestures (fingers spread apart) may suggest passiveness or your forceful gestures (a clenched fist) may indicate aggressiveness. Assertive behavior includes many components that are easy to overlook. From *Your Perfect Right,* a manual of assertiveness training by Robert E. Alberti, M.D., and Michael L. Emmons, here's a checklist of some of the things you're likely to focus on in assertiveness training.

Eye contact. Look directly at the person you're speaking to and it will help communicate your sincerity and help you get your message across directly.

Body posture. You'll add assertiveness to your message if your posture is active and erect.

Gestures. You'll add emphasis, openness and warmth if you accentuate your message with appropriate gestures. If your movements are uninhibited, you will suggest openness, self-confidence and spontaneity.

Facial expression. Let your face mirror your message. You're sending mixed signals if you smile while delivering an angry message.

Evaluating Assertiveness Training

Dr. Diffendale says you should find yourself challenged by assertiveness training, but not at a level that overwhelms you. For some people, the therapist or group leader is easygoing and the person winds up not being stretched and doesn't learn any new behavior. That's no good because any learning you do in assertiveness training *should* be tough, he says. On the other hand, he points out that some therapists or group leaders push so hard that people get overwhelmed by the challenge. They get frightened and drop out.

In group settings, a good trainer will start out by helping people tackle situations that are not particularly threatening or emotionally intense, says Dr. Frank. This is the time you learn to ask your spouse to get you a glass of water if he's going into the kitchen. She adds that after training progresses and skills are honed, it's time to deal with emotionally laden issues.

How can you tell if the assertiveness training you choose is effective? Among the items on a consumer checklist drawn up by Dr. Gambrill and Cheryl A. Richey, Ph.D., a professor of social welfare at the University of Washington, are:

- Participants select their goals.
- Long-term as well as short-term consequences of changed behavior are considered.
- Personal and social goals selected are individually tailored for each person.
- Goals pursued are achievable.

Beyond that, ask yourself if you are aware of using new skills outside of the classroom in situations that would have otherwise had you hooked. Do you know your rights and how to enforce them?

Chapter 5

AUTOGENIC TRAINING

Imagine being able to simply tell your body to relax — and having it respond! That's the goal of autogenic training, a form of self-hypnosis that is among the best and most complete reducers of stress.

"Autogenic" means self-regulation or self-generation. It's a technique developed by Johannes Schultz, M.D., and Wolfgang Luthe, M.D., early in this century. Autogenic training is a combination of their medical research (particularly hypnosis) and Yoga. The result is a series of self-instructions that can help the body to rid itself of such diseases as high blood pressure, headaches, chronic pain, allergies, ulcers and general anxiety. It also can induce deep relaxation.

You tell yourself what you want ("My heartbeat is calm and regular") and you produce the desired physical results. As you practice the training on a regular basis, you'll discover it becomes easier to instruct your body to reply. Part of what's happening is that you get relaxed to the point where your body's self-regulating systems take over. Says Martin Shaffer, Ph.D., a clinical psychologist who runs the Stress Management Institute in San Francisco, "It's not the verbal cue but the relaxation that brings about the physical change."

There's a variation of the process that's perfectly suited to relieve stress: autogenic relaxation. It may take weeks or longer to use autogenic training to achieve a desired physiological result (such as increased thyroid production). But if you practice the method for relaxation, you're likely to get satisfaction in the first session.

How to Do It

As with other relaxation techniques, you do this one in a quiet room. Turn the lights down low and wear loose clothing. You should sit in an armchair that comfortably supports your head, back and extremities. Or you can lie down comfortably with your head supported, feet slightly apart, and arms at your side but not touching your body. You should be free of tension.

As Dr. Shaffer outlines in his book *Life after Stress,* here are the basic instructions for using autogenics to produce relaxation.

In your comfortable position, close your eyes and slowly recite the following instructions. Breathe deeply and evenly, and recite the verbal cues to yourself as you exhale.

1. "My hands and arms are heavy and warm" (5 times).
2. "My feet and legs are heavy and warm" (5 times).
3. "My abdomen is warm and comfortable" (5 times). (Omit this step if you have ulcers.)
4. "My breathing is deep and even" (10 times).
5. "My heartbeat is slightly calm and regular" (10 times). (Use of the word *slightly* in this step can help prevent the reaction of a rapid, irregular heartbeat some people experience when that word is omitted.)
6. "My forehead is cool" (5 times).
7. "When I open my eyes, I will remain relaxed and refreshed" (3 times).

Perform the following sequence of body movements.

1. Move your hands and arms about.
2. Move your feet and legs about.
3. Rotate your head.
4. Open your eyes and sit up.

All of this should be done with an attitude of passive concentration. Observe what's happening to your body, but don't consciously try to analyze it. By all means don't criticize yourself for having distracting thoughts. If your mind wanders simply bring it back to your instructions as soon as possible.

Dr. Shaffer advises doing two-minute autogenic training sessions ten times a day. "If you spend ten little times a day bringing your tension level down, it's unlikely to get up that high," he says.

Unexpected Results

You may experience "autogenic discharges." These can be tingling or other body sensations, involutary movements, pain or even a desire to cry. These feelings may be pleasant or unpleasant, but they will pass as you progress. "When this happens, simply do nothing," says Dr. Shaffer. "Tell yourself this is a normal discharge of tension in your body. What's happening is that your brain is dumping tension through your motor system."

Some people lie back, begin their autogenic ritual, but instead of feeling relaxed lapse into a panic of anxiety. "This happens with people who need tension as a defense," says Dr. Shaffer. "They're getting rid of their tension and up comes anxiety. Things they've not paid attention to are coming up to the surface." His initial advice: Let it pass and continue the autogenic formula. His secondary advice (if the agitation continues): Seek professional therapy to get to the root of your anxiety.

Because autogenic training produces physiological changes, it's not something to take lightly. If you have high or low blood pressure, diabetes, hypoglycemic conditions or heart conditions, you should consult with your physician before you even start. Those with severe mental or emotional disorders are discouraged from trying autogenic training. If you find yourself feeling restless during or after autogenic sessions – or if you suffer disquieting side effects – practice only under the supervision of a professional autogenic training instructor.

Bidding Migraines Adieu

Some professional therapists hook up people to biofeedback machines, so they can monitor the physiological changes that occur in autogenic training. It's a first step in learning voluntary control of certain functions. This combination of autogenics and biofeedback can be a powerful tool to get rid of migraines. At the Menninger Foundation's Biofeedback and Psychophysiology Center in Topeka, Kansas, patients use the autogenics/biofeedback duo to learn to short circuit the onset of migraines. (For more information on biofeedback machines, see chapter 7.)

A biofeedback unit is attached to a patient's finger to measure skin temperature. The patient repeats an autogenic phrase ("My arms and hands are heavy and warm"). After about 20 minutes, he looks at the printed record of temperature changes and writes down a summary of his feelings, emotions and thoughts during the session. The point is to perceive body changes without having to rely on a biofeedback machine, says Steven Fahrion, Ph.D., co-director of Menninger's voluntary control program.

After practicing this method with a home machine twice daily for about a week, the patient begins to replace the autogenic phrases with personal visualizations designed to make hands turn warm – visualizing burying one hand in warm sand, for instance.

How does this prevent migraines?

The stress response causes a constriction of the body's arteries, among them the carotid arteries, which supply blood to the brain. When the brain senses it isn't getting enough blood, it releases neurochemicals known as neurokinins, which cause the carotid arteries to overdilate. The arteries are wrapped with pain receptors that are stretched; that's what causes the pain.

Some migraine sufferers get a warning – such as blurred vision – that a migraine will soon occur. By warming their hands as soon as they get this warning, they can use autogenic training to halt the painful sequence of events and stop the migraine. But most migraine sufferers get no warning. These folks are often taught to keep their hands warm all the time, to keep the stress response in constant check, says Jack Hartje, Ph.D., a professor of psychology at the University of North Florida, who trains therapists to use biofeedback. One practical method is a daily session of autogenic training until the hand-warming becomes second nature.

Chapter 6

BACK PAIN

It's definitely back there. The dull ache just above the hips. The biting twinge at midback. The soreness about your shoulders that's moved in like an invasion of termites – and seems about as likely to leave. Eighty percent of us have a backache at one time or another, and for 70 million Americans this pain is as regular as the mail.

What's in back of it all? Rarely disease or a structural problem. A big scientific study says that 83 percent of all back pain is caused by muscle problems. The muscles may be weak because of a desk job or a constant slouch or extra pounds or careless lifting. And if your back pain is of that variety, it probably has another ingredient in its recipe: stress.

Your muscles don't like emotional stress, explains Hans Kraus, M.D., author of *Backache, Stress and Tension.* They tighten up, and if they are forced to make a sudden movement, these rigid muscles can cause a spasm, which in turn can cause a knot that primes the muscles for *more* spasms. And tight muscles can work against you in other ways.

"Over a period of time, a chronically tensed muscle may lose its stretch and become shortened," writes coauthor Lawrence W. Friedmann, M.D., in *Freedom from Backaches.* This, he says, may "lead to awkward, jerky movements, which may make the muscle more susceptible to injury."

Ways to De-Stress Your Back

Several of the stress-management techniques described in this book may help prevent you from turning stressful situations into back pain. Many people respond well to massage (see chapter 39) as a means of relieving pain. According to Dr. Friedmann, a light, stroking massage at home can relax muscles and relieve spasms.

Certain relaxation techniques, if practiced properly and routinely, can work to eliminate muscular tension. For example, the use of deep breathing techniques (see chapter 16) is being accepted as part of relaxation training in some pain clinics. One method suggested by James F. Loehr, Ed.D., and Jeffrey A. Migdow, M.D., in their book *Take a Deep Breath,* may be especially helpful to release the tension that contributes to your back pain. They call it "The Controlling-Pain-with-Imagery Breath."

1. Keep your eyes closed throughout.
2. Begin abdominal breathing (breathing with your belly instead of your chest).
3. Imagine tension leaving your body, like a vapor or stream of color, with each exhalation.
4. Imagine relaxation coming in with each inhalation.
5. Move parts of your body as you breathe, if it helps to release any general tension.
6. Imagine your incoming breath traveling to the area of pain and filling it with calmness.
7. Imagine the pain flowing out with each exhalation.
8. Allow yourself, through crying or sighing, to release any emotion related to the pain.
9. Continue steps 5 through 8 for five to ten minutes.
10. Feel the movement of your breath again.
11. Stretch your arms and legs.
12. Open your eyes when you feel better.

All these techniques are good — but using two or more of them in combination may be better. Robert G. Addison, M.D., of the Center for Pain Studies at the Rehabilitation Institute of Chicago and author of *Living with Your Bad Back,* says that people who suffer from stress-aggravated back pain should use a variety of stress-reduction techniques. In addition to physical techniques and exercise, people might consider using relaxation, exercise tapes *and* biofeedback, for example.

Dr. Addison also says people with chronic back pain should "examine what is causing the stress." Or who. According to one study, family conflict was often the cause of lower back pain. In the workplace, lack of a feeling of camaraderie with co-workers was cited as one cause of the problem. And the person who's stressing your life may be you. Another study concluded that people with chronic lower back pain tend to have a negative self-concept. In this case, a professional therapist may help you improve how you view yourself — and get you back to normal.

Chapter 7

BIOFEEDBACK

Want to know exactly how much you're sweating?

You probably don't. But maybe you should. Because if you hook yourself up to a GSR 2 — an inexpensive, hand-held biofeedback machine that emits a pleasant hum in response to tiny decreases in the perspiration levels of your fingertips and a near-whistle when your skin becomes more moist — you'll know exactly when you're stressed and when you're not. And you'll be able to do something about it.

That's the principle of using a biofeedback machine. It reports on one or more of the physical functions that increase with stress: heart rate, breath rate, muscular tension or the moisture produced on your skin. Once you're aware of stress, you can reduce it. And there's no question about its reduction or its lack. Your body can't lie!

Just a Tool

But don't think a biofeedback machine is a relaxation robot you can command to de-stress you. You've got to practice a relaxation exercise (such as any of the techniques described in this book) until the gadget indicates that you're relaxed. After enough experience, you'll begin to get a clear sense of when you're relaxed and how much of what technique gets you there.

A biofeedback machine, whether a hand-held model or the elaborate doctor's-office variety, is only a tool. "People may have an exaggerated expectation of what they can accomplish with biofeedback," says Alan Glaros, Ph.D., a psychologist at the University of Florida, Gainesville, who uses biofeedback in conjunction with other methods for stress management in his practice. "Some people think biofeedback, with the stroke of a magical wand, will transform their daily, troubled existence into a Cinderella-like fairy tale. The reality is that it takes work."

Even though you may get yourself to stop sweating, he says, that's only a first step. You still have to examine and understand the stress factors that bring on the sweating.

That's why the biofeedback patient has to become a personal scientist, says John Corson, Ph.D., a professor at Dartmouth Medical College in New Hampshire. "Biofeedback allows you to collect data on your psychological strengths and weaknesses, on what upsets you and what calms you down."

Hum, Sweet Hum

The advent of hand-held biofeedback units opened up biofeedback therapy to do-it-yourselfers. No longer do the overstressed have to rely on $50 to $100 sessions in the physician's office.

Let's tune in to one person's experience with home biofeedback, as reported in the "Regenerative Living" column of *Prevention* Magazine.

"A couple of months ago a package came in the mail from a company called Thought Technology. Inside was a hand-sized piece of machinery with the enigmatic label 'GSR 2.' It was a biofeedback unit.

" 'The GSR 2 biofeedback unit,' explained a doctor I asked about the product, 'monitors the skin's perspiration level and emits a tone, which rises in pitch as more moisture is produced or drops as the skin becomes drier.'

"The actual unit fit easily in my hand and had a small elastic band that held my fingers snugly against two smooth metal plates. Upon contact, a small earphone began humming softly in my ear. I closed my eyes and started purposefully thinking about a stressful situation: my next deadline. Sure enough, within three seconds, the tone started climbing the scale until it resembled the high-pitched whine of a mosquito. No doubt about it, I was definitely worked up.

"Bringing the tone back down took a little more work. Over the next two weeks, I practiced regularly with the unit while listening to a tape of relaxation exercises that came with the package. Soon I had the unit humming a low complacent tone that was a virtual one-note hymn to relaxation. If I heard the tone rise, I stopped and examined my thoughts to see what was bothering me. In this way, I not only learned correct relaxation techniques but also discovered hidden stressors that I never realized were upsetting me.

"If you're thinking of giving biofeedback a try, be prepared for some serious work. To start, you've got to find a good relaxation technique and really concentrate on making it work. 'The unit itself only tells you how you're doing, not what to do,' says the doctor. I put in a good half hour a day at feedback. But the doctor says even 10 to 20 minutes daily, done regularly, can have a beneficial effect. 'Besides the promise of daily relaxation, I've found that biofeedback in conjunction with stress-management training often delivers other bonuses, such as better sleep and relief from stress-related high blood pressure,' he says.

"Eventually, when you've learned proper relaxation techniques, you can wean yourself from the feedback unit. But again, to make it work, you still must practice your exercises regularly. Otherwise your body will forget everything you taught it. 'Occasionally it's a good idea to go back to the biofeedback unit to make sure your skills are in good order,' says the doctor."

Professional Help

The ease of home biofeedback doesn't mean you should overlook the role of professionals. Physicians or professional therapists who are certified by the Biofeedback Certification Institute of America can give you direction and clear-cut goals in your stress management. They can tell you what to reasonably expect and can help you figure out what some of the other factors are that contribute to any stress-related ailments you may have. They can offer suggestions or remedies.

If you decide to go the at-home route, here are the addresses of two companies and descriptions of the units they manufacture.

> Thought Technology, Ltd.
> R.R.1, Route 9 North #380
> West Chazy, NY 12992
> 1-800-361-3651

Or in Canada:

> 2180 Belgrave Avenue, Suite 693,
> Montreal, P.Q. Canada H4A 2L8
> (514) 489-8251

1. The GSR 2. GSR stands for "galvanic skin resistance," a measure of your perspiration and resistance of skin to electrical flow. The tiny unit described above costs $49.95 (and comes with a relaxation cassette). For $79.95 you get the unit, four cassettes and a 48-page stress-control workbook.

2. GSR/Temp 2. It's the GSR 2 with the added ability to measure the temperature of your fingers to within $1/20$ of a degree Fahrenheit. (Stress causes cold and clammy hands. The temperature measures the cold, the GSR measures the clammy.) The unit is designed so that you don't have to hold it in your hand. A meter registers temperature changes. Cost: $99.95
3. Calmset 3. In addition to GSR and temperature functions, this unit has an electromyograph that registers your level of muscular tension. You listen in on headphones. Cost: $249.

A note for lovers of computers. All of the above can be hooked up to a computer via a software program named Calmpute. That way you can check out your responses in patterns or bar graphs on your computer terminal.

Thought Technology also sells an electronic gadget named Calmtone that lets you connect any of these biofeedback units to your stereo. Your favorite music will get louder or softer in sync with your relaxation.

Bio-Feedback Systems, Inc.
2736 47th Street
Boulder, CO 80301
(303) 444-1411

1. EDR-002. This unit measures skin conductance, which may help determine your level of stress. Metal contacts on two Velcro strips wrap around your fingers. A cable connects your fingers to the unit, which is the size of a hand-held calculator. You check out your conductance level on a digital display. Cost: $175.
2. Mini-Relaxometer. If you prefer to *hear* how well your skin conductance changes, this unit monitors your conductance and tells you what's happening via earphones. Pulse/clicks increase in speed when you get sweatier, slow down as you get dry. Cost: $110.
3. DT-002. Similar to the EDR-002, this machine checks out your temperature and displays the news in Fahrenheit on a meter. Cost: $175.
4. PE-020. Want to keep track of your muscle tension? Attach the electrodes from this unit to your lower back, forehead or any other muscle area that tends to tense up. This unit provides both visible and audible feedback. Cost: $395.

Chapter 8

BOREDOM

Do you find yourself eating everything in sight or perhaps not eating much at all?

Are you waking up earlier and staying up later or can't you drag your head off the pillow?

Is your mind a blank or swirling with random thoughts?

Are you peevish with your loved ones, taking dumb risks or having a lot of little accidents?

If you answered yes to any of the above, your problem might simply be a case of boredom. Stress experts are waking up to the broad range of physical and psychological symptoms that result from being understimulated by the challenges of our daily lives.

Boredom can make it virtually impossible to perform simple work tasks, tasks that are ordinarily part of our regular job. That's why boredom is among the major stress-related reasons we fail at our jobs, according to Arthur Witkin, Ph.D., an industrial psychologist at the New York career counseling firm of Personnel Sciences Center and professor at Queens College of the City University of New York.

"Most articles on stress deal with the overload side of stress, people being overwhelmed," says Augustin de la Pena, Ph.D., associate professor of psychiatry at the University of Texas Health Science Center, Dallas. "But the *underload* side of stress in adults is the predominant side of stress." What Dr. de la Pena calls underload, most people call boredom. *Why* are so many of us so bored?

As we grow, our brains gain the capacity to process ever-increasing amounts of information. It's kind of like computer software that helps us deal with or predict our environment. But when we're bored, the understimulated brain structure signals itself to increase the input of or sensitivity to information.

This continued growth and its resulting demand for ever more stimulation explains why what excited us as kids bores us as adults. "Most people try to get back to that intermediate range of information flow, to regain the fun and interest, and wind up on the overload side," says Dr. de la Pena.

Without conscious restraint, our brains will go to any length to combat boredom and seek new challenges. Boredom, for example, can increase the possibility of illness and/or the complaint of illness. Back pain, some eating disorders, high blood pressure, some kinds of cancer and other problems can be created by the brain to make its work more interesting, says Dr. de la Pena. Some people respond to boredom by becoming sleepy, but for others insomnia is a by-product. According to Dr. de la Pena's research, the chronically bored brain pursues the stimulation of an increased level of REM (rapid eye movement), or dreaming, sleep. "The more boredom, the quicker one gets into REM sleep," he says. But since REM sleep signals the brain to wake up, those who fall rapidly into REM sleep also find themselves waking up earlier than they want.

Keeping control of the physical results of boredom may be a simple matter of systematically increasing our daily challenges (and thus also increasing our brain-satisfying information flow) without overdoing it. If you've been playing dominoes for years, it might be time to take up chess. Forsake the television set to play the piano, study a foreign language or go out on the town. In other words, make a conscious effort to feed those hungry brain structures something fresh and meaty. Meditation can teach you to increase your sensory awareness if you are understimulated.

Put Some Fun in Your Life

When patients of Arthur Freeman, Ph.D., a psychologist at the University of Pennsylvania's Center for Cognitive Therapy in Philadelphia, complain of being bored, he instructs them to do two things. First, they are asked to determine their level of boredom on a scale of one to ten. Then he tells them to make a list of things that are mildly stimulating, moderately stimulating and very stimulating. "They have to determine for themselves what their needs are and what they find stimulating. Then they can be helped to go after it," he says. "For one person it might mean inviting someone over to dinner and creating an elaborate meal; for another person it might mean working out at a gym. Someone else might find it stimulating to rent a movie. They have to very consciously set goals for them-selves that will alleviate the so-called boredom. I find doing selected activities helps almost immediately."

Be sensible, however, when selecting your antiboredom activity. "A person who is bored may decide to drink; a person who is bored may decide to use drugs," says Dr. Freeman. "Eating, too, is something people do to arouse themselves when they are bored."

Boredom with work is the result of the same understimulation that causes physical ailments or sends people into eating binges, and with 40 hours or more of it a week, it is something that should not be underplayed. The number one complaint among 9,000 workers surveyed for the book *Stress in Organizations* was "feeling isolated and bored" at work.

Testing for Tedium

The first thing is to identify boredom – as opposed to a temporary "situational" emotional problem – as the culprit. At a very minimum, some of the symptoms of occupational boredom include a fluctuation of attention, absenteeism and irritability, which industrial psychologist Dr. Witkin describes as "the neurotic conflict that comes with being forced to do what you don't want to do." At its maximum impact, bored workers find themselves – without reason – to be helplessly incompetent. (In Dr. Witkin's words, "The inability to do what you're supposed to be doing.")

Those of us who are employed in large organizations, where the work can be dreadfully routine, are often in the best position to tackle occupational boredom. Over the past several decades business management has developed some sound psychological procedures such as aptitude testing to determine growth potential for employees who are in jobs or occupations that bore them. Most major corporations employ a human resources department whose function is to ensure that round pegs are in round holes, that employees' skills are best utilized in jobs that interest and challenge them.

For those working in such organizations, the advice is simple: Ask your employer to test your aptitude and, if the results warrant, find you another job within the company. If it turns out that you are well suited for your current job and no other, ask about the possibility of being given additional responsibilities.

Employees in smaller organizations will probably have to take matters into their own hands. The first step is to contact a career counselor. The International Association of Counseling Services (5999 Stevenson Avenue, Alexandria, VA 22304) is the accrediting organization for counseling centers, and it will provide a list of accredited counseling centers state by state (send a stamped, self-addressed envelope). Career counselors are listed, but only as part of a larger group. B'nai B'rith, YMCA and a few other nonprofit organizations offer career counseling on an ability-to-pay basis.

"A professional counselor may help you discover new options," says Dr. Witkin. "These options might include adding new responsibilities, getting a second job that is more challenging than your boring one, or taking on a hobby." At the absolute worst, a psychologist can teach a bored-to-tears employee how to adjust to the situation. A little scheduling, for instance, can go a long way toward alleviating boredom. Tedious tasks can be grouped together and accomplished in the morning, leaving the afternoon free for more interesting projects. Whatever the specific strategy, the advice of professionals is the same as that offered to those suffering from off-the-job boredom: Set realistic goals for yourself and go after them.

Dr. Witkin asserts that "there is no such thing as a boring job." He would probably be scoffed at by anyone who has spent time on an assembly line. But many individuals are attracted by the challenge of successfully completing an assembly task and by the camaraderie of participating with a group of friendly co-workers. In jobs, what's boring to one might be engaging to another. The same rings true for people.

The People Who Bore You

Mark Leary, Ph.D., an assistant professor of psychology at Wake Forest University in Winston-Salem, North Carolina, is coauthor of a report that lists the qualities that make a person boring. (It even established a "boringness index.") It has made Dr. Leary one of the nation's few experts on dealing with uninteresting people.

The Wake Forest study suggests that the people who are most boring are those who complain about themselves and their lives, as well as those who mutter trivialities. These bores are even more annoying than people who overuse slang or try too hard to be nice, according to the research.

"They interfere with communication and deprive us of rewarding social interaction," says Dr. Leary. "The frustration comes from not being able to interact as easily as we would like. We'd like to have rewards from our relationships just the way we'd like to have rewards from our jobs." In Dr. Leary's opinion, boring jobs are easier to change than boring people. "There are certain things you can do to change a boring job; you can often make it more interesting if you can get your employer's cooperation. But when it comes to changing a person, you need to change the way they interact." You need to teach them interpersonal skills.

To help convert boring acquaintances into tolerable ones, you could focus discussions on interesting things. If you both root for the home team, by all means discuss the repercussions of that error in the seventh inning. For friends and lovers, the advice is not as simple. "If you're really trying to bring out a spouse or a loved one, one of the best techniques is also one of the hardest – letting them know when they're being boring," says Dr. Leary.

He suggests you establish a manner of communication in which they encourage you to point out to them when their discussion treads mercilessly into areas that most people don't find interesting. Can you imagine yourself saying, "Dear, I'm so happy you could repair the brakes yourself, but I'm just not interested in the details"? Can you imagine your loved one's reply? Be aware that it's touchy telling someone he's a bore. "Unfortunately, it's much easier to tell a loved one or friend that they're untidy," says Dr. Leary.

The crusade against boredom has become a cottage industry for Alan Caruba, a writer and public relations consultant in Maplewood, New Jersey, who has given birth to The Boring Institute. A self-professed expert on boredom, Caruba sells a $2 poster that lists "25 Ways to Avoid Boredom" (they range from number 1, "Read a Book," to number 25, "Turn Off the TV"). And he is endlessly pursuing publicity for National Anti-Boredom Month, his designation for July. "It's July because if the first six months of your year have been boring, July is an opportunity to examine what aspects of your life have been boring – job, school, housework, whatever – and spend the other months changing it, to get yourself out of the rut of boredom," he says. For Caruba, at least, the crusade itself is one antidote for boredom.

Chapter 9

CAR TROUBLE

Sometimes it seems as if car ownership must have been written into the Bill of Rights. With more than 130 million of the vehicles on U.S. roads, Americans drive more than one-third of the world's cars. But our transportation of choice is also one of our biggest headaches: It's an engine that fails to start as you try to head to work on a blustery Minnesota morning, a tire that blows out as you enter the Lincoln Tunnel, the overheated engine during the freeway backup.

In the scope of the universe, these troubles are trivial, but as far as everyday setbacks go, they are among the most costly and, because they are seldom anticipated, among the most frustrating.

So the strategy for reducing the stress of unforeseen car trouble is to take charge of your vehicle. As much as possible, it should be you who controls the car, not vice versa.

Start out by avoiding the trap of driving beyond your means. "Amazing as it seems, it's possible to be happy driving a $6,000 car," says Andrew Tobias, a financial writer and author of *The Only OTHER Investment Guide You'll Ever Need*. He says, "Rather than buy a $16,000 car that you have to finance, buy a $6,000 car that you can afford. You'll get ahead of the game and get off the stressful treadmill."

Trading down helps you avoid the stress of car trouble in two ways. First, the most expensive models are generally costliest to maintain and insure. And second, if you are not forced to meet monthly payments for the car itself, you might be in better financial shape to maintain your car properly and even weather the unexpected. "If it's embarrassing to drive up in a $6,000 car," says Tobias, "just tell people your Jaguar's being repaired."

Triple-A Troubleshooting

One of the simplest, smartest and least expensive ways to reduce the stress of car ownership is to join the 27 million car owners who belong to the American Automobile Association (AAA). Annual membership ranges from $14 to $70 (average is $35), depending on which of the 161 affiliates you join and which services you select. At the very least, you will get emergency road service and towing, as well as such travel services as route advice and free maps. The membership fees include discounts on lodging and rental cars, insurance and financial services. (Contact your nearest AAA affiliate or call the AAA toll-free at 1-800-336-4357.)

And even if you don't ever intend to raise your car's hood, it makes sense to shell out $13.50 for the *Chilton Repair and Tune-Up Guide* for your model. Their basic repair guides cover every aspect of 125 car models. For non-do-it-yourselfers, these books unravel the mysteries of your automobile's innards and can make you more conversant with — and less intimidated by — your auto mechanic.

The people who feel least in control when car trouble occurs are those of us who don't budget for it. "A prudent car buyer will factor such expenses as insurance, taxes and standard maintenance into the price," says Daniel Kegan, Ph.D., a Chicago organizational psychologist who has researched the topic of the psychological meaning of money. He suggests car buyers check published reports on their model, particularly the data that indicate which parts are likely to wear out. That way a car's owner can save toward anticipated repairs. "Figure out how many miles you drive a year and estimate when you'll need new tires. Or look at other people's experience and see what's coming up," Dr. Kegan advises.

To get in the habit of planning realistically for car surprises, Dr. Kegan recommends that car owners make an estimate of what they think they will spend on their cars for a six-month period and then see how close they come to the projection. Those who budget 10 percent of their general expenditures for unexpected expenses will find themselves better prepared for car trouble.

"If you know you're the kind of person who takes that 'stitch in time,' who changes the oil regularly, you'll have fewer surprises. If you're not that kind, expect surprises and expect to spend more of your time and money on repairs," he says. "The more you can think ahead, or force yourself to, the better off you'll be."

A single example: Those of us who live in the North should designate a car winterization day sometime in mid-November and arrange to take the car in. Does mid-November seem too early? It's not, according to Dr. Kegan. His reasons are more "motive" than "automotive," however. "By planning ahead," he says, "you're more likely to be prepared when bad weather hits."

Chapter 10

COGNITIVE THERAPY

Picture yourself in a crowded elevator. Someone is standing on the back of your shoes. You're wondering who this obnoxious person is, and you're getting angrier and angrier by the second. Suddenly you turn around and see that it's a blind person, complete with sunglasses and a white cane.

Instantly, your anger subsides. You *thought* that person was intentionally abusing you, and your distorted thought produced a negative feeling.

That one simple example illustrates the basic principle of cognitive therapy, explains Fred Wright, Ed.D., of the University of Pennsylvania in Philadelphia. The principle is that thoughts determine feelings. And *negative* thoughts, or cognitions, almost always contain gross distortions. If we can identify our distorted negative thoughts, we can learn to change them. And if we can learn to change our distorted negative thoughts, we can change the bad feelings they produce. While thoughts aren't alone in creating bad feelings, they certainly have a major impact.

Dr. Wright, the educational director for the University of Pennsylvania's Center for Cognitive Therapy, explains that the way we interpret events has a powerful impact on the way we feel and the way we behave.

"If, when I hear a siren, I simply say to myself that a fire truck is passing, I'm not going to cause myself any difficulty," he says. "But if I say to myself that a fire truck is passing and my house may be on fire, that's going to have a strong emotional impact. So in cognitive therapy, we look for distortions in people's perceptions. Assuming that your house is on fire because you hear a fire truck siren is a distorted way of looking at something," he says.

Dangerous Assumptions

Carry the example a bit further. Every time your boss indicates he wants to see you in his office, do you jump to the conclusion that he's about to fire you? Your heart pounds and your stomach sinks. Every time you attend a party, do you assume that everyone will be criticizing your taste in clothes? You end up being defensive and critical – in advance – and get invited to fewer and fewer parties. Every time your daughter is late from a date, do you expect the worst – and find yourself fuming and infuriated, when there always seems to be a legitimate reason for her tardiness?

By using cognitive therapy, people can learn to be more objective and thus more realistic in the things they say to themselves. Cognitive therapists train us to sift through the rubbish that floats around in our minds, especially those thoughts that upset us and cause us to get into problems with our behavior.

Think how much better you'd feel if each time your boss told you to come into his office, you said to yourself, "I don't know what's going to happen, but it'll be new and different." Or if you went to parties saying, "Some people may not like my taste in clothes and maybe some people do not like me, but people won't dislike me simply because they don't like my clothes. Also, there are lots of people who like me – and some of them will be at the party." And when it comes to your daughter coming home late, wouldn't life be less stressful if you could say to yourself: "Well, my daughter's been late before and there always has been a reasonable excuse. Maybe I should explain that it's best to call, no matter what the hour is, if she knows she's going to be late. I've never told her how much I worry about her."

Your Cognitive Distortions

Cognitive therapists teach skills to identify, monitor and replace distorted thoughts that make you unhappy. The first step: When you are having negative feelings, look for the thoughts that may be lurking in the background. When you find your mood changes, when you suddenly discover that you are angry or anxious, do an instant replay. What was going through your mind, what were you saying to yourself that could have caused the change in mood? Says Dr. Wright, "Ask yourself if there is anything you could be saying to yourself that could possibly be a distortion or a dysfunctional thought, one that isn't serving a functional purpose."

We'll explain how you can answer these questions for yourself, but first you have to see what sorts of distortions may be reigning over your feelings. Which of the following are your personal favorites?

All-or-nothing thinking. Either the situation is right or it's wrong and there's nothing in between. If your careless driving results in a car accident, you blame yourself as being totally incompetent. If you lose your job, you blame yourself as being a total failure. It's unrealistic — not to mention stressful — to view the world in such black-and-white terms. It works the same way with your feelings. You may say you're stressed to the max and it's awful and terrible and you can't stand it, or you may say you don't have a care in the world. In reality, anxiety exists in varying levels all the time.

Jumping to conclusions. You have one bit of evidence (your car won't start, for instance), and you jump to the conclusion that the day is going to be a never-ending pattern of bad events. The results of your crucial lab test are held up by the hospital, and you jump to the conclusion that you're in for catastrophic news. In reality, the lab technician never showed up for work.

Mind reading. In this type of distortion, you assume you know what another person is thinking about you, and you almost always assume those thoughts are unkind. Take the following stressful situation: A waiter delivers a steak to a dissatisfied customer and is told to take it back to the kitchen. The waiter can make this stressful situation even more stressful by saying to himself, "The person at the table thinks I'm an idiot because I didn't get his order right."

"Catastrophizing." You take a situation and you blow it out of proportion. You grossly exaggerate the importance of a single mistake, saying, for example, "I forgot to mail the monthly payment. The bank is going to auction off my home." Think how much easier life would be if you said to yourself, "Okay, so I forgot to mail the mortgage payment; I'll take care of it right now."

"Awfulizing." "I'll never be able to make new friends in the new city and that will be awful."

Mental filtering. You take an experience, filter out the positive things about it and let only the negative things through. You focus on the fact that your son forgot your birthday (for the first time) and feel he is an ungrateful louse. You overlook his good qualities and all the nice things he's done for you over the years.

The tyranny of "shoulds." Also called "the fallacy of fairness," this distortion is based on the belief that things should be fair. "My boss shouldn't treat me that way." "My sister's kids shouldn't take advantage of her so often."

Overgeneralizing. "All of the neighbors don't like me all of the time." Just because one neighbor doesn't like you — or even several neighbors don't like you — doesn't mean they all do, and that all your friendships will be doomed. It's unrealistic to think you're locked into a never-ending pattern of defeat.

"Crystal-balling." "I know I'm never going to be happy in my new job." "I know the group will elect my opponent to be chairman." "I know our vacation will be a disappointment."

A Systematic Approach

Now that you know some of the major distortions, hunt them down in your thinking. You may find it difficult to become aware of how your vague, negative thoughts are producing feelings. So if you're feeling down in the dumps, for example, or if you're experiencing some of the physical symptoms of stress (the old butterflies-in-the-stomach syndrome, for instance) drag out some paper and a pencil and jot down three things:

Your situation ("My friend hasn't called").

Your feeling ("Sadness").

What you're telling yourself at the time ("He doesn't like me anymore. I'm worthless").

This little exercise will get you into the habit of understanding the connection between thoughts and feelings. The next step is to determine if what you're telling yourself is true. In this process, you may suddenly remember that your friend told you he was planning to be out of town this week. Or you may realize that your friend often is out of touch with everybody, not only with you.

Now you have to challenge your way of looking at the situation. That doesn't mean you should simply replace negative thoughts ("I'm worthless") with ones that are just as distorted, albeit positive ("I'm tremendous"). Accept that your worth as a human being doesn't depend, in this example, on hearing from your friend.

To get into the routine of answering negative thought patterns, divide another sheet of paper in half. On the left side, write out your negative thought ("I'm miserable because I'm never going to make friends with my daughter-in-law"). Then give it some serious thought and jot down a constructive answer ("That doesn't mean I'm an unworthy person. I've got lots of friends. Besides, my daughter-in-law is overwhelmed in a new job and has two infants to care for").

If you find that by arguing with your negative thoughts you are reinforcing them and becoming more anxious, you may be overdoing it, says Gary Emery, Ph.D., a Los Angeles cognitive therapist and author of *Rapid Relief from Emotional Distress.* If that's the case, he suggests you stop arguing. "Let the negative thoughts go and try to concentrate on what will produce a good feeling," he advises.

You can still work distorted negative thoughts out of your system, he says. "I'd have people buy a golf counter and every time they have a distorted thought, they click it and let go of the thought. Or make a mark on a three-by-five-inch card. And let go of the thought. Something about the counting allows you to distance yourself from the thought. And it reinforces that it's just a thought," he says. Another idea: Write down what your thoughts are and, when you're in a better mood, look at those thoughts and realize that they have no basis in reality.

When Negative Thoughts Are True

But your negative thought may turn out to be true, in which case you must look next at the realistic consequences and possible solutions.

Put things in their proper perspective. You may be disappointed that your daughter-in-law just plain doesn't want to be your friend, but it's not the end of the world.

If possible, try to problem-solve. Most therapists suggest you take small steps. Try to understand the daughter-in-law. Listen to her. And if the reality is that you won't be friends, accept the reality.

Finally, whether what you are saying to yourself is true or false, you must consider the disadvantages of continuing to say it. Examine the long-range impact on your feelings and behavior. The Pygmalion Effect dictates that people tend to get what they expect. "If someone tells you that a person you're about to meet is really bright, you'd tend to notice the bright things they say in a conversation," says Dr. Wright.

So if you're anxious and think you'll be awkward in a social situation, that will make you more anxious and you will be more awkward. If you expect the worst in any situation, that may be what you'll notice. Advises Dr. Emery: Focus on the positive, on what you want to see happen.

If thought are true, then try the 3 P's
1. Permanent - will last forever
2. Pervasive - colors everything in your world
3. Personal - your fault

Chapter 11

COLITIS

When it comes to life-disrupting ailments, colitis can be among the worst.

The most prevalent version of this disease is known as ulcerative colitis – inflammation of the colon lining. And as structural abnormalities go, this one takes quite a toll. Not only are its symptoms painful, but when flare-ups occur, regular day-to-day activities scarcely can go on as normal. For one thing, you spend most of your time enthroned on the nearest toilet.

A 46-year-old Philadelphia woman recalls her agony: "On two separate occasions I spent almost a year of my life in bed. I spent all of my time – that's *all* of my time – either in the bedroom or the bathroom."

In the acute phase of the disease, you have severe diarrhea, usually with blood, and up to 24 stools a day. Your inflamed bowel makes it difficult to absorb the nutrients in your food, so you may experience nutritional deficits – and possible weight loss. If you lose too much blood, you may become anemic. On top of that, there is abdominal pain – usually *lots* of it. And fever.

According to the National Foundation for Ileitis and Colitis, between one and two million people suffer from the ravages of Crohn's disease (or ileitis) and ulcerative colitis. These are often baffling – and sometimes genetically inherited – diseases.

At least ten times as many people are afflicted by a less severe condition that may be confused with colitis. It is called irritable bowel syndrome, or IBS, but it has been known by other names, too. (Sometimes IBS is referred to as spastic colon. And because its sufferers may pass mucus, it was once poorly termed mucous colitis.) "IBS is not a form of colitis," says Richard Johannes, M.D., a gastroenterologist at Johns Hopkins University School of Medicine, Baltimore, Maryland.

Irritable bowel syndrome, which hits 50 to 75 percent of us at one time or another, involves the alternating symptoms of diarrhea and constipation. And as its sufferers know well, there are abdominal pains. The mystery about IBS is that there's no known cause or associated disease responsible for producing the annoying symptoms (unlike colitis, where colon inflammation is the source of the problem).

What is known, however, is that the symptoms can be aggravated by stress. "It's not too uncommon that the symptoms are worsened with physical or mental stress," says Sidney Phillips, M.D., professor of medicine and gastroenterology at Mayo Medical School, Rochester, Minnesota. He adds that "stress makes it less easy to tolerate the symptoms."

And while doctors prescribe everything from anti-inflammatory agents to antidiarrheal drugs to iron medication to dietary changes to treat the symptoms of colitis and IBS, there is a movement to treat patients through stress management.

Stress Management to the Rescue

And why not? Here's a look at some of the evidence that stress management helps keep these ailments in check.

First, colitis.

In a study conducted by faculty members at the University of British Columbia School of Nursing, Vancouver, researchers determined that a stress-management program can greatly boost the physical and psychosocial well-being of colitis sufferers. Of 80 people in the study, half participated in a stress-management program and half were designated as a control group. The stress-management group attended 18 hours of classes that combined autogenic training (see chapter 5) and progressive relaxation. Also, they were taught communication skills such as assertiveness training and active listening in a group setting. And they were given instruction in personal planning skills—worry control and time management.

"Worry control was important because when you have a condition like this [ulcerative colitis], it becomes understandable that you become worried about recurrences and about coping when you're in an acute episode," says Barbara Milne, R.N., an assistant professor of nursing at the University of British Columbia School of Nursing and one of the study's authors. (The participants used some of the worry-control techniques outlined in chapter 60.)

Time management also is crucial. If you've got colitis, chances are you're not going to get around to doing everything you want to do. And the resulting pileup of chores and commitments can overwhelm you and contribute to your symptoms.

This is a lesson learned by one colitis sufferer, who says, "Over the years I realized that when I had so much to do, so many commitments to fulfill, I would get sick so that I had an excuse not to do them. Later I learned that my life would go on if I say no to commitments. I can relax and free my mind of the worry of not doing them."

In the Canadian study, the group that practiced stress management watched happily as their disease activity dwindled. They also discovered a boost in their mental health. For the other group, there was no reported change.

Hypnotherapy May Help

A separate study showed that hypnotherapy may help colitis sufferers. Edward Taub, Ph.D., a professor of psychology at the University of Alabama at Birmingham, and Alan Ginsberg, M.D., director of the gastroenterology clinic at George Washington University School of Medicine in Washington, D.C., tracked 25 patients from that clinic. The patients underwent eight hypnosis sessions that searched for the events that triggered colitis flare-ups. Under hypnosis, it was suggested to the patients that they could handle the illness and its symptoms. The hypnosis also included some suggestions for relaxation, according to Dr. Taub. The results? There was a general reduction in symptoms among half of the patients receiving hypnotherapy.

There's also hope in massage and deep breathing therapies. Both of these techniques helped colitis patients to cope with their plight. In a study of 15 people by Gloria Joachim, R.N., an assistant professor of nursing at the University of British Columbia School of Nursing, a majority were able to get to sleep more quickly and feel they had some control over pain. They also discovered ways of quickly calming themselves.

Experts suggest that a colitis sufferer find a stress-management program he or she can live with. "The point is to develop a personal plan that gives the body a break and helps relieve the stress for a certain time every day," says Milne. "The best stress-management technique is the one you can do every day and can incorporate into your lifestyle." Adds Dr. Phillips, "If you can make some modifications in your lifestyle so that physically and mentally you may be under less stress, it's a useful thing to add."

An important first step may be to learn all you can about colitis. For information, write to the headquarters of the National Foundation for Ileitis and Colitis, 444 Park Avenue South, New York, NY 10016. And if you've got colitis, keep this important fact in mind: Patients with colitis have a higher-than-normal risk of developing cancer of the colon or rectum. So you should be examined regularly to detect early treatable cancers.

Self-Help Groups for IBS

New Jersey psychologist Rosemarie Scolaro Moser, Ph.D., works with a lot of IBS sufferers and has built a repertoire of sound advice.

Education. Very often people with IBS are convinced they have the more serious colitis or worse yet cancer. Dr. Scolaro Moser advises that if your doctor diagnoses IBS, you should learn all you can about the disorder. The knowledge that you're suffering from a problem, not a dangerous disease, will go a long way toward reducing anxiety. This in turn may help reduce flare-ups. (To learn more about IBS, write to the American Digestive Disease Society, 7720 Wisconsin Avenue, Bethesda, MD 20814, or phone 301-652-9293.)

Groups. Wouldn't it be great to discuss your ailment without embarrassment? Self-help groups for IBS sufferers, while hard to find, can provide support and maybe a few coping strategies. Imagine laughing with friends who suffer from the same discomfort. To start a group, contact your gastroenterologist and ask to post a notice in his office. You may want a professional psychotherapist to lead the group. If your physician can't recommend someone, try your local mental health agency or the psychology department of a nearby university hospital.

Relaxation techniques. Virtually any relaxation technique that works for you will help you manage your IBS, says Dr. Scolaro Moser.

Therapy. Don't get the impression that all IBS sufferers need to pour out their souls to a shrink, but if your IBS is out of control, a therapist might guide you to the proper stress-management technique. A cognitive behavior therapist may show you how cognitive restructuring – such as learning to challenge the belief that you have to be perfect – can help alleviate IBS.

Chapter 12

COMMUTING

Freeway crawlers in Southern California's San Fernando Valley can tune their car radios to KWNK-AM for instant temporary relief from the morning rush. Sometime around 7:45, radio personality "Sweet" Dick Whittington spins exercise music and leads commuters in "aerobics" for the rush-hour bound. "Lift your left bun. [Pause] Lower your left bun. Lift your right bun...." For more than a decade, Whittington's "The Aching Buns Boogey" feature has created a rare, pleasant diversion from the tense monotony of commuting to work by car. But it's not much.

Whatever the mode of travel, there's no question that commuting is stressful. It's particularly vexing when travelers find the situation out of their control. The traffic jam or the stalled subway train are likely to bring out the worst in even the least aggressive folks. In fact, it is "laid back" Type B personalities, not the traditionally competitive Type A's, who are more sensitive to traffic stress, according to Daniel Stokols, Ph.D., a University of California, Irvine, social ecology professor. He studied 100 traffic-congestion-plagued commuters and determined that the Type B personalities among them performed worse and had higher blood pressure readings when they arrived at work than did the Type A commuters.

In 1984, anxiety over arriving at work late caused 27,619 subway riders to phone New York City's Transit Authority for official "late slips" to take to the office. To reduce the number of individual telephone requests for subway delay verifications it received, the Transit Authority in 1986 began signing up major New York employers, who are now informed when subway trains are late.

Take Control

Such programs help a little, but there are stress-reducing steps commuters can take even when the train runs on time or the traffic is a breeze. *The key is in seizing as much control of the commute as is possible.* Jerome E. Singer, Ph.D., a professor of medical psychology at the Uniform Services University of the Health Sciences in Bethesda, Maryland, studied train commuters in Sweden and car commuters in the United States and determined that "the extent to which people feel they can control the situation is more important than the physical characteristics of the route."

In his study of rail commuters, for instance, he determined that those whose trips lasted 1½ hours experienced less stress than those who rode for 45 minutes. The reason: The longer riders boarded earlier and had the opportunity to choose well-located seats; those who boarded later saw that the territory had already been carved up and felt they had little control.

How to take control of your commuter stress?

Drive your car alone. If you like to exercise control over the route you take, your traffic behavior or the atmosphere in the car, it makes sense to go alone. But if the social atmosphere is more important than controlling the ride, travel in a van or car pool.

Make some conscious stress-reducing driving decisions. "Don't contest everybody trying to change lanes. If you let someone in, you are exercising some control. By doing so, you make it less stressful for yourself," says Dr. Singer.

Get a mobile phone. That way you can phone ahead if you're running late.

Sign up for a flexible work schedule. If your company offers it, a flexible work schedule will enable you to commute during non-rush hours.

Ride trains in a group. While you may not enjoy having others in your *auto,* riding on a train with your friends will establish the internal atmosphere of the car, suggests Dr. Singer.

Sleep on the train. New York's Metro-North commuter rail ferries 180,000 riders each day and figures a lot of them use the time to catch up on sleep. The color-coordinated interiors of its cars combine shades that are calming to the senses.

Read on the train. In one busy commuter train station, the DeKalb Public Library and the Metropolitan Atlanta Rapid Transit Authority installed a prefabricated, modular, 160-square-foot kiosk—a special library for commuters. The "read and ride" library branch is open during the commuter rush (6:30-10:00 A.M. and 3:30-7:00 P.M.). "Many of our users are commuters who would like to read but don't have time to get to the library," says Barbara Loar, the library director responsible for the project. "People are hungry for information. Whenever they have a spare moment, when they ride a train or ride a bus, it's an ideal time to add to their knowledge."

Chapter 13

COMPETITION

"The world is not a football game," says Elliot Aronson, Ph.D. This simple sentence sounds like the practical advice of a caring grandparent who knows better, who knows that for many people the world *is* a football game but knows also that life would be less stressful if it weren't viewed as such.

The University of California, Santa Cruz, psychology professor once conducted several experiments on elementary school classes. In the experiment, students were taught to cooperate, not compete, on projects. The clear results were superior performances, as detailed in his book *The Jigsaw Classroom.* "They achieved better grades on exams, their self-esteem improved, they liked each other better, ethnic stereotypes diminished and absenteeism decreased," says Dr. Aronson.

The evidence against competition is growing rapidly. In 1985, Robert Helmreich, Ph.D., of the University of Texas, Austin, and his associates studied seven different groups of people, groups as diverse as scientists, undergraduates and airline reservations agents. Dr. Helmreich, a psychology professor, determined that on a consistent basis, in work and in school, the participants who exhibited the most competitive personality traits were those who performed worst.

Interesting news. But how does this information help those of us who try to seek out a living in workplaces that are only slightly less competitive than the Army-Navy game? How does it help those of us who find our friendships soured by an undeclared contest? How can we keep competition in proper perspective?

"It's hard to," answers Dr. Aronson, "because the whole society, from kinder-garten on up, is geared toward competition." Dr. Aronson's the-world-is-not-a-football-game advice is a start in the long task of putting stressful competition in its place. Robert L. James, M.D., an assistant clinical professor of psychology at UCLA, adds, "A person needs to ask 'What's really at stake? What's the worst thing that could happen if I lose?' "

He echoes the sentiments of many health professionals who believe competition is not uniformly unhealthy. "It depends on each individual's reaction to competition," says Dr. James.

"Acknowledge that there's nothing wrong with competition unless you're out to annihilate the other person," says Lillian Rubin, Ph.D., psychologist and senior research associate at the Institute for the Study of Social Change, University of California, Berkeley, and author of *Just Friends: The Role of Friendship in Our Lives.*

Keeping Up Is Hard to Do

Among the most irksome forms of competition is the unspoken rivalry with friends and neighbors over status. The sports car, the backyard pool, the new dinette set – these possessions often aren't bought because we *need* them. They're bought to use like flashing neon signs signaling to the Joneses, "RICH, RICH, RICH." Then we can only hope they don't buy a sign that says "RICHER, RICHER, RICHER."

Once trapped in such a game, it can be stressful, frustrating and *expensive* to keep up. "If people are in such a competition, it's important for them to recognize it and to know what's motivating them," says Lillian Rubin, Ph.D., psychologist and senior research associate at the Institute for the Study of Social Change, University of California, Berkeley. "Such behavior can be controlled and devalued," she says.

Paul Wright, Ph.D., a psychology professor at the University of North Dakota who has studied male friendships for nearly two decades, says, "Try to adapt a more balanced perspective in what is important in life. Recognize that there are rewards in life other than material successes – like having friends and keeping friends. I know, it's easy to say and hard to do."

So count your rewards and seek your own rewards. But don't worry about measuring up to the folks next door. "In most situations, another person's gain does not have to be our loss," says Elliot Aronson, Ph.D., a professor of psychology at the University of California, Santa Cruz. "That's something that has to be taught in elementary school."

Initially, those of us who are concerned that competition is too pervasive could take a survey of our own competitive impulses. This involves understanding what kind of competitors we are, why we compete, and what's at stake when we do.

Sam Osherson, Ph.D., author of *Finding Our Fathers,* explains that our competitive behaviors are rooted in childhood experience. The patterns of competition we learned as children competing with parents and siblings are revived in the workplace family. So we have our backgrounds to blame for the manner in which we compete – or how well we compete. Then we have employers who often deliberately pit workers against each other in the belief that everybody's performance will be improved.

Calling for Time Out

At its harshest, competition stirs up basic fears of survival, fears that are not realistic in some work environments. For those who don't want to compete or who don't feel comfortable in such an atmosphere, the wisest move often is to get out before too much damage is done. Even if you survive the job, you might lose your health. "If survival in the workplace is on the line, then competition will lead to chronic elevated levels of stress that certainly can be related to causing illness," explains Dr. James.

"The art of living involves finding what kind of lifestyle is most suited to a person. There are people who are not well suited to highly competitive environments. Bow out of a competitive line of work if it doesn't fit your personality," he says.

But that doesn't necessarily mean you have to find a new job because, in your current one, you're routinely "tackled" by fellow employees. Instead, you might try learning how to deal with and control the competition rather than be shocked when it occurs. "Accept it as something that's normal and learn the skills for managing it," suggests Robert E. Lefton, Ph.D., an organizational psychologist and president of Psychological Associates, Inc., in St. Louis.

"In the workplace, a lot of stress is produced by competitive interpersonal relationships. So you can teach people how to have better people skills," Dr. Lefton says. Consider how you handle disagreements with co-workers.

"When it comes to routine disagreements, you've got a choice," he continues. "You could squelch it, going along as though a disagreement doesn't exist. Or you could treat it lightly. Or you could acknowledge it, which involves probing and problem solving.

"Suppressing, smoothing over or avoiding can spin up to a very high degree of stress. Problem solving is the most effective means of dealing with a disagreement. It can be stressful up front, but the long-term results are good," he says.

Here are Dr. Lefton's solutions to a touchy, competitive workplace problem. Suppose you frequently find yourself arguing with someone at work. You could confront that person in a negative "win/lose" manner, warning that "If you try to get me, I'll get you." Or you could smooth it over, saying, "Well, we argue, but it's really not *that* significant." Neither of these responses will lessen stress. The first is a declaration of war, and the second just submerges the tension and feelings of distress. Instead, you might try a third option. You could openly state your concern, saying, "I'm very upset and concerned about our constant arguing. As a result of our bickering, our discussions deteriorate and our work suffers. What can we do to solve this problem?"

According to Dr. Lefton, "Anything that requires confrontation requires courage and assertiveness. For some people that's stressful. But when you weigh it against possible long-term gains, you can save a great deal of stress. There's no magic. All you can do is increase the probability that you'll relate better."

A Buddy System

Business consultants tell employees to try to have good relations with workplace competitors. But if that notion sounds contradictory, consider the awkward — and often destructive — role that competition plays in friendships.

In her book on friendships, Dr. Rubin explains that in male friendships, "The competitive thrust is overt and direct; with women, it's hidden from view, too often covered with a smile, a veneer of warmth and friendliness that bodes ill for the kind of trust a friendship requires."

The bottom line is that most men, because they are openly competitive, have difficulty forming intimate friendships. Most women, because they are unwilling to acknowledge competition with friends, may destroy the intimate friendships they have. "Women's inability to deal directly with competitive feelings is a source of difficulty in their relations with each other. For whether the motive is to compete or to avoid competition, it creates a similar distance between friends."

There's another problem. Dr. Rubin points out that it's particularly stressful to compete against someone with whom you have an emotional involvement. "You want to win," she says, "and don't want to win."

One step toward keeping competition between friends from getting out of hand: Acknowledge the competition, acknowledge the feelings of jealousy and guilt. And acknowledge the affection. Dr. Osherson says that between men, at least there's a strong undercurrent of affection beneath the competitive surface.

"Healthy, mature relationships include mixed feelings toward those whom we love," says Dr. James. "Real maturity, real intimacy requires working through these feelings, embracing these feelings and coming to terms with them as a normal, healthy part of the human experience, rather than denying them, throwing them out the window." As with the competitive co-worker, tell your friend how you feel.

The outlook for competitive friendships does not have to be bleak. Paul Wright, Ph.D., a University of North Dakota psychology professor who has collected data on 5,000 male friendships since 1968, says, "When men become really good friends, the competitive element disappears. It's a matter of just gradually lowering guards and becoming more secure with one another."

But developing such friendships with "strong security value" takes time, he says. And they are not limited by gender.

Dr. Helmreich warns that it's "darn hard" to view the world in noncompetitive terms if the people we encounter are relentless competitors. Still, you can set a cooperative tone by relaxing.

"Look at one another as being on the same team rather than needing to beat one another," says Dr. Aronson. "In most situations, doing well does not have to be consistent with beating someone. Relax," he says. "Do the best you can and cheer for the others to do as well."

Chapter 14

CORONARY ARTERY DISEASE

You probably won't be surprised to know that coronary artery disease is the major health problem in the industrialized world today. Yet the five biggest risk factors – high blood pressure, high cholesterol, diabetes, overweight and smoking – fail to explain half of the worldwide cases of coronary artery disease. Stress accounts for a good portion of the rest.

Is heart disease the price we pay for living with twentieth-century stress?

"We have the bodies of our ancestors, yet we are living in a world they never dreamed would exist," says Robert Eliot, M.D., director of the cardiovascular unit of the Swedish Medical Center in Denver, Colorado. "Mankind has been around for 1,600 generations, 1,300 of which we spent in caves. The major stresses were physical and triggered physical reactions, including higher heart rate and blood pressure. Today's stresses are more often mental than physical: We face 30 or 40 mental 'saber-toothed tigers' a day that may trigger the same sort of physical reactions. So those who interpret mental stress the same way as a physical threat are activating out-of-date ancestral responses that can be suicidal," says Dr. Eliot, author of *Is It Worth Dying For?*

Like most people, you probably assume that a sudden, overwhelming shock can send your heart into a dither – and you into the nearest coronary care unit. And a major upset can trigger a heart attack. But what you may not realize is that *chronic* stress also threatens your heart in other, less obvious but equally threatening ways, either directly or by increasing risk factors such as cholesterol levels.

What Gets Your Goat, Gets Your Heart

Did you know, for example, that nervous tension can raise your cholesterol levels as easily as eating a ham and cheese omelet? Or that giving up in the face of a stressful event is as bad for your blood pressure as getting fighting mad? What's more, a low-cholesterol, low-salt diet doesn't cancel out the effect.

One of the most significant effects of the acute stress response is the damage it can wreak on heart muscle fibers. "[The stress reaction] actually takes bites out of the heart muscles," says Dr. Eliot. "It can overcontract the small muscle fibers until some of them rip." This leaves the heart vulnerable to arrhythmias – a heart spasm that can cause sudden death.

Pulling the Plug on Stress

The difficulty in overcoming this problem is that different types of stress affect different people in different ways at different times. "That's why there is no objective definition of what a stressful event is or how many events add up to 'too much' stress," says Dr. Eliot, who also directs the National Center of Preventive and Stress Medicine in Phoenix, Arizona, and serves on the Prevention Committee of the American College of Cardiology.

"Identifying the sources of stress in your life is simple," says Dr. Eliot. "Just ask yourself, 'What three things bug me the most?' Right off the bat, most people say it's something like traffic, deadlines or a relationship. Once you identify and deal with the Big Three, you can uncover – and deal with – less obvious secondary sources of stress."

Dr. Eliot compares stress with overloaded circuitry. "If you have six or seven appliances plugged into an electrical outlet and unplug three, you lighten the load considerably."

Another simple way to assess your stress levels and therefore your heart disease risk, according to Dr. Eliot, is to ask yourself, "Am I working, or am I struggling?"

"A famous physiologist from Sweden, Dr. Bjorn Folkow, discovered that when animals struggle and perceive they can't win, their metabolism changes and they roll over and die," explains Dr. Eliot. "Similarly, if you work hard yet feel you're getting somewhere, you'll feel fulfilled, your blood pressure will usually be fine, your immune system will coast along smoothly and you'll be okay. But if you struggle and don't feel you're making any headway, you could be in big trouble. Being caught in the 'struggle/defeat syndrome' is a tough way to get through the day, let alone your whole life.

"In other words, if you feel that deadlines will kill you, they probably will. But if you feel they're unreasonable yet probably won't kill you, they probably won't," says Dr. Eliot.

Mastering Stress

Sometimes, life seems to be just one big "in box" for stress. Here are seven ways to manage that stress – and your reaction to it.

Don't overreact. Some people call it "making a mountain out of a molehill." Dr. Eliot calls it "burning a dollar's worth of energy for a dime's worth of trouble." Call it what you will, chronic overreaction grossly overworks your heart and arteries.

Talk yourself down from the brink. Psychologists use a technique known as cognitive therapy that deals with "self-talk" to help people cut down on self-induced stress when things don't go their way. Suppose you're waiting for friends to pick you up for dinner, for example, and they're 15 minutes late. Irrational, negative self-talk – saying that "People should always be punctual" or "Lateness shows that a person doesn't care how you feel" – creates unnecessary stress. Positive self-talk, on the other hand – saying, "That's okay, I'll use the time to finish a project I'm working on" – is a positive, less stress-producing reaction.

"The most important conversations you'll ever have are with yourself," Dr. Eliot quips. "So watch your language!"

Stand back and consider all your options. According to Dr. Eliot, managing stress actually means managing the anger and anxiety you feel in a stressful situation so that, rather than being overwhelmed, you can see options available – and solve the problem.

Learn to say no. Dr. Eliot says "no" is the most lifesaving word in the English language, especially for heart attack candidates, who tend to try to do more than is realistically possible.

Set realistic expectations for yourself and others. "Much self-induced stress – especially guilt and perfectionism – arises from expectations that cannot be met," says Dr. Eliot. "So ask yourself, 'Am I asking more of human performance than can be expected?' Aim for excellence, not perfection. After all, not even machines are always perfect."

Make friends. "The data are definitely in: Social support reduces the impact of stress on the heart," says Dr. Eliot. "And that includes having a spouse and friends you can confide in or count on in the face of uncertainty. So ask yourself, 'Do I know someone who would lend me money if I needed it? Who would give me a lift if I needed a ride? Who would let me spend the night at their place if I had nowhere to go?' With friends in the wings, you'll survive."

Find a relaxation technique that suits you, and practice it daily. "Relaxation methods are like music: We all like different kinds," says Dr. Eliot. "Most people can learn and use deep breathing, for example, but not everyone can do visualization. So try various methods, and adopt the ones you like best."

And remember, says Dr. Eliot, that learning to control your emotional responses to everyday stress – just like learning any skill – takes practice.

A Prescription for the 21st Century

Small adjustments in coping style can make big differences in heart health. "Like aiming for any target, one small adjustment can determine whether you hit the bull's-eye or miss the target entirely," says Dr. Eliot.

"People who've completed our preventive program can control their blood pressure without medication," he adds. "Their cholesterol levels dropped. They feel less anxiety, hostility and depression. They have fewer arguments, headaches, backaches or sleep interruptions. In short, their physiology cools off, even among people in high-pressure, commission sales jobs. What's more, their incomes have risen anywhere from 40 to over 200 percent – yet they work an average of 50 hours a week instead of 70."

The benefits to your heart and to your quality of life are tremendous. No wonder one doctor calls Dr. Eliot's prescription "medicine for the twenty-first century."

Chapter 15

DEADLINES

Tia O'Brien, a political reporter for Philadelphia's KYW-TV, arrived at work at 10:00 A.M. and immediately traveled crosstown to cover a relatively routine and predictable assignment. She would have enough time, she figured, to gather tape, do her interview, travel with her cameraman to different parts of the city to get on-camera reactions and then return to the television station to write her story, shoot a "stand-up close," edit the story and fight for time on the 5:30 or 6:00 P.M. newscast. It was to be an easy, well-paced day.

But shortly after noon the day was thrown into a frenzy. The state treasurer — recently convicted of bribery – killed himself during a news conference.

O'Brien instinctively knew that her original story was now nothing more than a ten-second announcement for the news show. She had to shift gears quickly and rearrange her day in order to meet the same 5:30 deadline, but with a vastly different and exceedingly more difficult story.

First she mentally calculated how much time it would take to gather and produce the breaking suicide story. By 1:00 P.M. she knew that her new assignment was to produce the "reaction" story and that she would have to begin the final editing stage by 5:00.

She had to factor in the snow-covered roads, unavailable sources, the difficulty in tracking down "background" film of the late state treasurer and the reluctance of other politicians to offer taped reaction to the suicide. And as happens every day, she had to be realistic in accounting for other possible setbacks: tape editing machines that are being used by other reporters or faulty camera equipment — a bad battery, for instance — that could send her mercilessly behind schedule.

"I always keep a mental timetable as the day goes on. I have to calculate backward how much time each process could take. In other words, by 1:00 P.M., when I started out on my new assignment, I knew I only had four hours left before I had to start editing," she says.

Given the city's snow-paralyzed streets, O'Brien opted to do telephone interviews. "When the blizzard intensified, I knew that I would jeopardize my whole piece if I left the building," she says.

In the end, it all worked out because O'Brien, like most successful people, has mastered the difficult art of meeting deadlines. As the example suggests, meeting deadlines – and reducing the stress of deadlines – is often a matter of setting up priorities, scheduling your time accordingly and making an effort to stick to both priorities and schedule. The strategy is the same for a television reporter's minutes-away deadline as it is for a bookkeeper's quarterly deadline or an academician's years-long deadline. By prioritizing and scheduling, you gain control.

Being Realistic about Your Time

"Many people are unrealistic about time. They either overestimate how long something will take or they underestimate," says Jane Burka, Ph.D., a Berkeley, California, psychologist. "The first thing to do is anticipate realistically how long a task will take and how much time you can spend on it. For instance, if a project is due in a week and you're feeling optimistic about that deadline, check your calendar. Are your in-laws coming to visit on one of those days? Do you have an all-day meeting another day?"

"You have to take steps now to ensure that you'll complete what you have to do. For instance, tell your secretary *today* that you have to be uninterrupted tomorrow while you work on your project. Working without interruption would be difficult to do when it's already tomorrow and your phone's ringing all day," adds Ronald Drabman, Ph.D., professor and director of clinical psychology at the University of Mississippi Medical Center.

If you've set aside the time to work, you should also have a clear sense of your priorities, suggests Dr. Drabman. You have to consider all the tasks you have to do, then put them in order of importance. And chances are, if you don't get to some of the lower priorities on your list, they weren't very important – or they were things you couldn't possibly have done, given your timetable.

In addition to putting tasks in order, you also should prioritize your deadlines. "One thing that is helpful in reducing the stress of deadlines is to make up in your mind which deadlines are really important and which ones are flexible," says Dr.

Burka. "On one hand, you might say you want to finish reading a book by Friday, or you want to get a new job by Christmas. These are self-imposed deadlines, which can be flexible. Then there are deadlines of real consequence – such as the date by which you must pay your traffic tickets or register your car. These deadlines are inflexible. Meet them first."

Gaining Control

To gain control, think of doing the project in very specific steps. "Rather than saying you have to have the quarterly report completed by Thursday and proceeding blindly, break down the project into very small and manageable tasks. For a six-page quarterly report, you might have to gather the financial data, talk to three people in your department and look at the last two years' worth of reports. Realistically assess the time required for each," says Dr. Burka, coauthor of the book *Procrastination: Why You Do It, What to Do about It.*

To minimize the stress of a deadline, Dr. Burka suggests you pick out the first step you can accomplish within 15 minutes and do it. "A person can stand almost anything for 15 minutes," she says, "and you may feel better that you're on your way to meeting your deadline. Then make a note to yourself about what you have to do next."

Breaking up a project, making a deal with yourself to work only 15 minutes and rewarding yourself for completing a task are methods of seducing yourself into working toward your deadline. There are others. "I simply turn on my computer," says T. Thorne Wiggers, Ed.D., a counseling psychologist at George Washington University, Washington, D.C. "That way, I figure that I might as well write just the beginning of whatever it is I have to write, since the computer is already on. Or if I'm preparing my taxes, I'll collect all my receipts. Then I say to myself, 'Now that I've got all the receipts together, I might as well sort them into categories.' "

The Procrastinator's Profile

Such tips are fine, but a person plagued with a tendency to procrastinate should also look below the surface to understand why he or she has trouble meeting deadlines.

Some procrastinators take *every* deadline so seriously that they can't distinguish between those that are rigid and those that are flexible. Such people "have to question their assumption that they are being judged by every challenge that they face. They need to realize that doing everything is impossible and that the stress of perfectionism is very costly," says Dr. Burka.

Other people procrastinate out of rebellion. For instance, they may delay paying taxes because they are angry about having to do it. Still other procrastinators operate out of a fear of failure. They figure that if they procrastinate and then they don't do well, they can blame the procrastination rather than their ability. "What they're doing is protecting themselves from finding out if they would or wouldn't fail if they didn't procrastinate," says Dr. Wiggers.

Then there are people who use deadlines as motivators. These folks might do well at meeting deadlines, but the process takes its toll. These are people who cling to the motto, "I can only work under pressure."

Dr. Wiggers is skeptical of such a statement. "I ask those people how it feels working under pressure and to describe to me how it would feel if they did the work over a long period of time relative to a short period of time. I ask them what the quality of their work would be like if they took the time instead of jamming it up against a deadline. For some people it might be fine. But for others, there are signs that it isn't. They complain of ulcers, headaches and of drinking too much to deal with the stress."

For some, however, cramming really is best. Dr. Drabman divides most people into two groups in terms of how they accomplish tasks: plotters and crammers. Plotters chop off sections of work and proceed accordingly. Crammers wait until the last minute and work in a panic.

"Parents often tell children they have to be plotters. That makes sense except that lots of successful people function fine doing things at the last minute," he says. "So sometimes we try to be a way we are not, to be plotters instead of crammers, and that causes stress. Our natural inclinations could be successful. So the first thing you should do is whatever comes naturally to you. If what comes naturally doesn't work, if it provides stress, then you'll have to change.

"If you're a natural crammer, for instance, and you need the tension cramming induces but you find your cramming is causing too much stress, you could at least set some subgoals. That is, cram for parts of a project at a time."

Chapter 16

DEEP BREATHING

Ever notice how a newborn baby breathes? Deep and slow and rhythmic. A baby's tiny abdomen is relaxed, and he pulls air into his lungs easily and fully.

Now how do you breathe? Chances are your breaths are shallow, and it's your chest that rises and falls with each breath, not your gut. Sorry, but after all these years you've forgotten how to breathe in a way that will increase your oxygen supply and revitalize your body's tissues and organs — and keep you naturally relaxed and at ease.

Stress takes a long-term toll on your breathing. "Under stress, rather than breathing all the way down to your abdomen, your breath becomes short and shallow," says Jeffrey A. Migdow, M.D., Lenox, Massachusetts, holistic physician and coauthor of *Take a Deep Breath.* Your breath probably only goes as far as your upper chest and then stops. Or you hold your breath. Or you do panting breaths.

Even if you were perfectly calm to start, such breathing automatically produces stress and reinforces stress. And what's worse, you become used to it.

Dr. Migdow says that when you breathe shallowly, the oxygen level of your blood drops and the carbon dioxide level takes a jump. To get rid of that carbon dioxide, you feel the need to breathe harder. But stress tenses up your breathing apparatus. "As the diaphragm tenses, abdominal and intercostal [between the ribs] muscles constrict and you lose the ability to inhale deeply and naturally at the very moment you need it most," he says.

If you don't believe it, try breathing with quick, shallow breaths for a minute and see how tense you feel.

The Abdominal Breath

So before we offer some special breathing exercises for the times you feel stressed, let's give you a simple refresher course on how nature intended you to breathe all the time. It's called "abdominal breathing," and it's so simple a newborn can do it. Here's how Ronald Dushkin, M.D., of the Kripalu Center for Yoga and Health in Massachusetts teaches the method.

1. Start by sitting in a relaxed position with your spine straight and shoulders back (but down and loose) to allow your lungs to expand. Rest your hands on the arms of your chair or in your lap. Put your feet flat on the floor.
2. Breathe in slowly through your nose as you expand your abdomen. Imagine that you have a balloon inside your abdomen and, as you inhale, you're slowly inflating it, causing the abdominal area to swell.
3. Breathe out slowly through your nose. Pull your abdominal muscles in as you press all the air out of your lungs.
4. Continue breathing in and out as your abdomen rises and falls. Establish a natural rhythm. (Hint: Place your hands on your abdomen just above the navel with fingertips pointing toward each other and just touching. If you're breathing correctly, your hands will rise with your abdomen as you inhale, and your fingertips will separate. As you exhale, they'll touch again.)

Eventually, you'll get in the habit of breathing this way all of the time. And you will find yourself more relaxed and pleasantly energized. But for those moments of high stress, take the time to reverse the fight-or-flight response with some special deep breathing exercises from *Take a Deep Breath*.

The cleansing breath. This is a good, quick exercise you can practice anytime you want to release tension.

1. Inhale deeply through your nose.
2. Exhale through your puckered mouth, as if you were blowing out a candle.
3. Repeat steps 1 and 2 three times.
4. Issue a few sighs. Inhale deeply, then sigh. Again. Again. With each sigh, drop your chin to your chest and droop your shoulders. Think of yourself as a tire letting all its air out. Think of the tension you are releasing.

The stress-discharging breath. Allow more time to do this exercise. It's perfect for after work.

1. Make sure you will not be disturbed.
2. Get into a comfortable position, lying down or sitting in a favorite chair. Loosen any constricting clothing.
3. Start relaxing with several abdominal breaths; breathe in to the count of four, then breathe out to the count of eight.
4. Take a deep breath through your nose and hold it. Tense your feet as long as you can. (Warning: If you have a history of heart disease, high blood pressure or stroke, consult your physician about this technique. He or she may suggest a modified version, with little or no breath-holding.)
5. Relax your feet as you exhale with a sigh through your mouth.
6. Take a few abdominal breaths with each count, as in step 3.
7. Breathe in deeply through your nose. Hold it. Tense your calves.
8. Relax your calves as you breathe out with a strong exhalation.
9. Repeat the sequence for each area of the body, working from the extremities to the center: feet, calves, thighs, buttocks, abdomen. Next, the upper body: fingers, forearms, upper arms, shoulders. (Hunch your shoulders up to your ears.) Don't forget your face; it may hold much tension. Work it in three stages: pull your jaw back so your mouth looks funny; scrunch up your nose; furrow your brow.
10. Take a few minutes to relax and let go.

The waiting (in line) peacefully breath. Banks and post offices should print copies of this exercise on index cards and distribute them to customers. It works!

1. Do the slow, deep abdominal breath with long, relaxed exhalation. Feel impatience drifting away. (In a traffic jam, don't breathe too deeply.)
2. Continue the abdominal breath. As you relax, realize that impatience will not get you to the head of the line any faster. Impatience only makes the time seem longer.
3. See those around you as fellow human beings also waiting and working to the best of their ability.
4. Hum or sigh to yourself for a while.
5. Imagine how pleasurable it would be if everyone around you were also relaxed and trying new ways to be patient and efficient.

Chapter 17

DELEGATING

Carol hates grocery shopping, but her family has to eat. So until recently, Carol would drag herself to the supermarket once a week and grudgingly push her grocery cart up and down the aisles.

Carol's 12-year-old daughter, Ann, loves to shop. She says supermarkets are "real neat." Ann also loves to search through newspapers, magazines and mail fliers for coupons to clip, organize and file.

Guess who does the grocery shopping at Carol's house now — Ann, with Mom's shopping list in hand and with Dad in the driver's seat. Carol discovered a way to get the shopping done — and done right — without doing it herself. She *delegated* the job — and relieved herself of the associated stress.

Why a Woman's Work Is Never Done

Whether you're managing a household of two, a small business or a major division of a large corporation, delegation not only increases your control but also takes a load of stress off your shoulders. Yet while the workplace is usually set up for delegating, the household may not be, leaving work distributed unevenly. And all too often, Mom carries the lion's — or lioness's — share of the load.

"Many women who are very capable at their paid jobs know how to delegate responsibility in the workplace, but they don't use those skills at home," says Kathleen V. Shea, Ph.D., a psychologist at Northwestern University in Evanston, Illinois. "If you don't delegate, you can dig yourself into a big responsibility hole."

"Evidence shows that in families where one spouse works, the other spouse [usually the wife] averages 8 hours of housework a day, and the working spouse [usually the husband] puts in 1.6 hours," says Ann Crouter, Ph.D., associate professor in the Department of Individual and Family Studies at Pennsylvania State University. "In households where both spouses work at jobs outside the home, however, the wife averages 4.5 to 5 hours of housework a day, yet the husband's time remains unchanged at 1.0 hours."

In other words, a lot of working wives are working time-and-a-half. There are limits to what even the most highly organized person can do. Yet many people try to defy the laws of time management and do it all.

How to Delegate without Distress

Many people would like to delegate but don't know how. Here are tips on how to delegate effectively, whether you're a business executive, a home executive or even the Chief Executive.

Decide which jobs you can unload. Make a list of routine tasks like watering the houseplants, walking the dog, folding socks and packing lunches, then decide what you can delegate. The idea is to delegate what you can (like household chores or office paperwork) so that you can devote your efforts to tasks that are too important to delegate (like hiring new employees for your company or interviewing full-time baby-sitters to take care of your children while you work).

Think beyond housework. Obligatory tasks like balancing the checkbook or sorting the mail can be a nuisance — unless you enjoy doing them. "Brainstorm about what has to be done, then decide who wouldn't mind doing it," says Dr. Crouter. One woman delegated to her teenage son the job of tracking birthdays and buying and sending cards. Another asked her husband to address the Christmas cards to his substantially larger side of the family, thus significantly flattening the stack of cards she had to write during the hectic preholiday season.

Give clear, complete instructions. You wouldn't give someone the responsibility of going to the supermarket for you unless you gave them a list of what you needed. By the same token, you'll be more likely to get satisfactory results if you tell people as precisely as possible what you want them to do. Just *how* specific your demands should be will depend on the age and experience of your helper.

"Rely on others' judgment somewhat," says Dr. Crouter. "You don't want to treat adults like very young children. With children, the older they are, the more discretion you can give them. For a teen, for example, cooking supper is more of a big deal if they can surprise you with what they've selected than if you've given them explicit, connect-the-dots instructions."

Set a deadline. "A project will almost always be completed sooner if it has a deadline than if it hasn't," says R. Alec Mackenzie, author of *The Time Trap.*

Don't be a dictator. "Allow a reasonable amount of leeway," says Dr. Crouter. "It's one thing to say, 'Clean your room once a week,' and another to say, 'You must clean your room on Saturday mornings.' Let your delegate do the job when it's convenient, within reason. You have to be willing to relinquish a certain amount of power, because if you set too-strict requirements, you're only delegating halfway."

Offer encouragement, not ridicule. Many people resist delegating because they are trapped by the feeling that no one could do the job as well as they could. Or they criticize their spouse's or children's first efforts at a task, then complain because they don't get enough help.

"Being too critical is counterproductive," says Dr. Crouter. "Accept the fact that errors and mistakes are bound to occur. Instead of criticism, give positive reinforcement. Rave about the meals your spouse cooks when they're good, for example, and don't say much when they aren't. No one is going to continue to do something if you belittle their attempts," she adds.

"At our house, for example, my husband does all the shopping and cooking, which relieves me of the responsibility," continues Dr. Crouter. "But it also means that I eat whatever is put in front of me, as graciously as I can. Similarly, if you ask a four-year-old child to sweep the walk—something a four-year-old can probably do without hurting anything—be sure to follow up with words of praise, such as 'Wow! Look who swept this sidewalk clean!' "

Make work fun. "If someone likes the task they're assigned, they're more likely to continue to do it," says Dr. Crouter.

"Does your teen like hamburgers? When you plan a cookout assign him to grill," says Dr. Shea. "Or get everyone into the kitchen together as a team: One person peels the potatoes, the other mashes them. The next thing you know, they'll *want* to help with dinner."

Rotate unpopular jobs. There are bound to be certain tasks that nobody wants to do. So take turns. "Children especially have to learn that sometimes we have to do things we don't like," says Dr. Shea.

Don't feel guilty. By delegating, you are teaching others self-sufficiency, not imposing on them. "Many parents, particularly mothers, feel guilty about working outside the home and try to compensate by performing at superhuman levels— doing all the shopping, cooking and laundry, for example," says Dr. Shea. "This encourages dependency in your children or spouse, when in reality they will be better off if they can manage for themselves."

"Without delegation, you have sad circumstances, such as when a husband, having depended on his wife to do the all the laundry throughout his adult life, enters widowerhood not having washed a shirt in 40 years – and not knowing where to begin," says Dr. Crouter. (By the same token, wives are better off if they have some experience in traditional male tasks like checking the oil in the car or filing a tax return.) So by delegating, you are not only absolving yourself of the sole responsibility for getting a job done, you are also teaching your whole family valuable survival skills they may need sooner or later. And the sooner they learn, the better.

Chapter 18

DIETING

We all know that stress can trigger the "nervous munchies." But can dieting itself leave you tense, irritable, angry and frustrated?

"No question about it," says Michael R. Lowe, Ph.D., director of the weight management program at Temple University Medical Practices in Philadelphia. "Trying to lose weight is both physically and mentally stressful.

"To begin with, the very fact that you are trying to lose weight implies dissatisfaction with your present shape. Pressures to lose weight are greater among women," says Dr. Lowe. "Being bombarded with image after image of ultrathin, high-fashion role models can reinforce the feeling that no matter how much you diet, you're not going to be thin enough or attractive enough.

"The physical effects of dieting are stressful, too, because evidence indicates that the body resists attempts to lose weight," says Dr. Lowe. "Feelings of hunger and lethargy triggered by food restriction are stressful, especially coupled with visual food cues like food stands, restaurants and magazine ads all around us. Altogether, constantly saying no to desired foods leaves you feeling frustrated, deprived and stressed."

Taking the Torture out of Eating Less

Short of abandoning all efforts to control your eating habits, what can calorie counters do to avoid dieting themselves down to a bundle of nerves?

Plenty. The following tips can counteract many of the feelings of resentment and deprivation that make weight control torture to body and soul.

Ask yourself if you *really* need to lose weight. "Many people who are dissatisfied with their size aren't really overweight, but they're either on a diet or feel they should be," says Dr. Lowe. If you have good reason to feel fat, though — if

you weigh 20 percent or more above the recommended weight for your height —
then you need to face some facts.

Accept the fact that you will never be able to eat whatever you like, whenever you like, in any amount, without gaining weight. "If people want to lose weight and keep it off, they first have to accept the fact that they will never be able to return to their eating habits of the past," says Dr. Lowe. "In our program, we find it useful to describe an overweight tendency as a kind of handicap. And as with other physical handicaps, the people who ultimately adapt best are those who can get past the feelings of anger and injustice, strive toward new goals and develop new feelings of pride at having overcome their 'handicap.' "

Don't cut back drastically. "Drastic efforts — a few weeks of strict discipline and extreme self-sacrifice — are usually followed by a return to old eating habits, leaving people feeling guilty and disgusted with themselves," says Dr. Lowe. "Instead, cut back gradually."

Don't adopt very odd or specialized diets. "Highly idiosyncratic diets that force you to eat only a few foods will also leave you feeling very deprived," says Dr. Lowe. You're apt to feel edgy and irritable. Odd diets are also hard to follow if you work outside the home, attend social functions and otherwise lead a normal, active life.

Build indulgences into your program. "If you say, 'I'm never going to eat ice cream again for the rest of my life,' you are aiming for the impossible and setting yourself up for failure," says Dr. Lowe. "Black-or-white, all-or-nothing thinking can undermine the very thing you're trying to achieve. So allow yourself an occasional stop for an ice-cream cone, but don't keep a half-gallon carton in the freezer."

Congratulate yourself on the victories and a healthier way of life. "If you lock yourself in a mind-set of, 'How much longer can I endure this?' you will feel upset, frustrated and angry," says Dr. Lowe. "But if you focus on the healthful benefits of weight control, feelings of inferiority and deprivation give way to pride, and your new diet becomes a morale booster."

Plan ahead. It's one thing to be obsessed with food (which many dieters are) and quite another to plan ahead in order to stick to your diet.

"Weight-conscious people need to be more mindful of what they're going to eat, and not make on-the-spot decisions at mealtime," says Dr. Lowe. Otherwise, you may end up eating high-calorie foods by default.

"Plan menus, shop for food, prepare for food-centered situations," says Dr. Lowe. "If you're going to a party, prepare to decline food when it's offered. Or set limits to how much you will eat. Or eat sparingly earlier that day." —or make your own

Don't let others coax or bully you off your diet. "No one, hosts and hostesses included, has the right to pressure you into eating or drinking something you shouldn't," says Dr. Lowe.

Losing weight is no piece of cake. But it doesn't have to be torture, either.

Chapter 19

DISAPPOINTMENTS

Consider the view from above. You are on the moon looking down at the earth. Somewhere below, a person's blood pressure is rising, his nights are sleepless. He yells at his kids, berates his wife, cannot concentrate at work and finds no joy in recreation. The reason for all this stress? He is disappointed that the new car he purchased is a lemon.

Sure, owning a car with flaws is frustrating. But consider the view from above: One car isn't going to mean much in the scheme of things. Ten years from now, it won't matter at all. So why should you let such a disappointment interfere with your health and emotional well-being?

Whether they are minor letdowns, like buying an unsatisfactory product, or major defeats, like discovering you are infertile, disappointments are always stressful. But the difference between letting them destroy you and letting them challenge you is a simple matter of attitude, and of understanding what disappointments show us about how we view ourselves.

Let's start off with a disappointment almost every working person has experienced at least once: the trauma of not getting an anticipated promotion.

What happens when you are denied a promotion, of course, is that someone is pointing out to you that you're not worth very much. And if that catastrophe has you feeling brutal about yourself, the big thing to recognize, according to organizational psychologist Maury Elvekrog, Ph.D., is how much your self-image, your self-interpretation and your values are totally tied to a promotion and to job prestige. He says, "Ask yourself, 'Do I have no value, no reason to feel good about myself except for the job?'"

In this case, as in most disappointments, the stress is basically a function of your own mind. It's not being passed over for the job, it's the meaning you attach to it that causes the stress. "It is almost never really the practicality of such a situation that causes problems, that the lack of finances will throw the person and his family into debtors' prison," he says. "The big problem is the blow to the ego."

So if you're feeling totally put down by such a disappointment, it's time for a little self-examination. People acquire values from our culture, from their parents and from peers, and they rarely look at them objectively. Start now. Sit back and ask yourself about your life values. Is there an overemphasis on job prestige? "One's values don't have to depend just on that. In fact, for people whose values depend totally on such external things as advancing at work, the stress never ends because you might never advance enough for your own liking," says Dr. Elvekrog.

Making It Hard to Rebound

The real key is the kind of message the person sends himself about the disappointment. If the person says to himself, "I must be a lousy person because they didn't hire me for the job," it's needless personalization. In fact, work by several researchers has shown that people who tend to blame themselves for misfortune are more susceptible to disease. And there is evidence that self-blaming types and other defeatist types create a self-fulfilling prophecy. It pays them not to be optimistic.

And people often make a catastrophe out of something that doesn't have to be a catastrophe. Someone who experiences any disappointment, even one as traumatic as losing a child through a miscarriage, should remind themselves that the sad event doesn't mean they can never be happy again.

"People say their life will never be satisfying again. And in communicating that feeling to themselves, they feel worse than just the experience of the loss. They've made the loss that much stronger," says T. Thorne Wiggers, Ed.D., a counseling psychologist at George Washington University, Washington, D.C. "It's sad when any disappointment happens, but it's not the end of the world." A doom-and-gloom attitude also makes it hard for the person to rebound in a positive way.

How you respond to major disappointments can have a profound impact on your life. John Snarey, Ph.D., conducted a study that examined how 52 men who experienced infertility coped with the problem over several decades. The results can teach people a great deal about the preferable methods for dealing with disappointments.

The men were divided into three groups, according to what kind of "replacement" they sought to cope with the stress of involuntary infertility. Members of one group treated themselves as their own babies, becoming preoccupied with activities such as body building, activities that Dr. Snarey describes as narcissistic. Another group's members found their replacement in objects, devoting themselves to a house, car, boat or the like. The third group's members became involved in vicarious child rearing by substituting the child of a relative, friend or neighbor for the one they couldn't produce.

By tracking the groups to midlife, Dr. Snarey found among the narcissistic group that 80 percent were divorced and 20 percent reported being unhappily married. In the group that found a substitute in objects, 50 percent were happily married, 25 percent were unhappily married and 25 percent were divorced. In the group that substituted vicarious child rearing, 90 percent reported being happily married.

For those who must bear the burden of involuntary childlessness, Dr. Snarey says, "Find important substitutes, other living human beings. I would caution people not to focus on themselves."

From Lemons, Make Lemonade

Solutions to disappointments aren't always easy. But Ronald Nathan, Ph.D., associate professor of psychiatry and family medicine at Louisiana State University School of Medicine in Shreveport, says to look for the opportunities that exist behind the disappointment.

Dr. Nathan is coauthor of the book *The Doctors' Guide to Instant Stress Relief.* And he's got a strategy for the age-old disappointment that accompanies lemon car models.

"The first step is to relax. Change your expectations and thoughts that the car will be perfect. Anticipate the inevitable problems, but not to the extent that you dwell on them," he says.

"A big part of stress comes from feeling out of control. So bring things under control as much as possible. Take out a pad and pencil and write down the things that are wrong with your car, when you want to bring it in for repair," he says, then adds, "Use this as an opportunity to employ your assertive skills."

Take the stress out of what you're telling yourself. Don't blame yourself. And see how this disappointment fits into the big picture from above.

Chapter 20

DIVORCE
AND MARITAL
SEPARATION

According to one widely consulted stress rating scale, only the death of a spouse ranks higher than divorce and marital separation as a major cause of stress. No wonder. After all, what is divorce but the death of a relationship, triggering not only a sense of emotional loss but the added burdens of guilt, depression, anger and feelings of betrayal? And, much like the death of a spouse, divorce catapults one into chaos, necessitating a change in living arrangements, income, standard of living and access to children – all stressful adjustments.

Nothing seems routine after divorce. Marital breakup is destined, it seems, to turn life into a melodrama fraught with uncertainty. What part do you play? Good guy? Rat? Martyr? What's going to happen next?

No divorce is stress-free. If you initiate the break, the guilt can devastate you. If your spouse initiates the divorce, hours of shock and disbelief give way to weeks of anger, which, in turn, can stretch out into months – and sometimes years – of bitterness and depression. Even the death of a loved one does not pummel the ego the way divorce can. When your marriage dies, the part of you that was Mr. or Mrs. John Doe dies, too.

Digging Out
from under an Avalanche of Stress

"Divorce can cause more stress than the death of a spouse," says Constance Ahrons, Ph.D., associate director of the Marriage and Family Therapy Program at the University of Southern California in Los Angeles, "because if your spouse dies, you have the immediate and often continued support of family and friends. Your self-image doesn't suffer. But with divorce, the stress *escalates* with the chain of events and circumstances that evolve." If you and your ex-spouse fight over child custody, for instance, or try to get the "best" deal in divorce court, stress becomes even more intense. And divorce, like the death of a spouse, all too often causes or coincides with other stressful life events, leading to what Dr. Ahrons calls "stress pileup."

"Take a middle-aged woman whose husband leaves her for a younger woman," says Dr. Ahrons. "Like a widow, she feels the stress of living alone, possibly combined with feelings of growing old and watching her grown children leave home. She may also have to face new career demands. But combined with all that is the added humiliation of being publicly rejected for another."

Not unexpectedly, this stress pileup takes a considerable toll on health. "There is a growing body of evidence that marital disruption [separation or divorce] constitutes a severe stress and that the consequences of that stress can be seen in a surprisingly wide variety of physical and emotional disorders," say Bernard L. Bloom, Ph.D., and his colleagues in an article published in *Psychological Bulletin.*

All told, the cost of divorce, in terms of money, emotions and health, can be devastating. What do you do when not only the rug but also the floor and the foundation are pulled out from under you?

While separation and divorce are never easy — unless there wasn't much of a marriage to begin with — you can survive with your self-esteem intact, without going bankrupt emotionally or financially. Coping strategies begin early on, when you find yourself entertaining thoughts of divorce or when you first realize that your marriage is not only in trouble but also finished. Psychologists we consulted had plenty of practical advice for coping with the stress of divorce proceedings — and for helping yourself recover emotionally when the divorce is final.

'Til Death Do Us Part (Maybe)

Divorce doesn't just happen; it evolves. For many couples, legal separation merely finalizes an emotional split that occurred months or years earlier. For some, divorce is unquestionably the way out. They're convinced that life apart couldn't possibly be worse than life together. But for many, the decision to divorce isn't so clear-cut.

"Sexual differences, change in finances, loss of a job, a career move, changing leisure interests can all stress a marriage," says Dr. Bloom, who has headed several studies of why marriages fail. "Some couples end up divorced, others stay married."

Agonizing over whether or not to break up your marriage can be – and usually is – pure hell. Wrestling with ambivalence – and your conscience – may be the worst part of separation. To decide *if* you should get a divorce, it helps to think about *why* you are considering divorce.

Judith S. Wallerstein, Ph.D., executive director of the Center for the Family in Transition, Corte Madera, California, has found that the decision to divorce usually falls into one of four categories.

Divorce as a rational solution. That is, divorce that is undertaken to undo an unhappy marriage considered unlikely to change, representing the culmination of years of visible unhappiness in which divorce had long been considered.

Divorce as a stress-related response. "Divorces occur in families where marital unhappiness had not been a special source of concern to either partner," writes Dr. Wallerstein in her book *Surviving the Breakup: How Children and Parents Cope with Divorce.* "Rather, the decision to divorce followed some stressful experience outside the marriage, which was profoundly upsetting to the person who then initiated the move toward divorce. The response to the external stress, in other words, ricocheted into the family arena." Examples of outside stresses that can influence divorce include the death of a grandparent, the diagnosis of a life-threatening illness, or a crippling accident to a child, says Dr. Wallerstein.

Why do events that mobilize some families, drawing members together in mutual support, rupture others?

"The psychological mechanisms that lead from such stress to divorce can be explained by the stressed person's need to take flight to ward off the depression that threatens to overwhelm him or her," explains Dr. Wallerstein. "One or both parents escape from each other and run from the marriage in a desperate effort to avoid the unbearable memory of the tragedy and so avert the threatened depression."

Impulsive divorces. Some divorces are initiated without really considering the consequences. A good example is the spouse who sues for divorce in outrage and jealousy in order to punish a partner who's been unfaithful or to secretly win back the partner. More often than not, says Dr. Wallerstein, the strategy fails, leaving the aggrieved partner raging for years.

Decisions encouraged by others. If marital distress is obviously to blame for physical symptoms or emotional distress, psychotherapists or physicians suggest divorce, says Dr. Wallerstein.

Generally, though, only you can decide whether you're better off unhappily married or unhappily divorced – undoubtedly one of the hardest decisions anyone can face in life.

"Yes, seeking divorce is a very emotional decision," says Dr. Ahrons. "You can start by asking yourself, 'Am I divorcing the person or the marriage?' Many young adults, married only a year or two, for example, split up because they realize they made a wrong choice – either they chose the wrong mate or married life wasn't for them. The mistake may become obvious rather quickly and they decide to get out before investing more time in the marriage or having children."

For people who've been married longer, the decision is usualy harder. "Motivation to continue is the key to whether a marriage will end or not," says Ann Leahy, a social worker and co-owner of the Marriage and Family Institute, a private clinic in the Washington, D.C., area. "Making the decision comes down to asking two questions: 'Am I interested in continuing this relationship or not?' and 'Are there enough positive benefits to enable [me] to live with the problems?' These kinds of questions take a lot of self-knowledge, but the answers help people to decide whether to stay married or to split up."

Mediation Is Less Stressful Than Confrontation

Once the decision to split has been made, more practical questions arise. Who will live where? Who gets the kids, the good car, the stereo? If you and your spouse take the customary, adversarial approach, you hire lawyers and square off over division of property, child custody and support, parental visitation rights, spousal support, tax considerations and responsibility for debts. Sad to say, money and children become the emotional currency of adversarial divorce. You find yourself caught up in a no-turning-back-now legal power struggle in which each spouse fights bitterly for all he or she can get. Adversarial divorce can make the unhappiest of marriages look like a picnic by comparison.

Few couples realize they have any choice, so they don their armor and sally forth, prepared for all-out war, when in fact there is a rational, humane alternative to adversarial – i.e., lawyer-negotiated – divorce. Mediation is a process of creative bargaining, facilitated by a neutral third party, by which divorcing couples work out a mutually aggreeable legal arrangement that's fair and equitable to both sides.

Unlike adversarial divorce, in which spouses are instructed not to speak to each other, spouses themselves negotiate their needs. The mediator is not the legal representative of either party but rather a trained professional (family counselor, psychologist, social worker or attorney) who sugggests various available arrangements to be explored. These arrangements are based not so much on emotion-fueled demands but on the legitimate needs and resources of each spouse.

As yet, only 3 to 4 percent of the divorces in this country are settled through mediation, but experience shows that, conducted in good faith, mediation minimizes the tension and crossfire generated by a legal power struggle. Mediation focuses, instead, on constructive problem solving, leaving fewer battle scars for all concerned.

In their book *Parting Sense: A Complete Guide to Divorce Mediation,* attorney Jack J. Shapiro and family therapist Marla S. Caplan point out six advantages of mediation over adversarial divorce.

It is less costly. Mediation runs roughly between $500 and $1,000, compared with up to $3,000 to $5,000 for an adversarial divorce involving children along with accumulated property and other encumbrances.

It is less time consuming. Mediation can take as little as two or three months, versus six months to one or two years for full litigation.

It is confidential. Neither party is forced to blame the other for divorce, and you don't have to air your unpleasantness in court.

It causes less wear and tear on children. Mediation avoids the emotional blackmail of a long, drawn-out custody battle. "It also reduces the traumatic period of time between the child's first recognition that his or her family is being torn apart and the moment when he or she can begin to see how it will be put back together again," say Shapiro and Caplan. "That reassuring moment comes only when custody agreements are clear, living arrangements are established, and the child can begin to predict his future."

It eases financial hardship and distress. More often than not, divorce leaves both parties poorer, but surveys show that women over 40 who've never worked full-time outside the home are hardest hit. Shapiro and Caplan have found that mediation creates the foundation for easier and more organized financial planning, especially for the spouse with the lower income. What's more, statistics indicate that absent parents are more apt to adhere to mediated agreements regarding child support than those that result from adversarial agreements. "Millions of dollars each year are not paid, and spouses are spending large sums of money on attorney fees to collect these unpaid support obligations, often without success," say Shapiro and Caplan.

It forestalls future problems. "Couples are more apt to adhere to a mediated agreement that they, not lawyers, made, and are less likely to return to court, time and again, to modify the settlement — and modify the modifications," say Shapiro and Caplan.

If you and your spouse couldn't get along during your marriage, you may have trouble imagining yourselves sitting down during divorce mediation and calmly discussing such highly charged subjects as finances and child rearing. But like the Geneva Strategic Arms Limitation Talks, mediation works when both sides are aware of the unpleasant alternatives.

"It's not a question of getting along," says Shapiro. "It's a matter of being able to sit in the same room and talk to each other through the mediator, in a neutral environment. Together, the mediator and the environment facilitate communication in ways the couple could never hope to communicate before.

"Also, knowing the alternative – what adversarial divorce involves and the enormous amount of time, money and emotional strain they're saving themselves – is a *big* incentive to cooperate," says Shapiro. If emotions are running too high to permit productive discussion in the same room together, you can try shuttle mediation, in which the mediator meets with the husband, then the wife (or vice versa) and so forth.

No marriage ends painlessly, but Shapiro and Caplan say that mediation clearly reduces the conflict that is otherwise present in adversarial divorce. "Mediation has enormous emotional and practical advantages over adversarial divorce," they write, "and is available to any couple who can resist the temptation to use divorce as a means of recrimination and punishment."

Marriage counselors can sometimes recommend a divorce mediator. Shapiro and Caplan suggest that when considering a mediator, couples should look for someone with a strong professional background in either law or social sciences and substantial mediation experience. "Ask how many divorces he or she has mediated and whether any previous clients are willing to discuss their mediation experience. Also, it's in the interests of each party to have the settlement agreement reviewed by a legal attorney before signing."

A Bright Tomorrow, but What about Today?

Mediation may address your economic needs, but what about your emotional needs? Like the death of a spouse, divorce can leave you feeling lonelier than you've ever felt in your life. But loneliness is only one of many emotions triggered, for divorce is a hydra-headed antagonist. You're probably also feeling resentful, scared, depressed, hostile – and paralyzed with anxiety and tension. Motivation evaporates. Preparing meals once shared with a spouse may turn from a source of inner satisfaction to a task done simply to survive. Activities once pursued together no longer seem worth doing. Why think about taking a vacation if you can't share it? Why plant the garden this spring if no one is nearby to enjoy it? Why get out of bed at all? Death is the loss of a spouse, but divorce is the loss of a dream.

Your task, if you are to survive with your self-esteem and sanity intact, is to grapple with the emotions one at a time. Only then can you leave your divorce behind and get on with life.

First Aid for Divorce Trauma

Don't wait until your marriage is officially over to start nursing your bruised psyche back to health. But deal with one emotional problem at a time, as they strike.

Friends make good shock absorbers. The first reaction to sudden loss is disbelief, shock, numbness. Like a steelworker suddenly learning that the factory is closing, you may find yourself moving trancelike through the day or putting yourself into a funk with alcohol or drugs.

"How you cope with divorce is related to how you cope with other crises," says Dr. Ahrons. "If somebody routinely reacts to stress by turning to alcohol or drugs, that's how they tend to react to divorce. But if they usually turn to close friends in a crisis, that's how they cope with divorce."

In fact, confiding in others is a legitimate way to deal with the initial feelings of, I can't believe this is happening to me.

"First of all, it's important to realize that divorce no longer carries the stigma it once did, mainly because so many people go through it," says Dr. Ahrons. "Knowing this makes it easier to turn to friends for support."

Don't get stuck in the "anger" phase. "If you hang on to anger and keep it alive longer than necessary, what you are really doing is masking or delaying depression," says Dr. Ahrons. "Granted, it's easier to be angry at a target – your ex – than to review your life together and give in to feelings of sadness and loss. Anger can keep you going but you won't adjust. Eventually, you have to deal with sadness to come out with a balanced view of the breakup. If you negate the sadness, you negate a big part of yourself."

Grieving is normal – and healthy. "Bereavement entails the work of emotionally disengaging yourself from your marriage partner, whether separated by death or divorce," explains Dr. Ahrons. "The person who initiates the divorce goes through this bereavement beforehand, while contemplating his or her decision. For the person left, bereavement is similar to mourning for a deceased spouse, with one big difference: The 'dearly departed' is still around and may have to be dealt with during the divorce procedure and possibly later, especially if you share child custody. So your grief is reactivated again and again.

"Allow yourself to feel pain," says Dr. Ahrons. "Divorce is painful enough; trying to deny the pain only makes it worse."

Don't pretend your "ex" doesn't exist. "If you've been married for 20 years you may be feeling angry, but chances are it wasn't all bad. You share a lot of experiences, memories, family and kinship ties that aren't severed with the divorce.

"What's more, it's not healthy to try to sever all ties," continues Dr. Ahrons.

"We have a stereotypical idea that that says divorce cuts all ties between two people. But in my experience, divorced people continue to have some kind of relationship, especially if children are involved. I see a pattern: People relate to their ex in much the same way they relate to other significant people in their past. People who maintain friendships with old suitors or high school classmates tend to continue to relate to their ex in some new way, despite the anger and conflict that broke the marriage.

"You almost have to build a new relationship, if only in your mind," says Dr. Ahrons. "It's unhealthy to have been married to someone and to have children together and then pretend they don't exist. Denying the relationship is like tearing 20 chapters out of the middle of your life and throwing them away."

Give yourself time. Divorce takes longer to get over than a bad haircut. Give yourself a couple of years to heal, says Dr. Ahrons. "I've found that it takes people an average of two years after a divorce before people start to feel excited about life and regain a sense of wholeness. Don't rush yourself."

Use divorce as an opportunity to improve your life. "For some, getting divorced is a growth period, a time to explore various options and take steps to make changes in your life that perhaps you should have made anyway," says Dr. Ahrons.

Resist any temptation to leave town, quit your job or make other rash decisions. Moving takes a lot of energy and would put extra strain on your already disrupted life. "Resist the urge to 'run away,' " says Dr. Ahrons. "If you move, you'll be anonymous. Stay where you are, where you have friends, where you know who the reliable dry cleaners, hairstylists and auto mechanics are, to maintain what continuity is left in your life."

Don't rush into a new relationship. "Work out your bad feelings about the divorce before you rush into a new relationship," advises Dr. Ahrons. In other words, resolve one relationship before getting entangled in another.

Consider counseling if you feel you can't go it alone. Surveys indicate that separated or divorced individuals seek mental health care more than single or married folks – usually within the year surrounding separation.

"Psychological counseling isn't always necessary after divorce, but it can certainly help, especially in finding out what went wrong with the marriage, what part each played in the breakup," says Dr. Ahrons. "Divorce is rarely one-sided, even when it seems to be.

"Once their anger has subsided, some ex-spouses go into counseling together, especially if they still have to confer over children." Think of divorce counseling as postmortem, to find out what killed the relationship and prevent future heartbreak.

In fact, counseling can reduce the emotional stress generated by divorce during mediation, as each issue is grappled with, says Shapiro.

"Sometimes counseling is imperative," says Dr. Ahrons. "If you're depressed for more than six months, if you're abusing alcohol or drugs or having suicidal thoughts because of divorce, you may need professional help to work things out.

"Like it or not, divorce is now a normal part of life," says Dr. Ahrons. "Yet it's important to realize that divorce is not the same for everyone. Divorce means different things at different stages of a marriage or at different ages. An early divorce is far easier to survive than a midlife divorce," she says, "mainly because it's easier to resume a single lifestyle if you've only been married a year or two. But midlife divorce is quite complex. We lose not only a partner but also a whole way of life. We have to allow ourselves time for recovery."

Chapter 21

EXECUTIVE STRESS

Question: What's the difference between an executive and a tightrope walker on a greased wire above the Grand Canyon with no net?

Answer: The executive's under more stress.

If you're nodding your head at this lame joke, you must be an executive.

Executives know that they have their own tightropes to walk, balancing between success and failure, vigor and exhaustion, recognition and blame, and that stress accompanies every step. Indeed, enormous stress is part of the image of the American executive. We picture this: a harried man or woman burning the midnight oil at a massive desk piled high with papers, perspiration on the brow, sipping the tenth cup of coffee, then, in another moment of frustration, snapping a pencil in two.

The image, of course, doesn't quite fit all executives. But there's no denying that stress is a big part of executive life and that it can have serious consequences, both physically and mentally. Ulcers, migraines, heart disease, fatigue, sleeplessness, depression, anxiety, anger, low self-esteem — these and other symptoms, research says, may be the executive's lot if stress isn't managed.

And managed it can be.

The heartening news from stress experts to executives is this: Even though stress is an inescapable part of your job, you can — with proper techniques — handle it effectively, and even turn it to your advantage.

Pushing the Stress Buttons

What are the sources of stress for the executive? If you can answer that one, you're well on your way to bringing executive stress under control.

In a study of 300 managers from 12 major companies, John H. Howard, Ph.D., of the University of Western Ontario, pinpointed four factors in executive jobs that seem to produce the most stress.

A feeling of helplessness. When executives are prevented from acting out their proper roles, they feel helpless – impotent – and this feeling engenders tremendous stress. For example, you may work hard to develop reasonable solutions to some tough problems but can't apply what you know because of constraints within the organization. The wielding of power, therefore, is a remedy for stress.

Uncertainty. When you're not sure of the facts (about company policy, the vagaries of proposed budget or anything else), decision making is hard, and stress increases.

Urgency. The executive's day is filled with tasks that demand great attention and effort – right now. "On average," Dr. Howard says, "managers do something different every seven minutes. Their jobs are characterized by brevity and fragmentation and stress."

Overwork. Like the executive in the popular mind, the real executive typically strains under a huge workload. Executive jobs, says Dr. Howard, are often "much work at an unrelenting pace."

As Dr. Howard's study reveals, these four stress producers crop up in all kinds of on-the-job situations. He groups these situations into categories that probably will sound disconcertingly familiar to most executives. Here are a few of the categories.

Poor management or boss. For the 300 executives in the study, having to deal with bad management was the single biggest stress-producing situation to be in. They said that what causes the most strain and tension is poor planning, bad direction and chronic indecisiveness.

Lack of authority or blurred organizational structure. As far as the executives in the study were concerned, the second biggest stressful situation is having a job to do with no authority to do it. Almost as bad is having to work where organizational boundaries are fuzzy – where job descriptions are too vague and bosses are too plentiful.

Promotion and recognition. When you're uncertain about future promotion or you never get any praise or recognition from top management, you're going to be stressed. Perhaps *very* stressed. Many of the executives in the study found these situations to be particularly painful and complained that they didn't know what criteria they were being judged by or what they needed to do to get promoted.

Company politics. When work becomes political it becomes stressful, especially when office politics influences promotions, the use of power, transfers and allocation of supplies and equipment.

Personnel problems. Executives must manage people. And when those people aren't doing their jobs or they have personal problems, the executive gets hit with a wave of stress.

Stress Inoculations

One obvious strategy against stress is to eliminate or change the situations that cause it.

But wait a minute. You can't always avoid stressful situations. Often you can't even *change* the situations, not even one little bit. So what's a stressed-out executive to do?

You build up your stress resistance. That, in effect, is what some stress experts are recommending. They say that by changing your approach to stressful situations (your perceptions of them) you can actually make yourself resistant to stress and its awful consequences.

"We think of stress as something that's 'out there,' " says Paul J. Rosch, M.D., president of the American Institute of Stress. "Well, it's not 'out there.' It's all in how you perceive it. Look at how two people might experience a roller coaster ride. One has his back stiffened, his knuckles are white, his eyes are shut, his jaws are clenched, just waiting for it to be over. The wide-eyed thrill seeker relishes every plunge and can't wait to do it again."

Researchers Suzanne Kobasa, Ph.D., and Salvatore Maddi, Ph.D., have taken a firsthand look at the link between executives' attitudes and stress resistance. They studied executives involved in the 1983 Bell System breakup and found big differences between executives who withstood the stresses of organizational change and those who knuckled under.

First, they found that executives bothered the least by stressful circumstances had fewer illnesses than executives who had trouble coping with the same circumstances. No surprise. But what was significant was that Dr. Kobasa and Dr. Maddi were able to pinpoint what seemed to "inoculate" many of the executives against stress.

The key stress-resistance factor, say the researchers, was "personality hardiness." "Hardiness is not the mental counterpart of a strong physical constitution," says Dr. Maddi, coauthor with Dr. Kobasa of *The Hardy Executive: Health under Stress.* "Rather, hardiness is a set of beliefs people have about the world and themselves and the interaction between the two."

According to these experts, these beliefs or attitudes enable the executive to defuse stress by looking at stressful situations in a unique way. The hardy (stress-resistant) executive thinks: "The situation is not completely unmanageable; it's something I can control, at least to a degree. And it isn't a trivial or thoroughly terrible problem – it's actually interesting and important. And I don't really think of it as threatening to me – it's a challenge.

Such a stress-defusing outlook enabled some executives in the Bell System breakup actually to enjoy stresses that were making other executives' lives a nightmare.

Fortunately, say Dr. Maddi and Dr. Kobasa, this outlook isn't something that you either have or you don't – it can be *learned.* They've already successfully taught executives the psychological techniques that embody the stress-busting outlook.

Here are some of the key techniques.

Focusing. This involves discovering what's truly stressful to you about a situation and why – the idea being that understanding your stress lessens it and gives you some control over it. The technique may sound simplistic, but often people may think they know why something is stressful to them but are way off base.

For example: John has a report to prepare on improving his department's efficiency, and he's getting nowhere. The deadline's closing in – so is stress. John thinks he knows the source of the stress: "They never give you enough time to do anything in this place," he says.

But then he tries focusing. He takes a closer look at his emotions regarding his predicament and realizes to his surprise that he feels fear. He traces the fear back to grammar school, where he was afraid of failure and often simply didn't do assigned work to avoid failing at it. He realizes that he's doing the same thing now. And this insight seems to cut his problem down to size, at least to make it capable of manipulation.

Situational reconstruction. This method disarms stress by putting a stressful situation in perspective. It's most useful when you run smack into a really big stressful event in your life, especially one that you become obsessed with.

After a stress-producing event, you try to imagine specific ways that the event could have been worse and better. Then you visualize what you could have done to make the better outcome a reality.

Often the result of this exercise is that you realize that you do have options, that you can exert some control, that you can use your imagination to head off future stresses. And, as Dr. Kobasa explains, "When you realize how much worse it could have been, you know you didn't mess up as much as you might have."

Compensatory self-improvement. This is the technique you use when you run up against the "executive stone wall" – the stressful situation that can't be changed.

Step one is to be realistic. "If no amount of situational reconstruction provokes a sense that a stressful event can be transformed," say Dr. Maddi and Dr. Kobasa, "then that event is a given, and is best accepted as such."

Step two is to realize that you can still have control and success in other areas of your life, then set out to prove this to yourself. Pick out an important personal deficiency that can be changed, and work to change it. If you're hitting the stone wall at the office, work to overcome your fear of skiing or your lack of poise when giving speeches or some failing in parenthood.

The technique takes the bite out of stress by giving you an added sense of

Stress First Aid for the Executive

It's only 9:22 and already the boss is steamed, your big project is snafued and you just got enough stress in ten minutes to last you all day. You'll eventually get the mess straightened out, but what can you do right now for on-the-spot stress relief?

A lot, say stress experts. Here are some of their best suggestions for rapid easing of the effects of stress so you can get on with the job of being a top-notch executive.

- Stretch yourself. Dissipate the tension in your muscles by giving them a nice long stretch. Select a muscle group (legs, arms, neck, back, whatever), gently and slowly stretch them until you feel a tug, hold for 10 to 30 seconds, then release. You can do this throughout your whole body or just in the muscles that are tensed up.
- Walk it off. When tension is high, don't sit. Get up and take your stress for a stroll. A brisk 10- or 15-minute walk can reduce muscular and nervous tension.
- Take a trip — in your mind. By visualizing a stress-free scene that appeals to you, you can actually unwind the tension you feel. Lock the door to your office, sit back and "see," as vividly as you can, the sandy shores of your next vacation, or a single magnificent rose. Use as many senses as possible to experience your stress-reducing vision.
- Take a breather. When you're uptight, your breathing becomes rapid and shallow. Decrease stress by deliberately breathing more slowly and deeply. Take seven seconds to inhale, then eight seconds to exhale. Then repeat this for five minutes — or longer if necessary.
- Practice executive P.R. The technique known as Progressive

power, by widening your scope of possible actions, by undercutting obsession with a hopeless situation.

The Power of Expert Coping

Like Dr. Maddi and Dr. Kobasa, other stress experts have investigated what distinguishes executives who cope well with stress from those who can't, and they've come up with some surprising data. Many researchers found that the

---

Relaxation is a perfect stress releaser for the office. The first time you try it you may need some privacy (in your office or the washroom, for example) so you can concentrate. But as you get better at it, you can use it to de-stress yourself anywhere.

First, sit down, lean back and close your eyes. Then clench your right hand, tensing the muscles in your wrist and forearm. Hold for five seconds, concentrating on the tension building in your hand. Then release, letting the tension drain away and paying close attention to the feeling of relaxation. Repeat this sequence of tension and release in your left hand, then your upper arms, shoulders, neck, back, face, legs, feet and toes.

- Open the pressure valve. If you're steamed up or stressed out about something, open your mouth and let out the pressure. No kidding. Talking is one way to do this. Sometimes the quickest way to ease tension is to discuss it calmly with the people involved in the tension-producing situation. If you can talk out the conflicts you're having with someone in a detached manner – without adding fuel to the fire – you'll be able to depressurize yourself and the whole situation. Even talking things over with friends outside the stressful situation can help.

Another way to open up the stress-release valve is to have a good laugh – or a good cry. Laughing at your predicament can restore calm and give you a more productive perspective. Crying – which every good executive wants to do occasionally but usually won't – may do its stress-easing by carrying away some of the body's potentially harmful chemicals in tears.

"competent copers" use simple antistress strategies that other executives ignore. Unlike those ravaged by stress, the coping executives:

- Postpone thinking about problems until an appropriate time.
- Easily detect fatigue in themselves and respond to it by cutting the workday short or taking time off during the week.
- Size up stressful situations and decide which aspects are worth worrying about and which can be ignored.
- Delegate tasks to others, especially when stress starts to increase.
- Know when perfection is possible and when it isn't.
- Get regular exercise.
- Take vacations.
- Aren't afraid to laugh at themselves.
- Talk to others — colleagues, friends, spouses — about job pressures.
- Expect the unexpected. They therefore try to allow time and energy to deal with the inevitable stressful events that come out of left field.

Chapter 22

EXERCISE

As you move through your day, chances are you'll have more than one opportunity to get angry. It might be a chance encounter with an infuriating person, a near fender bender in heavy traffic or an overcharge on your electric bill. If the rage subsides almost as fast as it came, you're probably no worse for the experience. But if your rage continues and you don't vent some steam, a part of your body is pumping out a potentially toxic substance called noradrenaline.

Along with adrenaline, noradrenaline is a hormone triggered into action by your brain when you sense trouble. The problem is, if you stay angry and don't vent the hostility, the brain continues to trigger noradrenaline, which threatens the heart and may hamper the immune system.

"Everyday stressors can cause the release of this hormone," says Redford B. Williams, M.D., professor of psychiatry at Duke University, Durham, North Carolina, and director of the university's Behavioral Medicine Research Center, who has studied the hazards of hostility. "In lab experiments, we've found that noradrenaline can be released when people are given a difficult math problem to solve. This hormone is very easy to discharge, especially in today's society, where there are so many potential irritants."

It's also easy to deal with.

"If you blow up and vent your feelings, then you're releasing your anger and, in most cases, everything inside will go back to normal and the hormonal release will stop," says Dr. Williams. "Any physical expression that uses up calories, such as exercise, burns up the hormones instead of allowing them to get to the stage in the body where they can do harm. In this case, physical exercise is actually relaxing."

"Exercise also may induce a kind of 'Relaxation Response' by flooding your body with endorphins, natural opiate-like painkillers released by the brain and other organs," says Daniel M. Landers, Ph.D., of the Exercise and Sports Research Institute, Department of Physical Education at Arizona State University in Tempe. "This theory is still under debate, however, because researchers aren't sure whether endorphins relieve tension directly, by traveling back to the brain, or indirectly, by slowing down your breathing."

The "Feel-Better Phenomenon"

Still another theory suggests that exercise relieves tension by taking your mind off whatever is bugging you – that exercise may be no different than such nonphysical diversions as reading. To test this hypothesis, Dr. Landers and Stephen Boutcher, Ph.D., measured anxiety levels in experienced runners and nonrunners before and after a vigorous run, then before and after a quiet reading session. The experienced runners felt less anxiety after running than after reading. They also felt less anxiety after running than the nonrunners did. Reading didn't seem to significantly reduce anxiety for either group.

"These data suggest that hard physical activity and a quiet reading session are not equally effective in reducing anxiety," conclude the researchers. "Thus, the effects of running may be more than just a 'time-out,' and physiological changes associated with recovery after exercise may also influence anxiety reduction."

Swimming has the same mood-elevating effects as running, say Brooklyn College physical education researchers. The researchers asked beginner and intermediate swimmers about their levels of tension, anxiety, depression and anger, then compared their answers with those of a group that didn't swim. The swimmers consistently reported better moods just after a swim.

Regardless of how exercise reduces tension, though, most researchers agree: People who take part in vigorous physical activity consistently report a dramatic increase in psychological well-being. They feel good not only after exercise but also in general, saying they have feelings of mastery, patience and a capacity for change. In fact, some doctors refer to this exercise effect as the "feel-better phenomenon."

Fit People Handle Stress Better

That heightened sense of peace and well-being can carry you through wave after wave of stress. "Increasing fitness may be a way of diminishing the effects of unavoidable stress," according to David L. Roth, Ph.D., and David S. Holmes, Ph.D., psychologists at the University of Kansas in Lawrence. They base their statement on a nine-week study of the moderating influence of physical fitness on the impact of stressful life events among 112 individuals.

First, the people being studied listed the stressful events they had experienced in the preceding year. The researchers then measured their physical fitness by recording their heart rate and estimating their aerobic capacity (an index of the amount of oxygen the body burns up as you exert yourself) while they rode on a stationary bicycle. For the following two months, the people studied kept a record of their physical health, depression, anxiety and general psychological distress.

The results: Among people who reported the most "bad experiences" over the year, only those who were physically unfit reported a significant number of health problems. In contrast, similar bad experiences seemed to have had little effect on the health of physically fit people. Physically fit individuals also reported less depression.

"With those people who cannot avoid or reduce life stress, increasing physical fitness may be an effective means of reducing the deleterious effects of stress on physical and psychological health," conclude the researchers.

A similar study, published in *The Physician and Sportsmedicine,* concludes, "Physical fitness is often associated with a feeling of well-being and reduced anxiety . . . regardless of the subject's age."

You Never Outgrow Your Need for "Recess"

You already may have experienced the "feel-better phenomenon" without realizing it. Remember elementary school recess? After drilling you on spelling and arithmetic all morning, the teachers released you and your classmates out into the schoolyard to play tag, kickball and hopscotch. That playtime helped you and your fidgety friends expend nervous energy and revitalized you for the afternoon lessons.

We never outgrow our need for "recess." Granted, it's rarely practical to go off and swim a few laps when you are straining to meet a deadline. Nor can you leave the scene to bicycle or shoot a few baskets every time toil and trouble bubble. But you can plan your activities to precede or follow anticipated stress, when exercise can do the most good. Schedule a workout for your lunch hour, after work or after you pack the children off to school in the morning.

The Exercise Prescription: How Much, for How Long

Researchers report that, generally, the best kinds of exercise for counteracting stress are continuous, rhythmic aerobic activities such as running, walking, cycling, swimming and cross-country skiing. Stop-and-go activities such as tennis, racquetball and basketball are less potent stress aids but are still worthwhile if you enjoy them. Or, as one doctor puts it, "Most anything that makes you sweat should work." (See the table below to find out how other popular forms of exercise stack up.)

Stress-Reducing Potential of Various Forms of Exercise

Some activities are better at diffusing stress and generating a feeling of relaxation than others. Daniel M. Landers, Ph.D., of the Exercise and Sports Research Institute, Department of Physical Education at Arizona State University in Tempe, has selected a number

Activity	Rating when performed at 70% or higher of maximum heart rate*	Rating when performed at approximately 30-40% of maximum heart rate†
Aerobics	5	2
Badminton (stop and go)	3	1
Basketball (stop and go	3	1
Bowling	1	1
Calisthenics	4	2
Canoeing	2	1
Circuit training	5	3
Cross-country skiing	5	3
Cycling	5	3
Dancing	2	1
Frisbee	2	1
Golf (foursome, pulling clubs)	2	1
Hiking	3	2
Hiking (with 10-pound backpack)	4	3
Ice skating	3	2

*By well-conditioned individuals
†By less-conditioned individuals

To get the optimum Relaxation Response from exercise, you should work out a minimum of three times a week, for at least 20 minutes, at a moderate or vigorous level (that is, 70 to 80 percent of your maximum heart rate, which is roughly 220 minus your age). Check with your doctor before beginning any exercise program.

of popular activities (listed below) and rated them for their approximate potential for reducing tension. Ratings range from 1 (minimally effective) to 5 (very effective).

Activity	Rating when performed at 70% or higher of maximum heart rate*	Rating when performed at approximately 30-40% of maximum heart rate†
Martial arts	3	1
Racquetball, handball, squash	3	1
Roller skating	3	1
Rope skipping	4	2
Rowing	5	3
Running	5	3
Softball	3	1
Swimming (crawl stroke)	5	3
Table tennis	3	1
Tennis (singles)	3	1
Tennis (doubles)	2.5	1
Volleyball	3	1
Walking	4	2
Water skiing	3	1
Windsurfing	2	1
Yoga	4	3

How soon after you begin an exercise program can you expect to feel a noticeable decrease in tension levels? That depends, in part, on your age and fitness level at the starting line.

"A healthy 20-year-old may begin to feel the effects in a matter of days," says Robert S. Brown, M.D., Ph.D., associate professor of behavioral medicine and psychiatry at the University of Virginia in Charlottesville. "People age 40 and older may not begin to feel the full effects for a month."

Attitude Adjustment

So far, exercise sounds like just the ticket for stress relief. But for many people, the mere thought of exercise can *cause* stress. Busy people struggling to meet existing demands on their time and energy may think of exercise as one more pressing obligation on an already hectic schedule. In one survey, "inconvenience" topped the list of reasons people gave for dropping their exercise program.

Other studies have shown that those who engage in sports do so because they are attracted by a variety of rewards, such as improving their skills, enjoying the excitement of competition, increasing their physical fitness, feeling a mastery of the sport and gaining the recognition and approval of others. People who shun sports or drop out blame excessive time and energy demands or excessive competitive pressures, among other factors. Some are simply put off by the "suffer, sweat and grunt" image of exercise. Or they feel self-conscious about baring their out-of-shape bodies to the world.

Any prescription for exercise has to take such anxieties into account, say doctors, because if you hate to exercise you'll defeat the purpose, which is to *relieve* stress.

"If you exercise grudgingly, you won't get nearly the boost in well-being as you would if you're enthusiastic, even if you pretend you're enjoying yourself," explains Sara Snodgrass, Ph.D., professor of psychology at Skidmore College in Saratoga Springs, New York. Dr. Snodgrass tested the effects of three different walking styles on 79 college students. Each student took a three-minute walk, either taking long strides, swinging their arms and fixing their eyes ahead, shuffling along and casting their eyes downward, or with a natural gait.

The shufflers experienced far fewer of the mood-elevating effects of walking than either the normal walkers or the striders did. Dr. Snodgrass feels that her study suggests that when we feel down, we can brighten our mood by purposely walking with vigor. In other words, if you approach exercise with the attitude that you're going to feel great, you probably will feel great!

Taking the Stress out of Your Workout

The key to stress-free exercise is to make it fun, convenient and suited to your personality.

Pick exercise you like. "If you dread your workouts and find yourself looking at your watch every five minutes, maybe you've chosen the wrong exercise," says Dr. Landers. "To benefit from exercise — and stick with it — you have to enjoy it and feel comfortable."

Make an appointment to exercise. Experts stress the importance of scheduling exercise into your calendar. "Then you've made a personal commitment to it, and you're less likely to miss your workout," says Dan Lynch, vice president of the Executive Fitness Center, New York. For some, this means exercising first thing in the morning, before you get swept up in the day's other activities.

Don't compete if it drives you to excess. Competitive sports are especially counterproductive for hard-driving Type A personalities. Also, don't play with highly competitive teammates or opponents unless you truly enjoy the pressure. (For further information on competitiveness and stress, see chapter 13.)

Choose more than one activity. "Variety is the key to successful exercise programs," says Dr. Brown. It prevents you from getting bored and dropping out. Giving yourself more than one option enables you to stick with your program if the weather or other factors interfere with your regularly scheduled workout.

Choose relaxing surroundings. Walk or bicycle in parks and trails, for example, instead of in city traffic or on busy highways.

Give yourself the "home advantage." Pro athletes know that they play better on their home turf. You, too, will be more likely to reach your fitness goals if you find a pool, track, route, court or club in which you feel comfortable. Where do your friends work out? Familiar faces will put you more at ease than a roomful of sweaty strangers. Or you can work out to exercise videotapes in the privacy of your own home.

Pack a week's worth of exercise clothes at a time. If you stash several sets of clean socks, underwear and other workout gear in your tote bag, car or locker, you won't find yourself scrambling for fresh clothes as you rush out the door in the morning.

Exercise to music you like. Music relieves the monotony of sports activities that involve the same kind of work for extended times, week after week, such as rowing, cycling, ice skating and long-distance running. Exercising to music, according to researchers, helps you to stay interested in repetitious activities, reduces anxiety and keeps you from looking at your watch every two minutes.

By integrating exercise into your family, social and work life, you can reduce any stress it may add to your schedule.

Chapter 23

FAMILY FEUDS

Most of us want a warm, loving family. We wish we'd get along the way the Cosbys do. So why do parents and children or brothers and sisters choose up sides and feud like the Hatfields and the McCoys?

It could be because we *expect* so much. "We want things from family," says Jacob Tebes, Ph.D., assistant professor of psychiatry and psychology at Yale University School of Medicine, New Haven, Connecticut. "We want things like intimacy, security and predictability." One big thing many of us still seek—even in our middle years—is approval. "The 'approval trap' is the major cause of nearly every dispute with your parents," says Leonard Felder, Ph.D., a psychologist in Santa Monica and author of *A Fresh Start: How to Let Go of Your Emotional Baggage and Enjoy Your Life Again* and coauthor of *Making Peace with Your Parents.* "That's when you each want the other to conform to your expectations and needs. It can block your feelings of love because you either wish your parents were different, resent that they're not, feel driven to defy or conform to their values or feel defensive and unloving when you are with them."

With brothers and sisters, the basis for a feud is often jealousy. In comparing ourselves with our siblings, we can help or hurt each other's sense of personal worth in achievement and success, sexuality and beauty, and social relations with others.

And with any relation, we can get locked into roles. "Children often give a lot of power to their parents and older siblings," says Dr. Tebes. "As they get older, they must learn to see their relatives through the eyes of an adult. They must recognize their own power and accept the limitations of their relatives. If they don't, they may be constantly disappointed."

The Nature of Grudges

Persistent grudges can leave you fuming after each phone call, dreading family get-togethers, yet feeling guilty if that relative becomes ill or dies.

Family feuds can even interfere with relationships that have nothing to do with family. "You may find yourself overreacting to anyone who reminds you of your brother, your cousin or any other family member you detest," says Dr. Felder. "When your spouse, friend or co-worker does anything that resembles the relative who gets on your nerves, you may unknowingly dump a load of resentments on that undeserving person."

And feuds can be self-perpetuating. "When a relative raises intense feelings such as anger, sadness and hurt, you may react in a negative way, such as yelling or accusing," says Dr. Tebes. "And that prompts the relative to act the same. So you get into a negative communication loop."

Backing out of a Feud

You may never be best friends with the aunt who bugs you, but you can let go of the hurt and anger. You can get out of the rut you're in and start enjoying this person more.

First, understand the other side. In most feuds, each of you is firmly convinced that the other guy is wrong. "Often, we assume that we should convert or reform our relatives to our way of thinking," says Dr. Felder. "We want to prove that we're right."

But in many cases, there's no right and wrong person. There are just differences in opinion – different religious beliefs, political parties, lifestyles, hairstyles, careers, moral values and personalities. And we each fight to prove our ways are right.

And the more we keep fighting, the worse it gets. "What you resist persists," says Dr. Felder. "Let's say your mother doesn't like your new girlfriend, and tells you so. The more you try to resist her point of view and try to convince her that she's wrong, the more she will persist in trying to convince you that she's right."

Instead, next time your relative says something you disagree with, try to understand his feelings, experiences and attitudes instead of attacking him. If necessary, do a little research on that person's behavior.

"I had a patient, Vicki, who married a man who came from a different religious and ethnic background," says Dr. Felder. "Her parents reacted so strongly, she eloped, and they remained distant for years. So I told Vicki to research their point of view. She talked to aunts, uncles and cousins and read several books on the subjects of intermarriage and religious identity. The more she understood about the personal and cultural reasons why her family had been so intolerant, the easier it was for her to work through her resentments."

Next, be assertive, not aggressive. Understanding the problem relative does not mean you must bow to his or her wishes. On the contrary, you should stand up for yourself. In fact, if you don't assert your own rights, you may perpetuate the conflict.

Let's say you have a mother who plays the martyr. "The martyr parent maintains control by making you feel inappropriately responsible for her suffering," says Dr. Felder.

With a parent like that, you may feel as though you can never win. You either comply with her wishes and feel resentful, or disobey and feel guilty. Either way you lose.

You probably can't change your parent's feelings, but you can give up your role in the melodrama. "Next time your dad says, 'If you love me, you'll do as I say,' don't yell," says Dr. Felder. "Instead, say, 'You've done your job as a parent by sharing your concerns, so now you can relax. Even though I don't always do what you like, I still love you.' "

And the next time your siblings make some snide remark that makes you feel inferior, don't burn up. Don't attack or hold your anger inside. "Stand up for yourself by saying, in essence, 'That hurt, here's why, and here's what I need so I won't be hurt again,' " says Dr. Felder.

Third, try to stay calm when you're under attack. Of course, it's not always easy to remain calm when your uncle tells you (again) that you'll never amount to anything. Here's a suggestion for keeping your cool.

"Try a 'guilt desensitization' exercise," says Dr. Felder. "Think of the five most common zingers your relative hits you with. It could be 'You're getting fat,' 'Why don't you call me more often?' 'When are you getting married?' 'Are you still wasting your life in that lousy job?' and so on. Record these phrases on a tape recorder and listen to them again and again. The next time you hear them, think to yourself, There it is, number three again."

Finally, discharge your rage. Despite all your efforts to be reasonable, you may still need to let off steam. "When you want to scream, and you don't do anything, your body suffers," says Dr. Felder. "Half your muscles tense as if to strike back in anger while the other half work doubly hard to suppress your reaction. It's like trying to drive with one foot on the gas and the other on the brake. I know people with family problems who get all sorts of physical symptoms — headaches, backaches and tension — when they visit their family for the holidays."

Suppressed anger can hold back your spontaneity and warmth and your ability to enjoy your relatives. But dumping it back on your relatives will just make the feuding worse. So dispel your anger by yourself. Write a scathing letter to your rival relative, listing every resentment, but don't send it. Yell at the top of your lungs into a pillow or in the car with the windows rolled up.

"Jump up and down and yell 'Get off my back!' But do it in private," suggests Dr. Felder. "It can be the quickest and easiest way to transform an oncoming 'downer' mood into laughter and emotional release."

Plan Smoother Get-Togethers

"Most family members see each other only at large group events," says Dr. Felder. "But when too many egos are gathered together, it's next to impossible to have a relaxed and satisfying conversation with any family member, especially the one with whom you've been having trouble. Too often, a few overbearing relatives dominate the conversation while the rest sit back and pray it'll be over soon."

Next time, try to do something both you and your problem relative enjoy. Take Dad to the ball game, go shopping with your sister. Ask your overly critical aunt and uncle to stroll in the park with you.

And try to notice the good points in this person. "If you're distant from a relative, try this exercise: Each of you tell the other 3 things you like about them," says Dr. Felder. "Then, instead of concentrating on the 50 things you hate about each other, try remembering those 3 good things."

Set new rules for length and frequency of phone calls and visits. "If your brother comes to visit for a month, and you drive each other crazy after five days, try a five-day visit next time," suggests Dr. Felder.

And make touchy subjects off-limits, if necessary. "If you just got a divorce and you don't want to be questioned about it, you can tell your relatives you don't want to discuss it," says Dr. Felder. "Tell them you need lots of love and support and you need the subject to be off-limits because you're so sensitive about it."

And keep working at the relationship, because it's worth the effort. Many people come and go in our lives, but our families are with us forever.

Chapter 24

FATIGUE

Everybody feels tired once in a while. Jet lag, shift changes, late nights and other schedule deviations can cause even the sturdiest of us to drag through a day – or two or three. But too often folks complain of feeling fatigue that has no clear cause.

Frequently it's stress alone – either an abundance or a lack of it – that can lead to this feeling. But your fatigue also may be a symptom of a physical ailment, your diet, your mental health or your sleep habits. Here's a checklist that can help you figure out what's causing your fatigue, and then work up a strategy for treating and preventing it.

Check Your Physical Health

Fatigue can be a symptom of disease. So if you find yourself dragging without apparent reason, first check with your doctor. Make sure you're not suffering from diabetes, kidney or liver diseases, anemia or any of the other illnesses that cause fatigue.

If illness isn't causing your problem, take a hard look at your physical condition. You've heard the saying "Fat folk fade fast." It takes extra work to carry around extra pounds. Begin a daily ritual of exercise. Your doctor can help tailor a routine to suit your physical condition and needs, but you can make the first step by taking a daily walk.

A lack of exercise ages the body and can contribute to fatigue. William M. Bortz, M.D., of the Palo Alto Medical Clinic in California, says that even though disuse is the opposite of stress, both produce the same impact: aging and the feelings of tiredness, weakness and feebleness. Dr. Bortz goes so far as to estimate that exercise is a 40-year age offset. "A fit person of 80 is as fit as an unfit person of 40," he says.

Check Your Diet

In addition to a lack of exercise, a nutritional deficiency also can cause fatigue. Some adults (particularly women in their childbearing years) barely satisfy the daily minimum requirement for iron, a mineral that maximizes the oxygen-carrying capacity of the blood. If you have only the minimum in your system, you can become deficient if you lose blood for one reason or another. People who regularly take aspirin lose blood from their stomach, menstruating women lose blood, nosebleeders lose blood, peptic ulcer sufferers lose blood. The Recommended Dietary Allowances (RDAs) are 10 milligrams for men and 18 milligrams for women, although some distinguished nutritionists believe the RDA may be too low, particularly for women.

Even stress itself can deplete you of some important nutrients – enough to wipe you out, according to Ray C. Wunderlich, Jr., M.D., a physician who practices preventive and nutritional medicine in St. Petersburg, Florida.

The cause of stress can be something very serious – childbirth, divorce, a court case – or just a dressing-down by your boss, but the response is the same. The event sends you into that adrenal overdrive of the fight-or-flight response. You initially experience a burst of energy as your hypothalamus signals the pituitary gland and then the adrenal glands to release stress hormones into the blood. But if you don't have the nutrients or adrenal sources to resupply those hormones, you may lapse into fatigue.

Dr. Wunderlich suggests you protect yourself from fatigue by building up the stores of such nutrients as thiamine (vitamin B₁), vitamin B₆, pantothenate, vitamin C, chromium, manganese, selenium, potassium, calcium and zinc in appropriate amounts. Your physician can help guide you.

Check Your Sleep Habits

Fatigued during the day and don't know why? Maybe you're not getting a good night's sleep. To ensure that you get sufficient sleep, practice what sleep experts call "good sleep hygiene." Stick to a regular bedtime and a regular wake time. Avoid substances such as caffeine or alcohol that interfere with your sleep. Don't spend too much nonsleep time in bed.

Set aside enough time to get the right amount of sleep for you. "Don't underestimate the amount of sleep you need. You may need ten hours of sleep a night and feel sleepy during the day if you only get eight," says Timothy Monk, Ph.D., a psychologist at the University of Pittsburgh's Western Psychiatric Institute and Clinic. And keep in mind that not everybody can supplement a bad night of sleep by taking catnaps. "People often believe they can 'snack' in their sleeping the way they 'snack' in their eating," says Dr. Monk. Don't cheat yourself of sleep.

Check Your Emotions

Sleep is very sensitive to our physical and emotional well-being. If something is bothering you, it can cause insomnia that results in next-day fatigue. David F. Dinges, Ph.D., co-director of experimental psychiatry at the University of Pennsylvania, estimates that psychological problems contribute to at least 60 percent of all insomnia. But it's not always easy to determine whether the sleep disorder is causing the stress or is *caused by* stress.

Just as you examine yourself for physical problems, look for evidence that your emotions may be keeping you in a state of fatigue. Donald Norfolk, a British osteopath and author of *Farewell to Fatigue,* writes, "Don't let emotional conflicts fester or allow doubts to lie unresolved. Take action. Face up to your fears, resolve your doubts, banish your hang-ups, conquer your inadequacies and make peace with your conscience. Learn to give vent to your emotions – frustration, laughter and tears – in socially acceptable, purposeful ways. Setting your mind at rest, you'll find, is an essential part of putting your body to rest."

Check Your Arousal Level

According to one theory, anxiety improves performance until a certain optimum level of arousal has been reached. Beyond that point, performance deteriorates as higher levels of anxiety are attained. How does this theory relate to fatigue? Dr. Norfolk writes that many sufferers of chronic fatigue have either too little or too much arousal. On the other hand, they may "have nothing to tap their energy stores or arouse their latent powers," he writes. "If they are to overcome their lethargy they must live more adventurously, be more competitive, take on extra responsibility, pursue new hobbies and tackle fresh challenges." On the other hand, there are those who have passed their peak of arousal and "need a temporary relief from stress to help them regain their normal vigor."

His advice: If you're bored, inject more variety and challenge into your life. If you feel tired from overstress, step back and slow down for a while. Learn your personal warning signs that you've overstepped your limits of stress arousal. They may be headaches, backaches, tooth grinding, increased consumption of alcohol or an escalation in your willingness to yell at your kids.

Dr. Dinges says that much fatigue is caused by three factors: the quality and quantity of our sleep at night, the state of our internal clock and how long we've been trying to work on a difficult task.

In fatigue, the brain loses some of its ability to function. When that happens, says Dr. Dinges, we become more dependent on our environment for stimulation. So if we're already fatigued – and at the same time our environment offers little stimulation – we're bound to be dragging. But when we're wide awake, there's no reason why we would fall asleep during a boring lecture or a long, dull drive, he says.

With good diet, regular exercise and a solid night's sleep behind you, even stress won't rob your energy.

Chapter 25

FRIENDS
AND FAMILY

If your monthly phone costs sometimes look like the Pentagon's budget for Star Wars, perhaps it's because that bill represents your own personal defense strategy. It may simply show that you have developed a good way to cope with stress: talking to those who are close to you.

Should your mother or father fall ill, do you automatically phone your brother or sister to enlist their support? If you get that big promotion, is the first person you call your old college roommate? (Good fortune can sometimes be stressful, too, according to psychologists.) When you're feeling out on a limb — and alone — remember that a friend is just 7 digits away (11 if you're out of town).

"People who have others with whom they can communicate about the tensions in their lives often find relief for those tensions," says Lillian B. Rubin, Ph.D., psychologist, sociologist and author of *Just Friends: The Role of Friendship in Our Lives.*

"Just knowing that you can turn to others is comforting," says Anthony D'Augelli, Ph.D., associate professor of human development in the College of Health and Human Development at Pennsylvania State University. "And when trouble does arise, friends can help you out and prevent problems from escalating beyond control."

In fact, some psychologists go so far as to say that many people may not necessarily need professional counseling to deal with certain kinds of problems, and that a good listener and trusted confidant can serve the same purpose.

"Friends can and do serve as effective counselors," says Dr. Rubin. "Feelings of loneliness and despair, for example, can be met and assuaged by a solid network of friends with whom you share your life."

The Amigo Factor in Health and Disease

"Close, confiding personal relationships have been found to reduce or buffer the stress connected with life's major changes [deaths, births, marriages, geographic moves, and so forth] as well as with the cumulative effect of daily hassles," concluded a study conducted for the California Department of Mental Health.

Medical evidence indicates that people in crisis who enjoy contact and support from others tend to maintain higher morale – as you'd expect – but also suffer fewer physical symptoms than those who do not. In one study, for example, pregnant women under stress who had access to supportive, confiding relationships had one-third the complications of women who were undergoing similar levels of stress but did not have supportive relationships.

One of the largest studies of the link between social support and stress relief was conducted by the Institute for Social Research at the University of Michigan in Ann Arbor. Researchers asked 2,000 people to rate how much they confided in others (friends, relatives, co-workers, supervisor) or sought their help. The people interviewed reported that social support helped to alleviate feelings of dissatisfaction, depression or anxiety generated by various types of on-the-job stress.

Should you lose your job, sympathetic comrades and kin can be of invaluable help – even if they can't solve your unemployment predicament. One study of urban and rural blue-collar workers, published in the *Journal of Health and Social Behavior*, found that people who lost their jobs but had no family, friends or neighbors to turn to for sympathy and help reported more symptoms of emotional and physical ill health than others who had people to turn to during the crisis. The people who found themselves both jobless and friendless had significantly higher serum cholesterol counts (increasing their risk of coronary heart disease), were more depressed, reported more illnesses and considered themselves worse off than those with strong social ties.

He Ain't Heavy, He's My Brother

If you belong to a close-knit family, you have an unconditional charter membership in an emotional support group wherever you roam. Many people consider close relatives – brothers, sisters, parents, grandparents or cousins – to be their oldest friends. For certain problems – especially those involving a major change or disappointment – no one is in a better position to provide a therapeutic shoulder to lean on than someone who knows how you got to be who you are, who shares many of the same childhood memories, good or bad (same house, same dog, same tuna casserole).

"The family can often be counted on to provide practical and concrete aid in times of crises – financial help, help with children, technical aid [cleaning or repairs, for example] and employment," says Cary L. Cooper, Ph.D., in his book *The Stress Check.*

"The person from a really supportive family doesn't have to go it alone," says one family counselor. "That person is part of something bigger – a family that cares enough to let him or her know he or she is okay."

"Probably the most obvious way family members can show support is by praising one another and by letting each member know how much he or she is cared for," says Dolores Curran, a family specialist, in her book *Traits of a Healthy Family.* In other words, a family who praises you when you succeed and supports you when you fail can go a long way toward helping you cope with mistakes, disappointments and other stressful events.

"Mutual support within a family in times of crisis is critical," says James J. Strain, M.D., psychiatry professor at Mount Sinai School of Medicine in New York. "Succoring one another, the family never feels alienated or alone. Instead, members feel useful, involved, in control, and able to adapt and reduce stress by pulling together."

"On the one hand, friends may be easier to establish a frank rapport with than family members because they're not as entangled in your life and can more readily adopt an objective point of view," says Dr. Rubin. "But kin still seem to most of us to offer a safe retreat, an anchor in an uncertain and unsteady world – the people who can be counted on when need is most urgent."

Family teamwork is probably one of the top ten means of reducing stress. Ask anyone whose spouse or children pitch in with dinner or chores after they've had a trying day. And never underestimate the stress-reducing power of having someone to hold your hand (figuratively and literally) through an emotionally trying time, an illness, a frightening hospital experience or other traumatic event.

(Of course, if your family resembles the Medicis more than the Waltons, your relatives may cause more grief than they relieve. If that's the case, see chapter 23.)

People You Can Count On for Better or Worse

A strong social network is too important a factor in stress control to leave to chance. Dr. D'Augelli suggests that people sit down and make a list of up to 20 people they feel they could turn to before stressful circumstances arise. Then ask yourself, "Of these people, who could I talk to about financial trouble? Marital problems? On-the-job stress? Who would be willing to give me a lift if my car breaks down? Who could I trust to pick up my child at day care if I can't get there in time? Who could help me if I got sick?"

This kind of practical help, along with emotional support, can make the difference between whether a crisis is manageable or catastrophic. And "preventive stress control" — having analyzed your support network *ahead of time* — gives you a person to call upon when trouble occurs, says Dr. D'Augelli.

When it comes to considering the supportive people in your life, quality counts more than quantity, says Dr. D'Augelli. The best candidates, of course, are people who've expressed concern and a willingness to help in the past, people whom you feel comfortable approaching again. And there are other traits common among your Who's Who of Helpers.

Good listening skills. "You need someone who will listen sympathetically but impassively, and not try to impose an answer on you or muddy up your thinking with their own views," says Dr. Rubin.

Dr. D'Augelli agrees. "Helpers are primed to rush in with advice, because they think that's what people want," he says. "To head off unneeded — and sometimes unproductive — advice, approach potential helpers by saying, 'I need to talk,' not, 'What should I do?' Ideally, the supportive friend will then help you sort out your feelings, set goals, and otherwise help you to make plans to resolve the crisis."

Open-mindedness. "Certain attitudes encourage us to open up, and others prompt us to back off, especially if we're distraught," says Dr. D'Augelli. "Judgmental, pushy or moralistic advice isn't constructive."

Trustworthiness. Needless to say, you should think twice about confiding in anyone who is apt to broadcast your troubles to others or use the information against you.

Give-and-take. Effective communication involves an exchange of both ideas and help, says Dr. D'Augelli. If you expect someone to take care of your kids at times, for example, be prepared to do the same for them.

"Reciprocity is the sine qua non [absolute essential] of friendship," says Dr. Rubin. "Otherwise, the person doing all the giving feels taken advantage of and will drop out of the friendship."

Shared fun. "People without a close family — whose relatives live out of town or single parents whose nuclear family has broken down — often develop a 'family' of friends with whom to share holidays," says Dr. Rubin. "Many good friends take vacations together."

Realistic optimism. Fatalistic, doom-and-gloom characters aren't likely to help you feel better or help you see possible solutions to a dilemma. "Also, people who are naive or offer simplistic solutions may mean well, but they won't really help you resolve the problem," says Dr. D'Augelli. "The best support comes from someone who has a positive yet realistic attitude."

To Make Friends, Be a Friend

Dr. D'Augelli offers two final tips for building a supportive social network.

Take the initiative. Show you care about your teammates. Look for subtle signs of distress and be ready to listen or help.

Say "thank you." Express your relief and appreciation for favors and help with a grateful word or a small gift.

Chapter 26

FRUSTRATION

Non possunt primi esse omnes in omni tempore.

—Laberius

Frustrations seem to come in three sizes.

Little frustrations: A busy signal on the phone; a red light; a quotation in a dead language, untranslated. Little frustrations come every day; they bug us but are quickly forgotten.

Middling frustrations: Driving 20 miles to your favorite restaurant to find it closed; driving 19 miles to your favorite restaurant and running out of gas; discovering your favorite restaurant is now a muffler shop. These midsize troubles really bug us, and can linger.

Big frustrations: Training rigorously for ten years in anticipation of the 1980 Olympics, only to see it cancelled. Kurt Thomas, 26, was then rated the best male gymnast in the country, a good bet for several gold medals.

"At first I didn't believe it," says Thomas. "My whole mind went blank. My body just gave up. I quit training."

Frustration is stress that comes when things turn out not quite the way we wanted them to, when we can't accomplish something we set out to do or when we feel cheated, foiled, thwarted or baffled.

Find your patterns. Although Kurt Thomas never went back to competitive gymnastics, he did eventually get over his enormous frustration. According to Richard Lane, M.D., assistant professor of psychiatry and psychology at the University of Health Sciences/Chicago Medical School, the way each of us handles frustration is partly genetic (we are not all born with the same temperament) and partly environmental (how well we have learned to deal with life's upsets).

Frustration isn't always cause for self-analysis. (In Thomas's case, it's hard to see how anyone would not have felt frustrated.) But, says Dr. Lane, "Intense reactions to something seemingly benign often resonate with important issues earlier in a person's life." He suggests the next time you feel overly frustrated you look within, and look back.

For example, if dealing with your boss constantly drives you up a wall, if your last parking ticket made you curse all cops, if nothing your elected officials do ever seems right – you just might have a problem dealing with authority figures. Could it all have begun with dear old dad?

Recognizing a pattern such as this one, says Dr. Lane, could be an important step toward overcoming your frustrations. If this pattern is yours, next time the boss rejects your work, ask yourself how this may mirror your dad's harping on you about schoolwork. Recognize the similarities in the situation and you can more easily recognize the differences – and this, says Dr. Lane, is the important thing. You are *not* still in the third grade, and your boss is *not* your father.

Take action. Allan Markle, Ph.D., a behavioral psychologist at the Veterans Administration Medical Center in North Chicago, believes there's a lot we can do about handling frustrations, regardless of their psychological roots.

He suggests the following:

- Decide if there's anything you can do about the situation, and if there is – do it. The light at 23d and Vine drives you crazy? . . . Take 22d Street.
- Don't "awfulize." If you must, consider the possibility of nuclear holocaust to understand that your puppy missing the paper isn't really the end of the world. Check your words: If you say "Oh God, this is a catastrophe," on a weekly basis, you're awfulizing.
- Don't ruminate. If your life's failures keep popping up in your mind – don't let them! A good exercise is to slap your thigh or snap a rubber band against your wrist every time you catch yourself dwelling on past frustrations.
- If all sorts of things get to you, consider learning various relaxation techniques.

Accept life's fizzles. According to William Knaus, Ed.D., author of *How to Conquer Your Frustrations,* frustration is not something that can be blotted out of our lives. Rather, it is something we must learn to tolerate.

"One must accept frustration as part of the price for getting things done," says Dr. Knaus. "There's no getting around it: You simply have to accept that things aren't going to be the way you want them to be all of the time. You can't always win."

Funny, that's just about what Roman playwright Laberius said 2,000 years ago. *Non possunt primi esse omnes in omni tempore* – "All cannot be first all the time."

Chapter 27

GRIEF

Our world is studded with monuments to grief. One of its most beautiful buildings, the Taj Mahal, was built by a grieving maharajah in memory of his young, dead wife. The sun never sets on the numerous memorials Queen Victoria dedicated to her beloved Albert. In our contemporary culture, however, grieving is considered a somewhat overblown emotion – even a waste of time. Rather, we tend to admire the stoicism of mourners who don't shed tears at funerals and people who "get on with the business of life" despite all sorts of personal trauma. Recent research suggests, however, that we should not be so quick to dispatch our grief. Psychologists say our cultural mind-set makes losing a loved one, for example, even more stressful than if we allowed ourselves to grieve, and places added burdens on bereaved people.

"Formal psychiatry suggests that 'uncomplicated bereavement' should be over and done with in two months. That's ridiculous," says Gerald Koocher, Ph.D., chief psychologist at Children's Hopsital in Boston and an expert on the emotional repercussions of grief. "A person can grieve continuously for a loved one for as long as two years, and intermittently for many years after. There is nothing wrong or unhealthy about it."

"In our society, we think a person who isn't 'back to normal' four to six weeks after a loss is somehow sick or wallowing in self-pity," says Stephen Goldston, Ed.D., a psychologist who also has worked with a great deal of research in bereavement. "This places a burden on grieving people, who then think they should 'snap out of it' after a few weeks. But people just can't recover from a major loss that quickly. And when they don't, they are made to feel abnormal or guilty about experiencing normal, understandable emotions. In fact, it takes most people a full year to resume life after bereavement, and it can take as long as three. They find ways to cope with a loss themselves, at their own pace. In fact, that is really the only way to handle grief."

The Spectrum of Grief

"Because we deny death and grief, most people don't know that bereavement unleashes a whole spectrum of emotions," notes Dr. Goldston. Feeling lost, sad and lonely during bereavement doesn't surprise most people. Feeling angry and guilty does. But these emotions, too, are part of grief."

"Many people are trapped by the myth that you must not speak or think ill of the dead. They feel tremendous guilt about being angry with the dead person for leaving them, or jealous that they have found peace, or oblivion, from worldly cares," says one psychologist. "Or they become obsessed with memories of little injustices they did to the dead person while they were alive. These are normal reactions. They happen when you are so wrapped up in your loss you can't think of anything else. With time, most people regain their sense of proportion, and realize the dead person didn't leave them on purpose, or to punish them."

One phenomenon that alarms grieving people terribly is aural or visual hallucinations of the dead person. "You'll be sitting in a room and imagine you hear the dead person's voice," says Dr. Koocher. "Or drive down a familiar street and think you see them. Bereaved people can be terrified that they're going crazy. They're not. This phenomenon is normal and common."

Pain that mimics the final illness of a loved one also can frighten a bereaved person and send them to the doctor convinced they, too, are dying. "Chest pains when a husband died of a heart attack, or abdominal pain when the person succumbed to colon cancer are frequent occurrences," reports Dr. Goldston. "A sensitive physician will discuss this with a bereaved patient before launching into a full-scale medical investigation. On the other hand, an examination can reassure a person that they are in fact healthy, and let them deal with their grief without worrying about placing a new burden on their family."

In the past decade there has been much research into the impact of bereavement on the immune system, but the findings are preliminary and tentative, according to Dr. Koocher. Some studies have indicated that people who lose a spouse are more likely to develop serious illnesses themselves in the year after their loss. "Does bereavement itself cause a depressison of the immune system? Or is it the stresses associated with dealing with illness, death and its aftermath, like settling the dead person's estate, that cause these illnesses? Right now, there is no clear answer," he says.

Even if the exact reason for illness in bereaved people is unknown, there are still good arguments for taking extra good care of yourself after the loss of a loved one. Eat regular, nourishing meals. Exercise is a proven tonic for depression. Don't attempt to drown your sorrows in alcohol or blur them with drugs. A report on bereavement done in connection with the National Research Council says many experts recommend caution in prescribing minor tranquilizers, sleeping pills, antidepressants or other similar medications for people who have suffered a loss. The researchers noted that there have been no studies or scientific evidence of the effectiveness of medication for coping with normal grief, and the danger of developing a dependence is very real.

Seeking Support

A person in mourning needs emotional support. It is vital not only immediately after a death but also in the months that follow. Both Dr. Koocher and Dr. Goldston have conducted studies in "grief intervention," which suggest the crucial time in bereavement is about two months later, when the shock has worn off and people are making their first tentative steps back into the world. Ironically, this time comes just when others who have extended their sympathy assume their support is no longer needed. Those who have suffered a loss may find the need to ask for help, or need someone to talk to. Often the best help comes from others who have experienced a similar tragedy.

One self-help and support source is the Widowed Persons Service program run by the American Association of Retired Persons (AARP). The AARP trains widowed volunteers of both genders and all ages to be "outreach" volunteers. Once back in their own communities, they contact widowed people and offer their support. Although the focus of the program is one-on-one, there are also group meetings.

For more information about the Widowed Persons Service, call the American Association of Retired Persons at (202) 728-4370, or write AARP, 1909 K Street NW, Washington, DC 20049.

Bereavement is a time to open or strengthen communications within your family. "People avoid talking about a dead loved one or how they feel about a loss because that usually causes tears, and that is perceived as stressful," says Dr. Koocher. "But talking and crying are helpful in coping with grief."

Some Guidelines for Coping

Although there is no pat formula for dealing with the stress and grief that come after the death of a loved one, the experts agree there are steps to take that can help people to cope.

"It is possible to prepare for bereavement," says Dr. Goldston. "A mature person realizes that life is a series of attachments, losses and reattachments. Accepting that can help you face a major loss without overwhelming despair." To further prepare, Dr. Koocher urges people faced with an imminent death to say the things they have always wanted to say to the dying person.

Afterward, they emphasize, don't expect to get over the experience quickly, even though society expects that you should. It is very important not to isolate yourself. Realize that you need support and seek it, from family, friends, clergy or self-help groups. Don't be ashamed to cry – tears provide emotional release and may even wash away some of the chemicals that stress builds up in our bodies. Expect to have overwhelming flare-ups of grief – holidays, birthdays and anniversaries can bring back powerful memories. Resume your daily routine when you feel up to it. Making a productive contribution to the world can be a source of comfort by helping you realize that life is going on. Recognize the signs of needing professional help, such as severe or prolonged depression, suicidal thoughts, an inability to find pleasure in anything, smoking or drinking too much, persistent pains or illnesses.

A Time to Cry, a Time to Grow

At some time, everyone faces the bleakness of bereavement. And for that we should be grateful, because if we grieve, it means we loved. The death of one who is dear opens up a black pit of emptiness that can seem inescapable and everlasting. By taking the time to grieve and by acknowledging death, we can become reconciled to our loss. With that accomplished, we then can move on to a full and happy life.

Chapter 28

GUILT

In the world of emotions, guilt has been given a bad rap. For a while it was in vogue among pop psychologists to dub it the "useless" emotion and to attempt to banish guilt and its many stressful side effects from the psyche. But recently, therapists have been working to restore guilt to its rightful place among our emotions. Without guilt, they ask, how many of us would cheat on our taxes? Without guilt, they ask, how many of us would never be kind to our parents or children or co-workers? "The sense of guilt you feel is what makes you human," says psychiatrist Willard Gaylin, M.D., author of *Feelings: Our Vital Signs.* "Be grateful you have it."

Guilt is a form of self-punishment. It is a reaction to an event or situation, and when it motivates us for constructive activity, it is both healthy and useful, says Salvatore V. Didato, Ph.D., a Scarsdale, New York, psychologist, syndicated columnist and author of *Psychotechniques: Act Right, Feel Right.*

Healthy Guilt, Unhealthy Guilt

Here's a simple example of the constructive nature of guilt. Say you were abrupt or abrasive to a co-worker. As a result of your words or actions you somehow bruised their self-esteem. You feel guilty, and to neutralize the guilt you apologize to the person, or you do a good deed to help the person, or you give them more of you and your time.

Here, on the other hand, is a typical example of unhealthy or unrealistic guilt. Say your mother dies. You search the past for situations where you may have offended her. You come up with a cluster of circumstances where you may have disappointed her – forgetting her birthday, not going home for Christmas and the like. So you lapse into a guilt pattern that causes you to behave differently. You mistreat people. You engage in self-critical thoughts. You find yourself becoming too passive or too unassertive in situations that you feel you don't deserve to win.

"Guilt is the agonizing sense that you have betrayed an internal value of your own, and its relief often requires – and invites – punishment," says Dr. Gaylin. And because it's akin to anxiety, it can cause stress. So if you're feeling guilty, the obvious issue to explore is whether your guilt is of the healthy or unhealthy variety.

The situations that make us guilty have their roots in our culture and in our families. Harry E. Gunn, Ph.D., author of *Manipulation by Guilt: How to Avoid It*, believes that all guilt originates from the fear that a parent will harm us for what we do – or even think. So the dynamics for guilt have been firmly established in childhood.

But many of the principles we learned in childhood – and by which we are dominated – are not appropriate for our lives today. And they can be a source of unhealthy guilt. Despite the widespread changes that have resulted from the women's liberation movement, for example, many women still feel guilt-ridden because they have careers, something that was taboo in their mothers' generation.

"The thing you would have to do in that case is to go back and track down the roots of your thinking," says Dr. Gunn. "Where did you get the idea that it's bad to have a career? Was it something your kids said? Was it an article you read? Very often in this search, people can trace their guilt to their parents. Then they have to ask themselves, 'Do *I* think it's wrong to have a career?' " he says.

Unadmitted Guilt

What made us feel guilty as youngsters often still can. As a result, many people are carrying around guilt that is no longer appropriate. And it is not always at the forefront of consciousness. Sometimes unhealthy guilt is so ingrained that it takes professional psychotherapy to flush it out.

Dr. Gunn gives the example of a former client, a young man with a talent for swimming who joined the Navy to become a frogman, but who experienced severe anxiety attacks when he embarked on solo scuba dives. In therapy it came out that at age 5 or 6 he loved swimming, but his parents were terrified of the water. His mother suffered from a heart condition and repeatedly implied that if he swam alone and needed to be rescued by her, it would result in her death. At age 25, his unexplained fear of swimming alone was as intense – although inappropriate – as it was at age 5. "If something is wrong at age 5, it is not necessarily wrong at age 25," says Dr. Gunn. It's a variation of a theme that surfaces repeatedly in his private practice. He counsels many women who feel guilt about their healthy sexual appetite, mostly because they were so warned against sex decades earlier.

Tracking and Treating the Cause

Unconscious guilt – the kind experienced by the would-be Navy frogman – is always manifested indirectly. So when you don't consciously admit your guilty feelings, you find yourself having unexplained problems. You may feel depressed. You may find work piling up that you somehow aren't able to accomplish. You may feel tense. You may have sleepless nights. You may lose your interest in socializing. You may lose your temper.

It may be a matter of not being aware of the guilt or it may be a matter of your not owning up to it. Say you get "called on the carpet" by your superior at work for continually making errors. You are told your job may be in jeopardy if you don't improve. You arrive home that evening feeling down on yourself, feeling threatened, feeling that you've lost the confidence of your boss and that you may also lose your job. You may not realize it, but you also may feel guilty – about not performing well and about not being secure in your ability to support your family.

So when you walk in the door, your son enthusiastically asks you to review his homework. You find two errors and immediately lash out at your child. "How can you make these errors?" you demand. "You've been watching too much television. Starting tonight, the TV goes off at seven o'clock." You are unconsciously repeating what went on at work. You are bringing your guilty feelings and feelings of self-defeat home.

The smartest method for determining if guilt is behind such a scene may be to engage in some reflection, alone or with the support of others. It helps to blow off some steam with a spouse. In the process, you may find yourself striking upon the real issue at hand. Or discuss the symptoms with a friend you trust. You may ask them if they've noticed that you haven't been your real self lately. Tell them how you've felt: withdrawn, lazy, anxious. A session with a counselor or therapist may be something that can get you to notice how guilt translates into problem symptoms and offer suggestions about what to do. It may be a matter of telling yourself – even aloud – that you're not feeling good about something and that you've got to guard against overreacting.

To Punish or Not to Punish

In his popular self-help book *Feeling Good,* David Burns, M.D., implores readers to examine the distortions that sometimes govern guilt. One possible distortion is the belief that your behavior is "bad." He writes, "Is the behavior you condemn in yourself in reality so terrible, immoral or wrong? Or are you magnifying things out of proportion?" Another possible distortion is that your behavior makes you a "bad" person.

Dr. Burns explains how the concept of "badness" distinguishes guilt from what he describes as the healthier feeling of remorse. "Remorse stems from the undistorted awareness that you have willfully and unnecessarily acted in a hurtful manner toward yourself or another person that violates your personal ethical standards. Remorse differs from guilt because there is no implication your transgression indicates you are inherently bad, evil or immoral," he writes.

So if you're experiencing remorse, you feel bad about your action, but you don't feel that *you're* bad.

Dr. Burns and other cognitive therapists ask clients to explore these potential distortions as well as a few others, among them the notion that they are inappropriately assuming responsibility for problems they did not cause. "If a person has a poor self-concept, not a normal amount of self-esteem, they'll seize upon any situation where they did something wrong," says Dr. Didato. "A counselor can get to the more fundamental issues and strengthen the personality and enhance the self-esteem."

More Warning Signs

Here are some other signs that you may be wallowing in unhealthy guilt.

- Feeling vaguely guilty, even when there's nothing to feel guilty about.
- Feeling guilty about being happy, or about something good that has happened.
- Turning your guilt into anger because it's easier to express anger than to admit guilt.
- Experiencing guilt over an incident that occurred 20 years ago.

How intense are these feelings? Are you virtually immobilized by some cruel statement you made to your spouse last week? And what kinds of behavior does the guilt cause? To explore that behavior, ask yourself:

- Does it get you into more difficulties?
- Does it cause you to lose friends?
- Does it cause people to reject you, to withdraw their love from you?

- Does it cause you to have self-critical feelings and attitudes?
- Does it diminish your drive for engaging in constructive behavior such as working and socializing?

Owning Up and Letting Go

Many therapists suggest that guilt is best dealt with quickly and efficiently. Once you realize you're feeling guilty, you should analyze the situation that triggered the guilt and decide whether your guilty feelings really are appropriate.

If you decide the guilt is appropriate, *own up to it.* Take responsibility for your actions by apologizing to a person you've wronged or resolving to change if it's yourself that you've failed.

And then let go of the guilt.

"It's better to let go and try to do better next time," says Julian Marder, M.D. He explains how people who cannot rid themselves of guilt often back themselves into a corner. Take the example of a person who said something to his wife that he regrets. He hangs on to the guilt feelings so that the guilt is a constant burden. Because of it, he may feel caged by the relationship. He becomes angry about the incident, about the guilt and about the burden. And his anger may cause him to repeat his behavior.

"He can't forgive himself. He can't take responsibility. There's no way out," says Dr. Marder. "In its own way the guilt reinforces the bad behavior. It becomes a vicious cycle."

So try to understand your guilt and let it go. And remember, says Dr. Marder, that we all make mistakes. After all, we're only human.

Chapter 29

HEADACHES

Headaches are symptoms, not diseases. Although they can be related to a physical ailment like a hangover or an allergy, many chronic, recurring headaches are brought on by stress, according to Seymour Diamond, M.D., author of *Advice from the Diamond Headache Clinic* and other books on the topic.

Among the varieties of headaches that have been isolated by experts, muscle contraction headaches are the type most directly caused by stress. More commonly known as "tension" headaches, this type of headache afflicts people when they transfer their tension to their muscles. What happens is relatively simple: As you meet your day-to-day challenges, frustrations and disappointments – watching your child dump a jar of jelly on the freshly scrubbed kitchen floor, having your boss make an impossible demand – the muscles in your head and neck begin to contract. As a result, they constrict blood vessels, the action that is believed to be the main cause of the discomfort, according to Dr. Diamond.

To escape from the grip of tension headaches, the most obvious solution is to pay attention to the sources of your stress and observe how your body reacts to them. For some people, the discovery that it's stress and not something physical that causes the headaches is enough to help prevent them from reccurring. So before reaching for an over-the-counter headache remedy, determine if you're doing all you can to release the tension in your muscles, where the headaches begin. (However, if the headaches become increasingly frequent and more severe, you should seek a doctor's help right away.)

The Electronic Headache Detective

You can rely on biofeedback techniques to discover which muscles contract to cause your tension headache and then designate a strategy for relaxing those muscles. Joel Greenspoon, Ph.D., a professor of psychology at the University of Texas at Odessa who has conducted research in the area of headaches, relies on biofeedback to help clients look to the activity of their muscles to predict when a headache is likely to occur.

Dr. Greenspoon attaches electrodes to various muscle groups of a headache sufferer and measures the electrical activity in terms of microvoltage. In a trial-and-error manner, he tries to pinpoint the muscle groups most affected. If he sees the normal limits of electrical activity are surpassed in a particular area, it's a good bet that those are the muscles involved. Most of the time, he says, it's the *frontalis* muscle (the muscle across the forehead) that tenses first. But it can also be the muscles in the back of the neck or in the jaw, with the headache eventually working its way up to the head.

But once a person realizes where the headache starts, he can engage in one of several strategies to relax the particular muscles. Dr. Greenspoon's clients employ Progressive Relaxation, deep breathing (see chapter 16) or autogenic training exercises (see chapter 5). For some, a warm bath works to eliminate tension. For others, stretching exercises (see chapter 53) loosen muscles in the neck or jaw.

Think Your Headache Away

Kenneth A. Holroyd, Ph.D., a professor of psychology at Ohio University, relies on cognitive therapy to help clients prevent and treat tension headaches. He instructs clients to keep daily records of headache episodes and to record the thoughts, feelings, activities and environmental factors that precede or accompany the pain. Once the clients understand how their thoughts and underlying beliefs contribute to headaches, they begin the task of changing those thoughts and beliefs.

So you get a tension headache every time your boss makes an impossible demand? Dr. Holroyd would have you determine whether the *perception* of the demand is impossible or whether the demand itself actually *is* impossible. If you determine that it's your perception that's creating the difficulty, Dr. Holroyd's next question is: What is the source of that perception (your own fear of failure, for example)? Another thought he has you ponder: How much of your perception is a reaction to something else about the boss? These new perspectives are a first step in changing the way you think and feel when a demand is made, and the first step in taking control of the stress — and the headaches.

Avoid Your Migraine Triggers

Migraines, by their nature, are more dramatic than muscle contraction headaches. They are technically considered *vascular* headaches. In vascular headaches, the blood vessels or arteries inside and outside the skull dilate or expand; thus, the walls of the blood vessels apply pressure on the nearby nerves and cause pain. Unlike muscle contraction headaches, which usually are felt on both sides of the head, migraines are often felt on one side or the other.

While migraines tend to run in families, there's no evidence that the problem is inherited genetically. "People have predispositions to migraines the way some people have predispositions to ulcers," explains Jack Hartje, Ph.D., a professor of psychology at the University of North Florida, who treats migraine sufferers with biofeedback.

Migraines occur when a person with such a predisposition is exposed to a trigger, such as certain foods or a stressful situation. As Dr. Hartje explains, the trigger activates the stress response. One result is that the carotid arteries – which supply blood to the brain – constrict. When the brain senses it isn't getting enough blood, it releases neurochemicals to dilate the carotid arteries back to normal. The problem is that migraine sufferers experience an overreaction: The arteries overdilate. Sensitive pain receptors that are wrapped around the arteries are stretched, which is what causes all that pain.

Physicians suggest migraine sufferers understand their physical or emotional triggers. Avoiding a food or substance that triggers the migraine is often the best way to control attacks. If emotional triggers are causing migraines, a therapist may be able to help you recognize the triggers and learn to avoid them or deal with them in a different way. According to one study, stress may play a role three or four days prior to the onset.

While many of the stress-reduction techniques outlined in this book may not cure you of your migraines, they may help you prevent them. Biofeedback, combined with various relaxation techniques (see chapter 7), has been successful in training patients to suppress attacks.

Chapter 30

HOLIDAYS

It's Thanksgiving Day. It's 5:00 in the afternoon. You have a houseful of very hungry guests eyeing the barren dining room table. As you check the turkey for what seems like the zillionth time, it finally dawns on you. The bird is not going to be cooked in time for dinner. In fact, it's *never* going to be cooked. The oven is broken.

Is your day spoiled? Are you going to fume and sputter and apologize until your last guest leaves? Or are you going to put out some lunchmeat and hope for the best?

If you're like Jerry Burnam and his wife, Pat, you'll head straight for the bologna.

"That's the kind of situation, where, if you're inflexible, or if you decide you're going to have a miserable time, you can be sure you will," says Burnam, a University of Illinois professor of leisure studies. He and his wife have learned to be just the opposite, to go with the flow. "We ate our bologna sandwiches, looked at slides, talked, laughed and ended the evening in a good mood." In fact, their dinner that day became a standing joke. Years later, their now-grown son still asks if the turkey will be cooked.

The holiday season offers its own special stresses. Most of us enjoy buying or making gifts, going to parties, baking cookies and seeing friends and relatives. Some of us even enjoy Alvin and the Chipmunks and mimeographed Christmas greetings. But too much, even of these good things, can generate a lot of stress.

And not everything about the holidays is pleasant. These particular days seem to magnify certain aspects of our everyday life. If we sometimes feel lonely, for example, we feel especially lonely during the holidays. If we miss a family member, we miss them most of all at Christmastime. And the marking of a new year brings into focus all the issues that have been bothering us year-long.

"This time of year is a milestone for people," says Lynn Rehm, Ph.D., a University of Houston psychology professor. "It's a time when we evaluate where we are since last year or earlier Christmases, and how we stack up to idealized images of family life. It can be a stressful and unhappy time for us when we feel our lives don't measure up in some way."

It's possible to plan ahead to eliminate at least some holiday stress. This is *not* the time to air long-term grievances or regrets, but it's important to make note of the issues that do arise, particularly in family relationships, so that you can deal with them later, *before* next Christmas!

Tradition versus Time

Remember the poppyseed cakes Mom used to bake for the holidays? Your mouth may water just thinking about them, but it's not easy rolling dough at night when you've been busy earning it all day. Women, especially, can feel guilty when they realize they just can't do everything they think they "should" to prepare for the holidays.

"Women need to realize they can't be the perfect wife, mother and worker all at the same time," says Herbert Freudenberger, M.D., a New York City psychiatrist and author of *Women's Burn-Out*. "People need to prethink the holidays, to anticipate as many problems as possible, and to make plans to avoid them."

Rather than trying to do everything themselves, for instance, or abandoning tradition altogether, women need to delegate holiday tasks to their husbands, children, friends and relatives. "*Do* have dinner at your house, if that's what you want," Dr. Freudenberger says. "But ask your guests to bring a dish. Most people actually like to contribute, and then you don't have the pressure of having to do it all."

And help the hostess if you're visiting for several days with friends or relatives, Dr. Freudenberger says. "Offer to take everyone out for one meal a day. That way, mother, sister or whoever doesn't feel tied to the kitchen throughout the holidays."

You can take some stress out of gift giving by shopping at off hours and ordering through the mail. Or don't buy gifts at all. Teenagers, especially, prefer money to a hastily bought gift.

Also allow extra time to deal with holiday hassles — getting stuck in traffic, driving to the airport, dressing for parties and wrapping gifts. And be sure to schedule some daily "down time" to take a bath, exercise or simply rest.

Plan time to do the things you really need or want to do, then write them on a big calendar. If you really want to make those poppyseed cakes, prepare the dough one night, the filling another, and bake them on a third.

And decide to enjoy yourself, even if everything doesn't get done. Things don't have to be perfect, as the Burnams will tell you.

Gifts versus Money

Are you still paying for Christmas in July? "Money is something people absolutely need to look at ahead of time and set limits on," says Dr. Freudenberger. "I regularly see people after Christmas who have run up $5,000 credit card bills and who are very distressed about it."

Spending so much money can represent something else. For one busy worker, who spent at least $1,000 on each of his children at Christmas, it meant making up for the time he hadn't given them during the rest of the year. "For others," Dr. Freudenberger says, "being extravagant at Christmastime is a way of denying to themselves the economic bag they are in," especially if they're in debt or have lost income.

If you're financially strapped, first admit it to yourself. Then talk with your kids about what gifts you can afford this year. "Unless they're totally spoiled, you'll be surprised how accepting they'll be," says Dr. Freudenberger. "Say, 'Daddy's been sick [or laid off, or whatever], and we don't have the money to give the same kind of gifts this year, so let's talk about what we *can* buy.'"

Being broke can be a good reason to start moving away from the notion that material gifts are the only way to express affection. Instead, give children some things that cost nothing but that they'll like – breakfast in bed, making their beds for them, teaching them to play poker. And suggest they do the same for other family members.

"We really learned what Christmas was all about the winter I lost my job," says Bob, a former steelworker. "You know that saying, 'We ain't got much, but at least we got each other?' Well, that's what it was like. We were real worried and all, but somehow that made us closer. We had to let one another know how much we cared, *without* presents."

Expectations versus Reality

Even in Hawaii, come December 25, people tend to dream about a white Christmas and riding to each other's houses in horse-drawn sleighs, Dr. Rehm says. "That image sure is hard to shake." So, too, is the childhood belief that everything is supposed to be just wonderful. We are primed to be full of great expectations, and so we're set up to be disappointed.

The antidote to disappointment is to make a good, hard reality check. "Your family relationships are going to be the same at the holidays as they are any other time of year," Dr. Rehm says. "Don't just magically hope that you'll get along better because you will see this person at Christmas. If you want to improve a relationship, make long-range plans. Make plans to get together during the year, or to write or phone more often. Do whatever it takes."

If you need to patch things up with someone, don't wait until they walk through the door on Christmas Day. Talk with them at least a month before the holidays, Dr. Freudenberger says. "Clear the air a little bit before you visit. Apologize for whatever it is, not calling or writing, and let them express their anger. Let them know you're happy to be talking it out and that you'll be glad to see them in a few weeks."

Is this the first Christmas since you were divorced? If so, it's very important to plan ahead for your children. Who gets them, and when? And will the children have a say in where they spend the time? If it's the first Christmas for you without your children, it may make sense to go on a winter vacation. Being with strangers who are in the same boat will help you take your mind off missing the kids.

If you're introducing your children to a new mother or father, or boyfriend or girlfriend, preparation beforehand is a must if the children are to feel comfortable in a new family, Dr. Freudenberger says. "Have photographs with the names written on them of the people the kids are going to meet. Sit down and talk about the people with your children." It's also important that the children have some routine during the visit. Give them quiet time to rest and talk, or just play by themselves.

Is this the first holiday since Mom or Dad or Grandma died? Don't wait until the holiday arrives to comes to terms with it. "Some of the young people I see feel like they don't have much of a family anymore," says Dr. Freudenberger. "But sometimes they can put together a real family Christmas. They'll invite everyone to their place [or take turns]. They're impressed to see how many people are just looking for someone to take charge. That tradition, that ritual, can continue if someone in the next generation is willing to pick it up."

Christmas is a spiritual time of year, whether we're Christian, Jewish or Moslem. And it's a good time to take a look at who we are and how we're living our lives. Try to get away from what you think Christmas "ought to be" and make it what you *want* it. What really gives you pleasure this time of year? How can you just relax and enjoy the company of friends and family? "That," Jerry Burnam says, "is what you should do with Christmas, *and* with your life."

Chapter 31

HOSPITALIZATION AND ILLNESS

A few days before his 60th birthday, Joe had a heart attack. Not a massive one, but cause enough for hospitalization. His wife, children and grandchildren – not ones to let a little matter of heart disease get in the way of a family celebration – persuaded an understanding nurse or two to look the other way while they smuggled birthday cake and party hats up to Joe's room. Counting five grandchildren and a patient with a broken leg in the next bed, 21 people helped Joe celebrate his birthday and forget about his ailing heart for the time being.

No one would be so naive as to imply that hospitalization can always be turned into a party. Treatment for illness or injury is inherently stressful. But a stint in the hospital doesn't have to be all doom and gloom, either.

How to Take the Fear and Anxiety out of Your Hospital Stay

"Much stress experienced by hospital patients is caused by feeling a lack of control," says Lynda Denton Lane, R.N., a clinical nurse specialist in the Department of Cardiovascular Physiology, University of Texas Health Sciences Center in Dallas. "But there are a number of ways to restore some control, thereby relieving much of that stress."

Learn about your medical problem and its treatment. A number of studies have suggested that the more psychologically prepared you are for hospital treatments, the less traumatic the experience. In one study, published in the *Journal of Stress,* a psychologist divided 80 women who were undergoing minor gynecological surgery into three groups: One group received routine care and nothing more, one received routine care and read a booklet briefly describing hospital procedure, and one received routine care and a highly informative booklet. Women in the third group experienced less fear and anxiety before the operation. Their heart rate and blood pressure were also lower. Plus, they reported less postoperative pain and recovered faster in the hospital. They also were able to resume normal activities sooner than the other women.

Similar studies have found that candidates for hernia repair, cardiac catheterization and other nonemergency procedures who received information, emotional support and psychological counseling experienced less distress or needed fewer painkillers or sedatives than those who did not.

"Patient education is the key to de-stressing medical and surgical procedures," says Lane.

Ask questions. If you don't understand what is being done for you or why, don't hesitate to speak up.

"In the past, if a patient questioned anything – 'Why do I have to use a bedpan?' 'How much medicine am I taking?' or 'Why won't you tell me my temperature?' – the nurse simply stated, 'Doctor's orders' and that was that," says Elizabeth Hahn Winslow, R.N., Ph.D., assistant professor of nursing at the University of Texas at Arlington School of Nursing. It was very much a parent/child sort of relationship.

"One big change in medical care is that nurses now view themselves as patient advocates rather than simply physician assistants," says Lane.

"The squeaky wheel gets the grease – or in this case, reassurance," quips Dr. Winslow. "The more assertive a patient is, the better able they'll be to take care of themselves."

Find out what the procedures you're about to experience will feel like. A number of studies have suggested that knowing what to expect reduces fear, anxiety and pain. "If a nurse says she's going to give you a shot, ideally, she should prepare you for what to expect by saying something like, 'I'm going to wipe your skin with a cool cotton swab; then you'll feel a burning sensation that will last a second or two,' " says Lane. "If it makes you feel better, prompt the nurse for the information."

Also, the less anxious you are before surgery, the less anesthesia you may need.

Less Pain, Less Stress

One of the biggest fears patients have is that they will suffer unrelieved pain after surgery, waiting hours between doses of pain medication. They also worry that doctors or nurses won't believe them if they say their pain medicine isn't helping. Rest assured, though: Pain relief is a mutual goal for doctors, nurse and patients alike.

If necessary, ask for an adjustment in your pain medication. "Nurses are governed largely by doctors' orders, but there is some degree of flexibility," says Lane. "Nurses *can* make you more comfortable. Giving aspirin or Tylenol in addition to Demerol, for example, can make pain relief more complete and longer lasting."

Ask your doctor about "patient-controlled analgesia." In many hospitals, doctors allow postsurgery patients to control their own painkillers – without risk of overdose – by means of a specially designed dispenser attached to an intravenous line.

"The nurse sets the IV [intravenous] pump to deliver a certain amount of painkiller per hour, based on the doctor's prescription," explains Cynthia Pastorino, R.N., clinical nurse specialist at Methodist Medical Center in Dallas. "If a patient feels the medication wearing off, all he or she has to do is push a button to release more.

"This alternative method of pain relief has some definite advantages," says Pastorino. "The patient is in control; the IV delivers the medication instantly, without the delay of calling the nurse, asking for more medication and waiting until she unlocks the 'medicine chest' and returns with the medicine; best of all, blood levels of painkillers are more consistent, without the peaks and valleys of relief experienced with injections given at conventional intervals." (In fact, studies have found that self-medicating patients end up using *less* medication than those who rely on injections from a nurse.)

"The best time to ask about patient-controlled analgesia is when you and your doctor decide on surgery," says Pastorino, "so that he or she can incorporate it into the hospital orders."

Practice "slack-jawed" relaxation. Anxiety sharpens the perception of pain. Consequently, relaxation tends to lessen the perception of pain. Toward that end, researchers at the College of Nursing, Wayne State University, in Detroit, Michigan, taught jaw-muscle relaxation to patients admitted for gallbladder surgery, hernia repair and hemorrhoidectomy. Their goal was to relax the link between the brain and the mouth, to rest the speech mechanism. Patients then used the technique as they first ventured out of bed to walk across the room and back, six to eight hours after surgery. Compared with surgical patients not taught relaxation, they reported less incisional pain and bodywide distress and needed less pain medication during the 24 hours after surgery.

Here's how to practice the technique. Drop your lower jaw slightly as though starting a small yawn. Let your tongue rest motionless in the bottom of your mouth. Let your lips go slack. Breathe easily and deeply – inhale, exhale, pause. Avoid thinking or forming words.

A Smooth Recovery for Body and Soul

Doctors and nurses have long noted that the more relaxed a patient is going into surgery, the more relaxed he or she is coming out. The rationale is, the more you know about what to expect, the less panicky you are afterward. Here are some suggestions to further smooth recovery.

Try to get up and around as much as your doctor allows. "The untoward effects of bedrest are horrible," says Dr. Winslow. "Studies have shown that patients who are allowed to get up and sit in a chair do better, physically and psychologically, than patients who lie in bed feeling helpless and powerless. Bedridden patients are susceptible to a variety of physical problems, including faintness, muscle atrophy and constipation, as well as depression."

Let family members help you. "Hospital patients are often too sick to verbalize their wishes, so they need a 'protector' or 'advocate' who knows and understands them to express their wishes to the health care team," says Dr. Winslow. If you need an extra pillow or blanket, ice water or more pain medication, it helps to have an attending friend or relative who can speak up for you.

Nurses also encourage interested and able family members to help a patient eat, wash or get to the bathroom. "Because so many hospitals are short on nurses, patients benefit tremendously from family helpers," says Dr. Winslow. Most patients also feel less self-conscious being bathed and assisted by their spouse or family. Plus, taking an active role in patient care alleviates some of the powerlessness that family members feel at seeing their loved one confined to an alien setting, she says.

With visiting hours stretching from morning until night in many hospitals, bedside helpers can be available to tend and comfort you for most waking hours. "That also gives nurses more opportunity to answer questions about postoperative care and teach the patient and his or her family the survival skills they will need to recuperate at home, after discharge," says Dr. Winslow. "That's especially important now, with so many patients admitted for short-stay treatment. We see them during the most acute phase of their condition only, then they're discharged," she says. "The patient and his or her family is more or less on their own."

Get discharge instructions in writing. "Patients and their families are told when to change dressings and so forth, but they're under so much stress they may not remember everything," says Dr. Winslow. "So we give them booklets or written instructions clearly explaining what signs and symptoms to look for, and when and if to call the doctor.

"From the moment you put on that hospital gown, you feel vulnerable, and the entire hospital experience puts you in a passive role," she adds. "So the whole idea is to make the hospital stay as homelike as possible."

Are Bedpans and Sponge Baths Obsolete?

Anyone who's served time as a hospital patient is probably familiar with two time honored hospital rituals: using a bedpan and taking a sponge bath. Both foster dread and loathing. As if being sick isn't stressful enough, using an awkward receptacle in place of a toilet adds insult to injury. And trying to wash and rinse from the same basin of water only leaves you shivering, soggy and disgusted.

Added to the sheer awkwardness of trying to relieve yourself and bathe in bed is the worry that a visitor will walk in on you. If you're not allowed to get up to go to the john, how are you supposed to get up and draw the curtain?

Doctors don't prescribe bedpans and basin baths just to be sadistic, though. For one thing, most have never used either one and don't realize just how disgusting they are. Rather, they assume that getting up to use the john or take a shower is just too much work for many patients, especially cardiac patients.

Well, it's high time to retire the bedpan and basin – or at least use them only when absolutely necessary, say two nurses who conducted research at the University of Texas Health Sciences Center in Dallas. Authors Elizabeth Hahn Winslow, R.N., Ph.D., and Lynda Denton Lane, R.N., measured oxygen consumption, blood pressure and heart rate in heart patients, other medical patients and nonhospitalized people. They discovered that except for a relatively few patients who are immobilized or severely debilitated, using a bedside commode is less stressful and more convenient and practical than using a bedpan or urinal. Their studies, published in the *American Journal of Nursing* and *Journal of Cardiac Rehabilitation,* also found that showering and tub bathing generally didn't cause any more physical stress in patients than the basin bath, and most patients preferred it.

If you're hooked up to a cardiac monitor, however, you may have no choice. But the nurses feel that many hospital patients should be permitted to bathe and relieve themselves in the least stressful ways possible.

"It's no wonder these rituals are stressful," says Dr. Winslow, assistant professor of nursing at the University of Texas at Arlington School of Nursing. "As a child, you're trained *not* to urinate in bed. Now you have to try to do what you've avoided all your life. It's basic things like this that make hospital patients feel helpless and powerless."

Now, if only hospitals would replace those dismal hospital gowns!

Chapter 32

HOUSEWORK

Most people hate housework. A survey of 3,600 people, conducted by researchers at the University of Michigan in Ann Arbor, found that, for most, housework ranked *last* on a list of 25 activities rated in order of preference.

When quizzed further, the few who didn't mind housework said they "felt good about having a clean house." It seems the best anyone can manage to say in defense of housework is that it's like beating your head against a wall – it feels so good when you stop.

How to Prevent Housework

"Fast, easy, orderly and *less* daily upkeep for the entire house, inside and out, will take pressure off the entire family and give you time to enjoy life again!" says Don Aslett, coauthor of *Make Your House Do the Housework* and several other best-selling books on housework. "The key to cutting housework is to look at each chore and ask, 'How can this be prevented?' "

The following tips are examples of how a little ingenuity can cut housework down to manageable levels.

Stop dirt in its tracks. Most dirt marches into your house on people's shoes. Once inside, it takes a fleet of mops, vacuum cleaners and carpet sweepers to get it back out. So install industrial entranceway mats at every door. Sturdy nylon fiber mats, often used in offices, supermarkets and other commmercial buildings, are best, says Aslett. "Nylon creates a static charge that actually helps pull particles from your shoes and clothes."

Keep your decor simple. "If pictures are hanging on a wall instead of sitting on a table, they won't have to be straightened, dusted around, worried about or picked up after they topple," says the author. By the same reasoning, one lovely vase is pleasing to look at; a table full of knickknacks needs a museum curator.

Clutterproof your house. One homeowner, tired of a messy tabletop in the entryway, removed the table. "There was no longer a handy place to set junk," says Aslett in his book. "At least half of housework is caused by clutter," he says. So removing "clutter magnets" can cut your housework by 50 percent.

Create a control center in each room. Keep keys, mail, grocery lists and phone messages in one area – a bookshelf in the kitchen, for instance. Then, instead of having the entire room to clean, it can be dealt with in one stop. "Plus, everyone will know where these things are," adds Aslett.

Stacked plastic bins make excellent clutter-control centers in the kids' rooms. Clearing up the obstacle course of toys, games and books won't be nearly as much of a project.

Rethink your kitchen work area for maximum convenience, floor to ceiling. Start by storing your cookware within easy reach of the main work area – the spot between the sink and the range – so you don't have to dart back and forth like a squirrel on amphetamines to prepare meals.

Demilitarize the toilet zone. Even if the tub has a bigger ring than Liz Taylor's, the bathroom will automatically look presentable in minutes if you can quickly clean the mirror and sink, says Aslett in his book. So clear the decks of hairbrushes, combs, shavers, toothpaste, makeup and hair dryers. Stash grooming paraphernalia in drawers, on shelves, on hooks or in one big crock on the corner of the vanity.

To eliminate soap scum "soup," use liquid soap from a pump bottle in the sink and the shower. And hang an extra towel rack to keep soggy towels and washcloths off the floor.

Democracy at Work

Short of hiring a live-in janitor, though, some housework will remain. To de-stress essential chores:

Ask for help. "Many people never get help with the housework because they don't ask for it," says Aslett. "And the truth is, 90 percent of housework is created by people – namely husbands and children – who are accustomed to having someone else pick up after them. So making each household member responsible for his or her own mess is a big help." Perhaps you could also persuade one of the neighborhood kids to vacuum or do windows in exchange for a ride to the movies or shopping mall.

Divvy up chores based on individual likes and dislikes. Everyone has some chores they hate less than others.

Decide what you can be flexible about and where you won't compromise. So says one busy lawyer and college professor whose husband, despite a combined household income in six figures, refuses to hire household help. Is it absolutely imperative that you can see a perfect reflection of yourself in the toaster? Probably not.

Easy Maintenance, by Design

"When furniture and fixtures wear out, or walls, floors and ceilings need repainting or re-covering, use low-maintenance materials," says Aslett. When choosing materials, ask yourself, 'Is it easy to clean?' " The last thing you want in the kitchen, for example, is flocked wallcovering, ornate hardware or other high-maintenance frills.

"Every room in your home can be changed to cut some need for cleaning," says Aslett. And every step that frees you from housework is a step closer toward a Home Sweet Home.

Chapter 33

IMAGERY

Try this. Command your mouth to "produce and secrete saliva." Bet it didn't work. Now try, as vividly as possible, to picture yourself biting into a juicy slice of lemon. Taste its sourness and wetness. Did that work any better?

Our autonomic nervous system — the system that kicks in when we're under stress — is linked to our *un*conscious mind. While we can use verbal commands to get our conscious mind to do things, we can't order around our unconscious mind the same way. What we can do, however, is communicate with it through images. Want to raise your heart rate? Think of something fearful — being chased by a snarling pit bull terrier, for example. Want to lower it? Think of something restful — swinging in a hammock, watching the leaves overhead. This powerful technique, sometimes called "visualization," has had well-documented and broad-ranging success. It has helped many women fight the pain of childbirth. It's eased the symptoms of some cancer patients, and even helped Olympic skier Jean-Claude Killy win gold medals.

There are a variety of uses of imagery to keep stress in check. One simple method suggested by Martin L. Rossman, M.D., a physician in Mill Valley, California, is to take a brief vacation in your mind.

A Trip to the Land of Relax

First, get yourself into a comfortable position. Take about six deep breaths. Breathing deeply and slowly, completely relax your body from toe to scalp. Think of relaxing each muscle in your body and feel the tension flowing out of you. Now count down slowly from ten to one, and feel yourself getting more deeply relaxed with each number.

Now that you're relaxed, imagine yourself in a peaceful, safe and beautiful place. It could be a place you've been to or an imagined spot you'll never really get to – like floating on a cloud.

Then, recruit your senses, and scout around for as many details as possible. Are there trees or plants in your paradise? Try to see the coconut palms. What time of day is it? Where's the sun in the sky? Feel the freshness of early morning. Now, what kinds of sounds do you hear? Chirping birds? What fragrances are there? Suntan lotion? The smell of the surf?

For stress-reduction maintenance, Dr. Rossman says to take such a mini-vacation for about 3 to 5 minutes a couple of times each day. If you suffer from a stress-related or stress-aggravated illness, he suggests you do it for 20 minutes twice a day for three weeks. Not only will it interrupt your stress cycle, it will also accelerate your natural healing process, he says. Have fun with the method. It may be the only vacation you ever take that doesn't include luggage, crowds, traffic and sunburned shoulders.

Talking to Dogs

If you are faced with a stressful situation you don't quite know how to handle, Dr. Rossman says you should ask a dog for advice. Or a towering oak tree. Or a wise old man or woman.

Dr. Rossman uses these and other images to help patients tap into wisdom that they already possess. First, he suggests you do a relaxation exercise to get you completely settled. Once you're calm, he says to imagine a place that is peaceful, safe and beautiful. Comfortably in place, you then have a talk with a "wisdom" figure that is close at hand. If you're imagining yourself blissfully lying on that Tahiti beach, it may be a friendly dog that happens by. But you can imagine yourself conversing with almost anyone or anything.

In that blissful state, you describe the predicament that's causing your stress and ask the inner adviser what to do. The result? If you're like many who have used the method, you'll learn, often by surprise, that you have the ability to under-stand and cope successfully with a stressful situation. To drive home the point and to transfer the advice to reality, you should keep a diary of the "inner-wisdom" discussions. (Nobody but you has to know it's a big black retriever who helped you out.)

Mind Games to Manage Your Anxiety

You can use Anxiety Management Training (AMT) if such emotions as anger get in your way whenever you are under stress. It's a method devised by imagery expert Richard M. Suinn, Ph.D., head of the Psychology Department at Colorado State University.

First, you completely relax yourself with a relaxation technique and abdominal breathing (see chapter 16). Then you imagine a circumstance in which you were highly stressed – returning an item to a store and having a salesperson give you a hard time, or walking into your boss's office and being turned down for a raise. "It must be a real circumstance that prompted a moderate level of stress," says Dr. Suinn.

While you're charged up from reexperiencing the stress, pay close attention to the emotional and physical upset you're going through. Then lower your upset by shifting to a relaxing image. You go from picturing the nasty salesperson to picturing a comforting friend. After some practice in making the shift, run through the exercise again, but this time imagine a *highly* stressful circumstance. After a period of time of working with this exercise, you should be able to shift to your relaxing scene at will.

Directing Your Own Show

While AMT is particularly useful for people who are paralyzed by emotional upset when they're under stress, others find it's their *behavior* that needs improving. In such cases there's another method that can offer help. Visual Motor Behavior Rehearsal (VMBR) relies on imagery to help you practice your coping behavior, it's much the same method used by pro golfers to visualize themselves sinking putts.

VMBR gets you to play the director of a stressful scene – let's say approaching your boss for a raise, and then test out different plots and dialogues. In this case, you'd picture yourself approaching your boss for the raise, but this time you won't be nervously entering his office. You'll be calm and self-assured. You won't blurt out your request. You'll present a well-organized case. And when he raises criticism, you'll respond with self-confidence.

You prepare yourself for every possible contingency. As a result, your reactions will be more automatic, and you'll find yourself more in control and able to be more spontaneous. "The imagery exercise reduces the chance that stress will happen," says Dr. Suinn. "And even if it does, you're better prepared to come out with the proper response."

The uses of imagery to motivate your unconscious mind are endless. By imagining something positive – that your relationships will improve, that you will see yourself as a happy person – you're taking the first step toward making your dreams come true.

Chapter 34

INSOMNIA

Way back around midnight you tried counting sheep. You couldn't muster anything more imaginative, like chronologically naming all the vice presidents of the United States. At 1:00 A.M. you got up and drank some warm milk. The only result? A scorched pot to clean tomorrow. An hour and a half later you poured yourself some Scotch. That knocked you out for a while, but it's now 3:30 and you're wide awake once again.

This is torture by sleeplessness, and even though the spouse beside you sleeps like the proverbial rock, you've got plenty of company if you ever suffer from insomnia. Some 30 to 35 percent of all Americans have trouble sleeping at least once a year. Among all symptoms reported to doctors, insomnia ranks second in frequency; only headaches are more common.

So what can you do?

First, stop doing anything.

If you're putting intense pressure on yourself to sleep, you may be contributing to the problem, says Edward Stepanski, Ph.D., director of the insomnia clinic at the Henry Ford Hospital Sleep Disorders Center in Detroit. The harder you try to sleep, the more aroused and more tense you are likely to become, he says. He offers some suggestions for folks who are light sleepers or who have periodic bouts of insomnia.

Stop trying to sleep. Get up and do something that relaxes you. Read. Watch the late, late, late movie. You may eventually fall asleep. But even if you don't, you'll set the stage for future sleep-filled nights by denying yourself sleep tonight.

Try a relaxation exercise. It just may work, particularly if your problem is stress or presleep anxiety. Try deep breathing (see chapter 16), autogenic imagery exercises (see chapter 5), progressive muscle relaxation or baths.

Don't hit the bottle. While alcohol may relax you, even enough to knock you out, it produces what sleep disorder researchers call "fragmented" (read: bad) sleep. You'll awake more frequently.

Don't try late-night vigorous activity. That, too, makes things worse. "Rigorous exercise tends to make the muscles more stimulated. It can lead to more fragmented sleep," explains Dr. Stepanski. And if all that tossing and turning wakes your partner up, don't think you'll be sedated by a round of sex. For many sleepless folks, the arousal that comes with making love only worsens the situation. "Don't do anything that is physically or cognitively stimulating," suggests Dr. Stepanski. These rules, of course, apply only to those who have trouble sleeping. "People who sleep well could do anything they want," he says.

Don't raid the refrigerator. Your body might get used to the idea of eating cold pizza at 3:00 A.M. It may crave food the next night at the same time, and you could be setting yourself up for long-term sleep trouble.

Don't build any "awake" activities into sleep time. Don't pick up that report you need to finish. Don't work on your income taxes. You may be setting a bad precedent for your body, says Dr. Stepanski. If you can't sleep, you can at least try to relax.

Start Relaxing Beforehand

Charles Dickens, the noted insomniac/author, suggested that one would sleep better if the bed faced north to take advantage of the pole's magnetic attraction. Benjamin Franklin recommended that insomniacs get up, remake the bed, walk around nude until they are thoroughly cold and then return to bed. More modern-day sleep researchers offer somewhat more believable tips.

Try some mild exercise between two and four hours before your bedtime. "Take a walk, a swim—nothing too strenuous," says Ernest Hartmann, M.D., a professor of psychiatry at Tufts University School of Medicine in Massachusetts and author of *The Sleeping Pill.*

Whether you exercise or not, set aside time to begin the process of relaxing toward sleep in the two or three hours before your bedtime, suggests Dr. Stepanski. This process can involve reading, watching TV—again, anything that will not overstimulate you.

If you're having trouble sleeping at night, avoid caffeine before noon and sugary snacks at night. Eat conservatively in the evening. Your body will be working overtime if it has to digest a big meal, and it could contribute to your sleeplessness.

Some physicians recommend pharmaceuticals to overcome temporary insomnia, either over-the-counter sleeping aids, which consist of antihistamines, or prescription drugs such as Valium. Pills may produce side effects – the dreaded next-day drowsiness, for example – and ordinarily are suggested only for short periods of time.

Those who have trouble sleeping because of temporary stress or emotional disturbances will often return to normal sleep once the stress disappears – when the check finally arrives in the mail, when the crucial exam is finally taken. But if the stress is not of a temporary nature, a vicious cycle can begin, according to Richard R. Bootzin, Ph.D., a professor of psychology at the University of Arizona in Tucson. "The stress may cause insomnia, and the resulting lack of sleep may make it less likely that the person will have the resources to deal with the factors causing the stress," he says.

Because your insomnia may be the symptom of a serious medical, neuro-logical or psychological problem, check with a doctor if you can't trace your sleeping difficulty to some specific emotional stress or physical cause. "The most important thing to remember about insomnia is that it's a symptom, not a disease," says Dr. Hartmann. "The question to ask is not what you can do for it but why you have it in the first place."

The Sleep Restriction Approach

Some chronic insomniacs are treated through sleep restriction therapy. It's a method that often works in cases of situational insomnia as well. Simply put, you establish a rigid schedule of denying yourself sleep.

The sleep restriction approach stems from the notion that chronic insomnia is perpetuated by several possible causes, among them irregular sleep/wake schedules, worrying about sleep, taking drugs and alcohol and spending too much time in bed. Arthur J. Spielman, Ph.D., a psychology professor at City University of New York's City College, has researched sleep restriction therapy and he explains how it works.

He has patients keep a log of the average amount of time they sleep each night and the average amount of time they spend in bed each night for five nights. If someone reports sleeping an average of 5 hours but spending an average of 6½ hours in bed, Dr. Spielman advises spending only 5 hours in bed each night. The point is to restrict the time in bed to what is ordinarily sleep time.

If a patient spends little enough time in bed, he or she eventually will increase the percentage of time spent asleep. When the sleep portion comprises 90 percent of the time in bed, Dr. Spielman permits the patient to increase, in 15-minute increments, the time in bed. The scheduling continues and more bedtime hours are added until the insomnia is treated.

Stimulus Control Instruction

Sleep experts Dr. Bootzin and Perry Nicassio, Ph.D., developed some instructions to help the insomniac acquire a consistent sleep rhythm. The instructions strengthen the bed as a cue for sleep and weaken it as a cue for activities that might interfere with sleep.

1. Lie down with the intention of going to sleep only when you are sleepy.
2. Do not use your bed for anything except sleep; that is, do not read, watch television, eat or worry in bed. Sexual activity is the only exception to this rule. On such occasions, the instructions are to be followed afterward when you intend to go to sleep.
3. If you find yourself unable to fall asleep, get up and go into another room. Stay as long as you wish and then return to the bedroom to sleep. Although you should not necessarily watch the clock, you should get out of bed if you do not fall asleep immediately. Remember, the goal is to associate your bed with falling asleep quickly. If you are in bed more than about ten minutes without falling asleep and have not gotten up, you are not following this instruction.
4. If you still cannot fall asleep, repeat step 3. Do this as often as is necessary throughout the night.
5. Set your alarm and get up at the same time every morning, regardless of how much sleep you got during the night. This will help your body acquire a consistent sleep rhythm.
6. Do not nap during the day.

Older People Need Less Sleep

As we get older, our sleeping patterns change: We sleep lighter and require fewer hours. Between the ages of 20 and 50, deep sleep is reduced by 60 percent, and the number of arousals in the night doubles. Keep in mind that it's normal to sleep less as you age. You're not suffering from insomnia unless your sleep patterns have dramatically and persistently changed or if you are experiencing such symptoms as lethargy, irritability, poor coordination and lapses of attention. If that's not the case, enjoy the news that your body needs less sleep. Physicians often tell older people to forget the myth of the required eight hours. Find pleasant activities for the extra waking hours you so rightly deserve.

In some parts of the country, you can even join an insomniac tour. In Baltimore, for instance, there's an Insomniac's Tour by the Sea, an Insomniac's Preakness Tour and a Halloween Insomniac Tour that includes a reading of "Annabel Lee" at the grave of that famous insomniac, Edgar Allan Poe.

Chapter 35

LAUGHTER

By 5:00 P.M., Celeste's nerves were shot. A dozen things had gone wrong – some even before noon. After that, things only got worse.

All Celeste could think of on the drive home from the office was how much she could use a glass of wine – or two or three. Waiting for her in the day's mail, though, was a videotape of a childhood favorite – Road Runner cartoons – that she'd ordered weeks earlier. Celeste forgot about the wine and popped the cassette into her VCR instead.

After watching the tape – an hour of back-to-back Road Runner versus Wile E. Coyote chases – Celeste was laughing so hard her ribs ached and she could barely see or speak. And the snafus at work didn't seem to matter anymore.

Do you, too, have days when, like Wile E. Coyote, the only light at the end of the tunnel turns out to be an approaching train? Maybe you need your own "humor first-aid kit."

A Laugh a Day Keeps the Doctor Away

"Laughter can provide immediate relief from life's daily pressures," says Joel Goodman, Ed.D., director of the HUMOR Project at the Saratoga Institute in Saratoga Springs, New York, and editor of *Laughing Matters* magazine. "But it also builds up immunity to stress for the long haul."

Other experts agree.

"The ability to get a laugh out of everyday situations is a safety valve that will rid you of tensions that might otherwise continue to build and damage your health," writes Laurence J. Peter in his book, *The Laughter Prescription.*

"Laughter is not only as good a method of stress relief as a massage, a hot bath or exercise, it's *essential* to stress relief," says Steve Allen, Jr., M.D., son of comedian Steve Allen and "a graduate of the Hawkeye Pierce school of medicine."

Assault with a Friendly Weapon

Playful humor (as opposed to derogatory humor) also helps to take the stress out of trying circumstances. Take the case of a couple who stopped at a roadside restaurant for lunch in the middle of a long drive from Boston to Philadelphia. After they had sat at a table for 20 minutes, the waitress still hadn't noticed them, let alone taken their order. So they toyed with the notion of sending her a postcard saying, "Having a nice time. Wish you were here." Instead of fuming, they giggled.

Slow service is only one of the many stressors that can get you riled up – if you let them. A good-natured sense of humor can make the difference.

"Situations like that aren't stressful in themselves; rather, our *perception* of adversity makes something stressful," says Katherine Ferrari, founder and president of the International Laughter Society, Inc., headquartered in Los Gatos, California. "By looking at a stressful event or situation in a new, absurd or slightly cockeyed way, humor changes our perception of the stressor and therefore can reduce tension and anxiety."

In other words, the problem hasn't changed – the waitress is still slow on the draw, the phone company still can't untangle the error on your bill, your car still needs a new muffler to pass inspection – but humor enables part of your psyche to step back and view the situation from a different perspective.

"And humor helps you move from venting frustration to inventing a solution – and preventing stress buildup," says Marjorie J. Ingram, director of the Creative Response to Stress Project at the Saratoga Institute.

Laughing, like aerobic exercise, also diffuses physical tension directly, according to gelontologists (people who study laughter).

"One theory proposes that laughing triggers a sequence of actions in which muscle tension first increases, then decreases – which explains why you can end up 'weak' with laughter," explains Dr. Allen.

At the same time, laughter seems to decrease the production of adrenaline and cortisone, the stress hormones, explains Dr. Allen, thus leaving you more relaxed. "And while it's hard to prove in the laboratory, experience indicates that these beneficial effects last."

Help for the Humor-Impaired

Caught up in the spinning vortex of life's commitments and conflicts, though, it's not always easy to stop and focus through the clear and detached lens of a "Candid Camera." Even the mental health professionals interviewed admitted that they, too, need reminders to lighten up once in a while. Here are their tips.

Remind yourself to have fun. When the going gets tough, just repeat to yourself, "Life is crazy" and "It's okay to be foolish."

Keep a "silly scrapbook." Collect funny cartoons, humorous anecdotes, remarks you overheard and other items that make you chuckle with amusement, say the experts. Then leaf through the book whenever you need a fix of laughter. (Your scrapbook is also a good place for mementos, like zany photos of you and your friends.)

Head off stress with regular doses of humor. "A shot of humor is like a dose of medicine; the effects linger, dissipating gradually, over several hours," explains Dr. Allen. "Say you see an Eddie Murphy or a Woody Allen movie on Friday night. You'll find yourself thinking about the movie as you leave the theater, after you get home, and often into the next day. Like medicine, at a certain point half the therapeutic effects of laughter will have been used up. Then you need another dose. So I tell people to gauge the 'humor half-life' of whatever amuses them and replenish their dosage as needed."

Take a "laugh break" instead of a coffee break. "Keep a 'humor first-aid kit.' Fill it with noisemakers, comedy tapes, a Groucho Marx disguise and other comic props to draw on when you feel the urge to be silly," says Dr. Allen, who's been known to retreat to his back office to juggle for 15 minutes if things get too hectic in his office practice.

Make a "silliness" check at 4:30 in the afternoon. "People around you need to see you smile, especially at work — we spend so much of our lives at it," says Dr. Allen. "If you haven't laughed yet, you should." A well-developed sense of humor is especially essential to avoid burnout for people in the so-called caregiving professions: doctors, nurses, teachers and writers of greeting card verse.

Lighten up. View would-be calamities through the eyes of your favorite comedian. "Say to yourself, 'How would Bill Cosby [or Erma Bombeck or Rodney Dangerfield] react to this?' " says Dr. Goodman. " 'What would he or she do in my shoes?' "

Spend time with those who help you see the bright side. "If you isolate yourself, you'll lose your perspective," says Marjorie Ingram. "Get together regularly with friends to share funny stories about daily disasters with an eye toward constructive solutions."

Heat up some "canned laughter." Every so often, you'll hear someone say,

"Someday you'll laugh about this." Ever feel like asking for an exact date? You know you need to laugh *now.*

"If you'd *like* to be able to laugh but can't – if you're feeling angry, afraid or grieved because of divorce, illness or other major stress, force yourself to laugh anyway; it will 'kick-start' your motor," says Annette Goodheart, Ph.D. (no kidding, that's her real name), who teaches classes in Beginning and Advanced Laughter at Santa Barbara City College in California. "Think about what's bothering you and try a 'tee-hee.' If that doesn't make you feel better, try a throatier 'heh-heh,' then a 'ha-ha' from the chest or a 'ho-ho' from the belly." (If your laughter ignition seems hard to start, think of something absurd – like George Washington in a pink tutu – to help trigger mirth.)

Practice makes perfect. "Like playing a musical instrument or any other skill, the more you practice laughing, the better your sense of humor becomes," says Dr. Goodman.

So when stress threatens to get the best of you, remember this: For every action there is an equal and opposite gut reaction. Make yours a belly laugh.

Chapter 36

LONELINESS

When Robert Weiss, Ph.D., a sociologist from the University of Massachusetts in Boston, who has conducted research on loneliness, delivers his classic line on the pervasiveness of that affliction, he conjures up a strong image. "Loneliness," he says, "has about the frequency of colds in the wintertime."

Why should loneliness occur so often? And who are the people who suffer this black emotion? Are they the elderly? The solitary widows wrapped in blankets, sipping tea? No. Not the old but the young, Dr. Weiss reports, complain most of feeling lonely.

"People have an image of the aged living alone, deserted by their family. That's not the case. The group most likely to experience loneliness are those in late adolescence, and it continues up to young adulthood. Just think of the music these people listen to, and how often loneliness is a theme," says Dr. Weiss. That loneliness tapers off during the years when people pair off in permanent or semipermanent relationships, or when they gain an increase in self-confidence, an acquisition that makes the world less threatening and thus makes them less vulnerable to loneliness, Dr. Weiss explains.

In the intervening years, until that self-confidence develops, many people blame themselves for feeling lonely. "People who are lonely, like people who are depressed, often attribute it to something being wrong with them. They say something like 'I don't have social skills' or 'I look bad,' " says Cecilia Solano, Ph.D., a professor of psychology at Wake Forest University, Winston-Salem, North Carolina.

Loneliness sometimes just develops because of a person's surroundings. Young people, for example, might easily suffer from "situational" loneliness. This feeling occurs when a person is separated from parents or from the high school gang. It's the same loneliness people of any age feel when they have recently moved, or when they are separating or getting divorced.

It's important for anyone who is plagued by loneliness to understand the cause of their loneliness, to connect it to their situation as a newcomer, widow, or any other changed status. "It's an extremely common phenomenon, so people shouldn't feel that it's something odd about them," says Dr. Solano.

Once you fully realize that there's a good reason for your loneliness – that it's natural, in fact – you should find ways to improve the situation. What you shouldn't do is fall into the trap of blaming yourself and feeling helpless.

Making Changes

If you've diagnosed your loneliness as a temporary thing, the process of making changes can begin. Start to focus your energy on activities that will put you in touch with both yourself and others.

First, push the loneliness to the back of your mind and devote some time, no matter how little, to a hobby, sport, spiritual pursuit or talent that you can pursue alone. That's right. Do something that will help you feel comfortable being by yourself. An absorbing and enjoyable activity will make you feel less desperate to meet people and will help you build confidence and self-reliance – traits others find attractive.

Next, find activities that will focus your attention on other people and relieve you of your temporary loneliness. Do some volunteer work at an organization where you are bound to meet like-minded people. Take a night school class in anything that interests you, whether it's Renaissance painting or assertiveness training. If you play tennis, check local tennis clubs for notices of tennis socials and attend one. "Try to pick an activity that you'll be reasonably comfortable with. It might be less anxiety producing than going to a bar," says Peter Stein, Ph.D., author of the book *Single Life*. His studies indicate that single people are relatively free from feelings of loneliness if they are hooked into friendship networks or are involved in professional counseling.

Suggestions for Older People

Widows, widowers, or even retired couples living miles away from family can consciously try to replace their departed or distant loved ones with friends. Among the solid suggestions in her book *The Survival Guide for Widows*, Canadian author and playwright Betty Jane Wylie offers a particularly imaginative one: "Make fudge with a child. If you don't have one the right age, borrow one."

Here are two more of her many suggestions.

"Crawl into a hole and pull the hole in after you. Sometimes it's so bad that's all you can do. While it's no permanent solution, it's okay to occasionally go ahead and brood. Wallow in it. Cry. Feel sorry for yourself. But don't try to share this with anyone. When you're fit for human companionship again, emerge, like a butterfly from a grubby cocoon."

And, "Forgive someone. There's a lot of residual anger flying around in you. When you're in one of these moods, pick out someone you really feel resentful of and forgive him or her. Do something for her: Bake her a loaf of bread or invite her for lunch or write her a note. Free of even a fraction of your burden of anger, you will feel much better."

This advice holds true for people of all ages. And when it comes to older people, research indicates that friends might actually do a better job than family at relieving the stress of loneliness. Ann Gerson, Ph.D., coauthored a study of 158 older people in Winnipeg and discovered that fact. "The older people who had a network of friends and no family felt less lonely than people who had family around and no friends," says the Salt Lake City psychologist.

So for older people, the message is clear: If possible, create a retirement situation where there is a built-in network of retired people that might be easy to fit into. For the families of older people, the study provides something new to consider. If you're thinking of moving an older relative in with you to take care of them, maybe you should think again. If the move deprives them of their friends, that consideration would be greater, perhaps, than the physical care you would provide, says Dr. Gerson.

Chronic Loneliness

Sometimes loneliness has nothing to do with moving to a new town, divorcing or aging. Sometimes loneliness is a chronic condition that lasts for years. It's a serious condition because the physical consequences can be deadly. In his book *The Language of the Heart,* University of Maryland psychologist James J. Lynch, Ph.D., writes: "All the available data pointed to the lack of human companionship, chronic loneliness, social isolation and the sudden loss of a loved one as being among the leading causes of premature death in the United States. And while we found that the effects of human loneliness were related to virtually every major disease — whether cancer, pneumonia or mental disease — they were particularly apparent in heart disease, the leading cause of death in the United States. Evidently millions of people were dying, quite literally, of broken or lonely hearts."

Seeking a Solution

The only way to end chronic loneliness is to make friends – an act requiring self-confidence and social skills many lonely people don't have. Both, fortunately, can be learned.

Among the more innovative forms of learning to make friends is something tailor made for chronically lonely or shy people: social skills groups. (Many of them exist in the United States, some of them even at the elementary and high school levels.)

In such a group, people can learn how to initiate a conversation with a stranger, how to conduct a telephone conversation, how to give and receive a compliment, and even how to ask for a date, says Karen Rook, Ph.D., of the University of California, Irvine. People "role play" how they would interact with others and try new ways of interacting. They get feedback on the order of "Gee, Bob, are you aware you looked at your feet during the entire discussion? Let's try it again with eye contact."

Sometimes videotapes are used. Sometimes group members are given homework to initiate a conversation on a bus, for example, and report on it. The lessons get increasingly difficult over the 10- or 12-week course, but the results are certainly worth the effort. For information on social skills groups, contact a community mental health center. If you live near a major university with a psychology department or clinical psychology clinic, inquire there.

If you want to change the way you relate to people but prefer doing it on your own, you can start by thinking about how to make friends in strategic terms. For instance, instead of going to a social function and standing in the corner, think about what you can do to take control of things you say and do. Remind yourself to ask questions and to listen to the responses, to be friendly and to be interested in people. And if possible, to try to make a friend.

The Intimacy Cure

Feeling really close to someone is tough for men in general and for college-age men in particular, according to Harry Reis, Ph.D., a professor of psychology at the University of Rochester in New York. "Men socialize as much as women, but women socialize more intimately. While men might be playing sports, they're not talking about their feelings and making intimate contact. It's intimate contact that helps avoid loneliness."

It's obvious, then, that Dr. Reis advises the lonely – regardless of gender – to try to become close to others. "Have interactions in which you open yourself up to other people and get close. Talk about how you really feel about the kinds of things most people don't usually talk about — fears and anxieties. And get into those discussions in some depth," he says.

How to determine with whom you should try to get so close? Carolyn Cutrona, associate professor of psychology at the University of Iowa, suggests you make a list of the people that are around and determine who among them are likely to develop as meaningful, rewarding friends.

If you figure you'd rather spend your time searching for the ideal lover instead of developing friends, figure again. Regardless of the fact that many chronically lonely people feel they must find a romantic relationship to overcome their loneliness, a perfect love will not necessarily make loneliness disappear. And Cutrona warns that by searching for the perfect lover, you might overlook the potential loneliness cure that exists in good friends.

Chapter 37

LOVE AND ROMANCE

Your author has found love to be the full trip,
emotionally speaking; the grand tour: fall in love, visit both
Heaven and Hell for the price of one.

—Tom Robbins, *Even Cowgirls Get the Blues*

A quick take of various *grand amours* reminds us that Shakespeare was right: "The course of true love never did run smooth." Witness the distress of Romeo and Juliet. ("She loves me, her family loves me not.") Or Lancelot and Guinevere. Or Elvis and Priscilla. Or Henry VIII and Ann Boleyn. (Please, no wisecracks about a lady losing her head over a guy.)

The special mix of fantasy, hope and uncertainty that constitutes romantic love can lead you to pure, unforgettable euphoria — or to the depths of despair.

Love can generate stress on any one of various fronts: longing for someone special; unrequited love; a romance gone sour; or when you suspect your honey has strayed. When psychologist Dorothy Tennov surveyed college students about their romantic relationships, most reported that they obtained great pleasure from love. But more than half said that they had been emotionally depressed, and more than 25 percent said that they had had suicidal thoughts.

Other psychologists report that people associate love with anxiety (would they be loved in return?), with emotional longing and with uncertainty, confusion and pain.

Adrenaline Makes the Heart Grow Fonder

Come to think of it, a certain amount of stress is what makes love and romance so euphoric.

"Obstacles lovers encounter in pursuit of their beloved often intensify love," say Elaine Hatfield, Ph.D., and her husband, G. William Walster, in their book *A New Look at Love*. "The passion of wartime romances, unrequited loves and extramarital affairs is fueled – in part, anyway – by frustration."

While *some* difficulty may add zest to a relationship, though, too much emotional stress can destroy you. "If you find yourself passionately attracted to [someone] who fills your life with pain only, stay away," say Hatfield and Walster, noted authorities on love. "In the not-so-long run, such relationships lose their passionate excitement and leave a residue of ugliness and pain."

Here are some tips from "love researchers" for taking unnecessary stress out of falling – and staying – in love.

If You're Looking for a Lover, Search for a Friend

Suppose you're not in love at the moment but want to be. The quest for love can be frustrating to anyone, but people who face dating again after a divorce or the breakup of any other long-standing exclusive relationship find the prospect of romance – or lack thereof – especially daunting.

"We all need to love and be loved, yet finding and sustaining an intimate relationship can be one of life's most difficult challenges," says Harold H. Bloomfield, M.D., in *The Achilles Syndrome*.

"If you hope to find someone to love, you had better arrange your life so as to have plenty of opportunity to associate with a variety of eligible men or women on a fairly regular basis," say Hatfield and Walster. They offer these tips:

- Don't spend your time longing for the "ideal" mate.
- Initiate contacts.
- Be extra-friendly to your neighbors and co-workers. They're the people most likely to become – or at least introduce you to – compatible mates.
- Get involved in an activity you genuinely like. Being involved in such activities allows people to learn your thoughts, feelings, attitudes and goals. It's a more efficient way to meet a like-minded mate than milling

about in singles bars, where people are often judged largely on appearance.

Learn to Shrug Off Rejection

Suppose you express interest in someone but get rebuffed?

"So what?" says Robert J. Sternberg, Ph.D., IBM professsor of psychology at Yale University, who is sometimes referred to as the "love professor" because of his research in this field. "Rejection is only a problem if people tell themselves it is.

"Let's put it this way: You have to take the attitude that dating is like shopping for a car or a house or anything else," explains Dr. Sternberg. "To see what's available, you expose yourself to many possible choices. Sure, you risk rejection in love. But if you don't, your chances of landing a less-than-optimal choice are higher.

"As the saying goes, 'You never know until you try.' If you try, at least you have a chance. But if you don't even try, you have no chance. And besides," he points out, "sometimes *you* will be the rejecter."

He/She Loves Me, He/She Loves Me Not

Cupid, with his unlimited supply of arrows, is bound to draw a bead on you sooner or later. And unless you marry – and stay married – to your first crush, chances are you will suffer the pangs of lost love at least once in your life.

"Feelings of loss are painful. We can accept them – we do not have to go crazy or become irrational – but they *are* painful. That is reality," says Nathaniel Branden, Ph.D., in his book *The Psychology of Romantic Love*.

"Even among mature, well-actualized individuals, love is not necessarily 'forever,' " says Dr. Branden. "As people continue to grow and evolve, their needs and desires change or shift as to emphasis. New goals and longings can emerge, causing rifts in relationships. This does not mean – or need not mean – that love has 'failed.' A union that provides great joy, nourishment and stimulation for two human beings is not a 'failure' merely because it does not last forever; it can still be a great experience that one is glad to have lived."

Even within successful, lasting marriages, passion usually ebbs eventually, its loss supplemented with highly rewarding yet less stressful companionate love – shared understanding, attitudes and interests (in short, intimate friendship). "Most couples find, happily, that a friend is really what they needed all along," say Hatfield and Walster.

Love Poison #9:
What an Affair Really Means

Perhaps the most stressful kind of love is that between people who are married, but not to each other. (This is equally true for romantic infidelity outside any exclusive love relationship.) Such affairs usually arise out of a desire for novelty and excitement or a desire to assure ourselves that we are still attractive. Sometimes an individual has an affair as revenge for something his or her mate did, or out of loneliness during long but unavoidable separations. But sometimes an outside affair – or a string of affairs – serves as a painkiller, to make marriage (or an equivalent relationship) more bearable. It can serve to distract you from or buffer the stress of dealing with problems within the primary relationship.

And, hard as it may be to believe, an outside affair sometimes has nothing at all to do with the primary relationship, but instead functions as a panacea for a generalized sense of tedium or boredom, or as consolation for some frustration not in our marriage but in our work or career.

"For those who are tempted by extramarital affairs, it can be very important to ask, 'How do I imagine I would feel about my marriage if I were *not* to have extramarital affairs?' " says Dr. Branden. At that point, ask yourself, "Is it worth jeopardizing my primary relationship?"

"One thing seems clear," says Dr. Branden. "It is an error to assume that if two people 'really' love each other it is impossible for either of them to have an affair – or to desire one – with anyone else."

"There are two issues with infidelity," says Dr. Sternberg. "First, was there infidelity, and second, what does it mean? The problem is, people focus too much on the first issue and not on the second. There's a big difference between a one-night stand with someone your partner doesn't particularly care about and an ongoing relationship with someone he or she sees every day." But if the relationship between two people is good, they'll get through the outside affair, says Dr. Sternberg.

Controlling Jealousy
Before It Controls You

If your mate has strayed, it's not easy to see the philosophical aspects of a fling. Mainly, you feel sick. Hurt. Angry. Distraught. Confused. Betrayed. Trapped. Paralyzed. *And undeniably stressed.* This is because jealousy is not one emotion but a chaotic jumble of painful feelings, according to psychologists. Most agree, though, that jealousy has two basic components: a feeling of battered pride and a fear of losing one's property.

"Healthy jealousy doesn't stem from your own poor self-image," says Roger Callahan, Ph.D., in his book *It Can Happen to You.* "It's focused on the loss of a romantic love . . . a perfectly healthy response to a terribly stressful situation."

Tempering jealousy – and panic – from the outset can prevent a bad situation from getting worse.

"If someone you love very much has stopped loving you and fallen in love with another person, it's likely that you'll feel jealous," says Dr. Callahan. "It's healthy and natural to not want to lose things you value highly, and there's nothing more valuable than intense romantic love."

Most people respond to jealousy in one of two ways. Some try to protect their egos by berating their partners or trying to get even. Others try to improve their floundering relationship by trying to improve their appearance, talking things out and so forth. Men are more likely to externalize the cause – to blame the partner or the third party. Women often internalize the cause – they blame themselves.

How can you relieve this stress before it devastates you?

"When you begin to feel twinges of suspicion and jealousy, the sooner you exorcise them – get them out – the less likely they are to drive you crazy and, in the process, ruin a relationship that might otherwise be in fine shape," says Dr. Callahan.

If you suspect an affair, be sure that you have good reasons. Seeking constant reassurance from an innocent mate can destroy an otherwise sound relationship.

What if your worst fears are fact? "You will be faced with a choice of either competing and trying to win back your lover, accepting the situation and waiting for its ultimate resolution or making the final break yourself," says Dr. Callahan.

Establish an Optimal Distance from the Start

The threat of a romantic rival isn't the sole trigger of jealousy between lovers. One may feel jealous of a mate's interest in friends, co-workers, sports or hobbies. Undue possessiveness can cause stress for both parties: One person fears being abandoned, while the other feels trapped.

If you and your mate are emotional Siamese twins – joined at the heart – you're more apt to suffer pangs of jealousy, warranted or otherwise, than people who maintain a reasonable distance between themselves.

"Many counselors have found that it's a lot easier for couples to maintain a close – while not excessively possessive – love relationship if they each maintain some separate friends and interests," say Hatfield and Walster. In other words, if you have your own identity – if you associate with others who like and admire you – you are far less likely to fear being abandoned by your partner, "and it's a lot easier to cope if you are," the researchers add.

What's more, it's unlikely that any two people – no matter how perfectly matched or how much in love – will fulfill 100 percent of each other's "minimum daily requirement" of attention. Think of your emotional needs as a pie chart. While your mate will probably fulfill the largest segment, other people are bound to contribute fair portions of affection and companionship. In fact, when one partner spends some time with friends outside the relationship, it takes pressure off the other to be the total means of emotional support.

"This is something that every couple has to work out individually, depending on their emotional needs. But expectations should be negotiated early in a relationship," says Dr. Sternberg. "Because if the road starts to diverge, it tends to continue to diverge. The longer you wait to address the issue, the more likely the other person will be to get defensive, and the harder it will be to resolve it."

Love can be stressful, yes. But falling in love needn't send you into a tailspin if you take measures to stay in control.

Chapter 38

MARITAL CONFLICTS

The object in marriage, according to myth, is to wed a mate who blends perfectly with your personality and temperament. Presumably, once this miracle occurs, you can set your marital cruise control on automatic and live in complete harmony happily ever after.

In reality, though, conflict and discord are bound to arise some time after the wedding cake is sliced. And it doesn't necessarily take a major calamity (like loss of a job) or a staggering blow (like infidelity) to strain a relationship. Everyday stresses can create considerable friction and fireworks, especially if you and your spouse can't discuss the most trivial of issues without acrimony.

"All stressors do not lead to conflict, but many do, particularly those that have to do with money, sex, children and shared responsibility in the family," writes Dolores Curran in her book *Stress and the Healthy Family.* And when these stresses reach a high level, they can damage the marriage, unless the couple has the skills needed to resolve conflict.

Bickering and Your Blood Pressure

Poorly handled, marital conflict can also jeopardize your physical health. Researchers in the Department of Psychology at the University of Michigan and School of Public Health studied 696 men and women for 12 years and concluded that an inability to express anger combined with marital stress can *double* the risk of death for people with high blood pressure. Apparently, *how* married people cope with anger makes quite a difference, say the researchers. "Anger-In" (suppressing your feelings) and "Anger-Out" (venting your anger on the spot) escalate internal stress, while "reflective coping" (waiting for the anger to subside and then rationally discussing the conflict) is easier on your health. The reflective coping style appears to be the healthiest choice because it restores a sense of control over the situation and helps solve the problem. (For more information on dealing with anger, see chapter 2.)

Further analysis showed a strong link between marital stress and higher blood pressure among women aged 30 to 44, who were more likely to either suppress their anger or feel guilty if they express it. The highest levels of blood pressure were found in women aged 45 to 69 who reported greater marital stress and were more likely to suppress anger. The researchers speculate that women who suppress their anger store up dissatisfaction and resentment.

Keeping your cool on the domestic front may boost your immunity and foster good health in general, according to a study of marital stress and immunity conducted by psychologist Janice Kiecolt-Glaser, Ph.D., and Ronald Glaser, Ph.D., professor of microbiology and immunology at the Ohio State University College of Medicine. Blood tests indicated that married women who rated their marriage as poor had weaker immune systems than those who said they were happily married.

How to Stop Arguing—For Good

When your spouse says or does something that makes you angry, do you: (a) swallow your fury and try not to "make waves," (b) tell him or her immediately — and quite vocally — how annoyed you are, (c) give your spouse the cold shoulder for two weeks, (d) take a few minutes to think about the situation, then raise your concerns calmly and rationally.

If you chose (d), give yourself a gold star: You probably resolve most of your difficulties without too much acrimony. The other options usually escalate stress levels.

Marriage counselors say that in many cases of marital conflict, the real problem is not the topic under discussion — money, sex, work, time or children — but poor communication style.

"Certain communication styles — blaming, placating, deciding by decree and dismissing issues or avoidance — don't solve problems but perpetuate conflict," says Lori Heyman Gordon, director of the Family Relations Institute, Falls Church, Virginia.

In contrast, "the couples best able to deal with everyday stresses are those who develop workable ways of solving their disagreements and a fat supply of coping skills," says Curran.

You can turn your arguments into constructive problem-solving discussions by learning to spot negative communication styles and correcting your course accordingly, suggests Gordon.

"Blaming is typical of the 'Virginia Woolf' type of marriage, where one person is very judgmental – always nitpicking, a constant critic or chronic complainer," says Gordon. "Blaming alienates a person and attacks their self-worth so that they end up either defending themselves, launching a counterattack or just tuning out the critic instead of dealing with the issue at hand."

Placating, or accommodating, your spouse is an easy way out that can eventually backfire, say marriage counselors.

"Saying everything is fine when it isn't leads to a situation where the placater just collects injustices until, much to his or her spouse's surprise, he or she just leaves," says Gordon.

Ignoring or dismissing feelings – either your own or your spouse's, also dead-ends a discussion.

"We call these people 'super reasoners,' " says Gordon. "They say things like, 'That's not the way you're supposed to feel, so I will ignore your feelings.' Or they will decide by issuing a decree or by deferring to higher authority, with statements like, 'This is the way my parents always handled it and this is how we are going to do it.' "

Still other people are avoiders who simply refuse to deal with the underlying problem. "It may seem easy just to make believe that what's happening isn't happening, to put your head in the sand like an ostrich and hope that when you look up again, the trouble will be gone," says Gordon. But it won't. (And it may get worse.)

Scratching the Marital Itch

Poor communication styles, like other bad habits, evolve over time and can often be traced back to earlier conflicts in life that condition us to react the way we do.

"You don't have to spend years in psychotherapy to realize that you may be reacting to your spouse the way you dealt with parental criticism," says Gordon. "Poor communication may be related to the psychological age of the person you're dealing with. If one or the other or both of you are stuck in the adolescent stage of 'Don't tell me what to do,' that person may hear a legitimate concern as an effort to treat them as a child, and react accordingly.

"Also, if you had a parent who deceived you, you may not trust your spouse and may question his or her honesty even if they are being truthful," points out Gordon. "I call that an 'emotional allergy.' We are programmed by early experience to react one way to certain similar triggers, like breaking out in hives when you wear any kind of perfume."

The key to reducing marital tension, then, is to modify your communication style.

To blamers, Gordon says, "Think about how you're going to be heard. Speak your mind without placing blame on the other person. Instead of saying, 'You are wrong' or 'You made a mistake,' say 'I feel bad when . . .' or 'I am hurt when. . . .' "

To placaters/accommodators, Gordon says, "Your spouse can't read your mind and will have no way of knowing what's bothering you or what you expect them to do if you don't tell them. Does it bother you, for example, that your husband waits until the last minute to buy you a birthday present and then ends up spending more than your budget can afford? If you don't act overjoyed, he'll be confused because he honestly thought he was doing something nice."

To super reasoners, the "Mr. Spocks," Gordon says, "Use your logic and reasoning powers to create solutions and solve problems the best you can, but also think about the impact of your reasoning on the other's feelings."

To avoiders, Gordon says, "Allow yourself a temporary cooling-off period, if necessary, but don't ignore a problem indefinitely in the hope that it will go away. Make plans to solve it."

More Tips for Peaceful Coexistence

"Many people avoid confrontation of any kind because they are very uncomfortable with the tension of conflict itself," says Curran. "And sometimes, avoiding conflict is appropriate. But generally, compromise and collaboration are better. Over time, couples find that the more they resolve, the better they get at it. But the less they resolve, the worse things get."

Curran offers two additional tips for resolving conflicts peaceably.

First, separate the issue from the person, so that you don't habitually think: If you disagree with me, you don't love me. "Disagreement is a normal part of life," says Curran. "We disagree with co-workers and still manage to get along. Why not at home? Couples need to establish early in the relationship that they can disagree, whether it's over where to spend Christmas or who to vote for in the next election, and not stop loving each other."

Second, fight respectfully. "That means don't attack one another's weaknesses or bring up past transgressions or unpleasantness," says Curran. "And no name calling."

"What all this boils down to," says Gordon, "is, speak in your own behalf, but also care about how the other feels and work toward a mutually beneficial solution. Because if your conflicts always have to have a winner and a loser, then you both lose."

Chapter 39

MASSAGE

The first bit of advice: Avoid massages in places that bear flashing, neon signs. You won't be relieving any stress in *these* establishments. Instead, put yourself in the hands of a trained masseuse or masseur, who will transform your uptight, knotty body into a completely relaxed puddle of pure bliss.

Swedish massage, also called Western or European massage, is the most common method used for stress management. It was developed by Per Henrik Ling as part of a medical program designed to treat disease. For bedridden people, massage often was used to take the place of exercise and to improve a patient's circulation. That's why some of the strokes are more stimulating than relaxing. All strokes are made toward the heart, to stimulate the blood supply as well as the lymph glands. "As blood flow is enhanced to the tissues, better oxygenation and cell nutrition results and more efficient removal of waste products, such as cell debris, is accomplished," says Gail Bell, an Arlington, Virginia, massage therapist. Pain or tension may vanish.

If you're visiting a massage therapist to counter your body's response to stress, you probably will receive a blending of Swedish massage techniques and a few other, more relaxing, methods.

Swedish massage relies on five basic strokes.

Effleurage. These are long and gliding strokes that relax tense muscles and stimulate circulation. This is the most common stroke.

Petrassage. This is a squeezing and kneading of the muscles.

Tapotement. This is the karate chop stroke. The masseuse or masseur hacks, taps or cups you with the sides of his or her hands or with fingertips. It's infrequently used in a relaxation massage.

Vibration. This is when the massage therapist uses two fingers to rapidly tap in either one spot or a series of spots.

Friction. This is created when a circular and rolling motion is applied to the muscle near the spine and the joints. It, too, increases circulation but in a more localized way than the other strokes.

These strokes form the basis of other hands-on therapies such as shiatsu (also called acupressure) massage, which is a finger pressure stimulation of acupuncture "meridians," which Chinese medicine believes correspond to the flow of energy in your body. Esalen massage, developed at the new-age Esalen Institute in Big Sur, California, is a free-flow relaxation massage, often done to the accompaniment of burning incense and soft music.

What to Expect

A full-body massage generally lasts an hour and takes place on a hard table. And a good massage therapist will, in addition to doing what's necessary during the treatment, send you out the door with homework, such as suggested exercises or instructions on how to massage your legs after a run, says Gene Arbetter, a Chicago massage therapist and chairman of the American Massage Therapy Association's (AMTA) department of information and inquiry.

The best way to receive a massage is in the nude, with a sheet covering the parts of your body that a massage therapist never touches: genitals and breasts. Even a modest amount of clothing will impede a massage and require a massage therapist to leave important muscle groups unmassaged. As a massagee, you may be told to focus on your breathing and on the parts of your body that are being massaged, and to relax. This is a time to let go of tension, and one time not to feel rushed. When the massage is over, it's often nice to lie still with your eyes closed.

When you go for a massage, the American Massage Therapy Association, the oldest and largest organization of massage therapists, recommends you check to see if the place is clean. Then ask for credentials. Certified members of the AMTA have completed 500 hours of approved AMTA in-class study or passed an entrance exam. A therapist who has completed an additional three years of professional work and passed another exam is a Registered Massage Therapist, or RMT. About a dozen states have licensing requirements for massage therapists. Check with a massage therapist to see that he or she has the proper state and, in some cases, local, licenses. Also note whether the practitioner appears confident in what he or she is doing. And finally, be sure to point out any injuries or health conditions the practitioner should be aware of. (He or she should ask you about them before beginning.)

For more information about massage, write to the American Massage Therapy Association, 1329 West Pratt Boulevard, Chicago, IL 60626, or phone (312) 761-2682.

Chapter 40

MONEY WORRIES

The evolution of piggy banks into automatic teller machines may have changed how we save our money, but how we *feel* about money is the same — stressed. Asked which emotions they most often associated with money, 71 percent of the 20,000 people responding to a survey conducted by *Psychology Today* listed anxiety. Fifty-two percent listed depression and another 51 percent, anger. (More than one response was allowed.)

Those most troubled by money — and they were not necessarily poor — complained of more fatigue, headaches, insomnia and other stress-related complaints than those least troubled by money.

And in researching her book *Stress and the Healthy Family*, Dolores Curran found that when asked to list their troubles, "the number one stress reported by respondents has to do with economics, financing and budgeting."

What makes money so stressful? Mainly the fear of what will happen without enough of it. Inflation, taxation, single parenthood and even increased longevity all threaten financial security. So no book on stress would be complete without some guidelines for gaining better control of your financial life and reducing the stress of economic uncertainty.

Breaking Financial Free-Fall

Are you going broke at the speed of light? No matter how hard you try to shake off debts, do bills seem to stick to you like Velcro? To bring your situation under control – and diffuse a lot of unnecessary worry – take some time to decide where you stand financially, where you want to stand and how to get there. Here are some suggestions to help you do that.

Make a budget. Say "budget" and most people immediately think of financial austerity – no steak, no movies, no fun. But a budget is simply a way to better meet both your needs (food, clothing, shelter, transportation) and your wants (restaurant meals, designer clothes, a spacious house and a luxury car).

"Sound personal planning has no more to do with belt tightening and crash budgeting than dieting has to do with self-starvation," say David M. Brownstone and Jacques Sartisky, coauthors of *Personal Financial Survival.*

Besides drawing a more realistic idea of what you can and cannot afford, a written budget can reveal where your oh-so-disposable money goes – those Bermuda Triangles of finance that swallow up hundreds of stray dollars every year. In that way, a carefully thought-out budget can relieve the stress of wondering why you always seem broke no matter how hard you work.

"Control is the key word," says Patricia Elder-Jucker, Ph.D., psychologist at the Temple University Counseling Center in Philadelphia. "A budget helps people feel that they control their money and that money doesn't control them."

Make a five-year plan. "To further avoid the anxiety of not knowing where you stand or where you're headed, decide on a goal," says Dr. Elder-Jucker. "Do you want to buy a house? A second car? Start a retirement plan? Then make a written plan of action stating how you will achieve your goal or goals."

Hold family business meetings. Most businesses, large or small, hold regular business meetings to evaluate their finances. Since a household is another form of small business, regularly reviewing household finances makes fiscal sense. "Regular, planned discussions about household finances take the sting out of the conversation, preventing conflict and blame," says Dr. Elder-Jucker.

Consider professional advice. If you need help establishing a budget or managing your debts, consider an accountant, banker, financial planning adviser or other person trained and equipped to deal with finances. Financial advice columnist Sylvia Porter also recommends the Consumer Credit Counseling Service, a nonprofit, community-sponsored group whose services are confidential and low-cost or free (depending on your income). To locate the office nearest you, consult your area telephone directory.

Brownstone and Sartisky caution against seeking financial advice solely from insurance sellers, stockbrokers or others who may have a financial interest in your decisions. Look for a financial adviser who will pay attention your needs, goals and desires, not dispense broad financial advice, they recommend. "You expect such concern from your medical physician – it is not too much to expect from your 'financial physician,' " say the authors.

How to Deal with Budget Breakdowns

Do you live from crisis to crisis? Do inevitable but surprise expenses like new tires, clothes for the kids and a broken water heater leave your "budget" shaken, to say nothing of your composure?

The key to coping? Expect the unexpected.

Establish an emergency fund. Dolores Curran advises putting a share of each paycheck into savings for unexpected repairs, replacements, trips and medical bills, *separate* from long-range untouchable savings for your child's education or your retirement. "When families have a cushion, they don't fall apart when something out of the ordinary happens," she says.

Other psychologists agree. "Sure, unexpected crises like job loss or car repair create anxiety," says Dr. Elder-Jucker. "But having money put aside to take care of them reduces the anxiety created."

Consider automatic payroll deduction. "An . . . excellent way to save is to authorize your bank to deduct a specified percentage from your paycheck when you deposit the paycheck in your checking account and to transfer this percentage to your savings account," says Sylvia Porter in her book, *Sylvia Porter's New Money Book for the Eighties.* "Make it 10 percent, if you can manage, or 5 percent – but make the transfer automatic and regular. The automatic, regular feature is the secret."

Weathering the Worst

Should the bottom fall out of your financial plan due to a major disabling illness, accident or legal difficulties, you can still land on your feet. There are some strategies you can use to survive the stress of a financial catastrophe.

Don't blame yourself. "Many things are beyond our control," says Dr. Elder-Jucker. "So when catastrophe strikes, it's okay to feel sad. But it's also important not to blame yourself or feel guilty or ashamed. Don't torture yourself by thinking, 'If only . . .' or 'I should have. . . .' "

Negotiate your bills. "Most doctors and hospitals are willing to discuss a workable payment schedule for unanticipated medical or dental bills," says Lisa Astor, adminstrator with the Health Benefits Research Center in New York City. "This reduces strain on family members who are already under considerable stress caused by hospitalization or illness."

Know your rights. Until you get back on your financial feet, bill collectors may start nipping at your heels, adding to your aggravation. To protect consumers from harassment, the Fair Debt Collection Practices Act prohibits debt collectors from contacting you at unreasonable times (before 8:00 A.M. or after 9:00 P.M.), bugging you at work or otherwise hounding you about money owed. For a copy of the law, contact the Division of Credit Practices, Federal Trade Commission, Washington, DC 20580.

Reducing Social Insecurity

Sometimes, even financially secure people don't seem to have enough money and find themselves driven to earn more and more money, creating a different kind of stress.

"For many, money – and what it buys – is a barometer of how they're doing," says Dr. Elder-Jucker. "But money is a precarious and inaccurate measure of self-esteem, since finances can change. Find something else in your life besides dollar signs to measure your worth."

Nonmaterial rewards – reaped through friendship, community work, teaching – can help balance financial concerns in your self-esteem ledger.

Chapter 41

MUSIC

When young David played his harp for troubled King Saul, he acted as one of history's first known music therapists, someone who knew the magical powers of this universal language.

Modern-day music therapists categorize tunes as either stimulating or sedative. Stimulating music – like an Irish jig or disco music – gets people clapping their hands, tapping their toes or dancing. Sedative music has a much slower, easier rhythm – approximately 60 beats per minute, and as regular as your heartbeat at rest. Calming music has been used to reduce distress and pain among people in dentists' offices, childbirth centers, coronary care units and migraine headache clinics.

"The right music can take you from a highly tense state to a relaxed yet alert state in as little as 30 seconds," says Steven Halpern, Ph.D., a pioneering composer, performer and producer in the field of music as it relates to health. By a fascinating and complex process, relaxing music seems to trigger the release of endorphins, opiate-like substances in the brain that make us feel less anxious, according to Dr. Halpern.

Andante for Relaxation

Instrumental pieces – notably those performed by flute, harp, piano and string ensembles – tend to be more soothing than vocal pieces, which can distract you. Surprisingly, studies have shown that not all classical music is relaxing. Look for sonatas and symphonies played *adagio* (in a slow tempo) or *andante* (moderately slow) that approximate the heart's natural rate at rest. (Some records now offer *adagio* or *andante* selections or movements only.)

Some jazz, blues or other traditional music may also instill calmness. As for background music, surveys show that many people find "canned" music irritating.

Dr. Halpern (and some new-age musicians) have been composing music with no dominant melody or rhythm. These compositions are intentionally designed to induce serenity. To measure the relaxation potential of the music you usually enjoy, pay attention to how your body responds. "If you feel yourself breathing more slowly and deeply, the music is relaxing you," says Dr. Halpern. "If, on the other hand, you can feel a slight tightness in the back of your neck or your solar plexus, it's not."

Chapter 42

NATURE

I went to the woods because I wished to live
deliberately, to front only the essential facts of life, and see if
I could not learn what it had to teach. . . .

—Thoreau

Thoreau filled a book with what he learned about the wonderfully regenerating effects of living alone in the woods.

If you too want to behold the same wonders of Mother Nature – and let go of stress – you don't have to transport your household to a log cabin by a pond. You don't even have to rent a weekend cottage by the sea or drag the family out to a picnic in the park.

The first rule for enjoying nature is to appreciate what's around you, wherever you are. Joseph Nold, director of Colorado Outward Bound School for 15 years, has spent a great chunk of his life in wilderness of the most serious sorts. But he appreciates the joys of nature virtually anywhere he goes – even in New York City. "I can recall walking across the George Washington Bridge at sunset and it being an almost mystical experience," he says.

What is it about nature that's so great for relieving stress? Scientists have studied the phenomenon, and when they report on their findings, they sound like, well, scientists.

One famous study divided the benefits wilderness vacationers enjoyed into two categories. "Health-related experiences" included "mental relaxation" and "feelings of receptivity and harmony with the environment." The other part, "aesthetic-transpersonal experiences" consisted of "awareness of beauty and flux of the natural world," "perceptual alertness," "personal insight," and "expanded identity."

Maybe a key to nature's ability to soothe lies in the simple fact that it transports us away from our chores and demands and worries.

Self-Medicating with Meadows and Clouds

"When we're overloaded with everyday concerns, nature takes us away from our problems," says David C. Glass, Ph.D., a professor of psychology at State University of New York at Stony Brook. "The break allows us to restore our energy. It could have tremendous benefits in alleviating negative feelings. And as self-medication goes, it's a lot better than the self-medication people too often engage in – smoking, alcohol and drug abuse."

Outdoorsman Nold, who now directs the wilderness program at United World College in Montezuma, New Mexico, calls it "a way of getting in touch with another reality.

"Life slows down for you in the outdoors. There's a very different view of life when it takes an hour to travel two miles than when you drive down the highway at 70 miles per hour," he says. "There's a whole different rhythm to life, and it's very different from the speed at which we usually live, which is stressful."

So you slow down. "You plod through decisions you have to make, questions you may have about yourself," he says. You put time in a new perspective.

Spend a half hour watching the waves crash onto a beach and think about how many centuries the waves have been crashing against the same shoreline. Study the layers of earth in the Grand Canyon – each layer representing a geological time period. Does that put your son's unacceptable new hairstyle in a different light? "If you're on the seas, if you're in the desert, you can't help but put your problems in perspective," says Nold.

Nature also gives you delights to look forward to. What greater encore to summer could there be than the autumn leaves? "The Japanese are very wise. They have a tradition of appreciating the changes of nature. Families go out for walks to observe the cherry blossoms when they come," says Albert Mehrabian, Ph.D., a professor of psychology at UCLA and author of *Public Places and Private Spaces*.

The Scientific Evidence

You can derive soothing benefits from nature even if you just look at a picture or a film of it, says Roger Ulrich, Ph.D., a University of Delaware geography professor who has studied the influence of the outdoors on people. In one study, a group of mildly stressed students who had just completed a two-hour exam were seated in a windowless room and asked to rate their feelings on a host of stress/anxiety measures. Immediately afterward, half of the students were shown pictures of beautiful outdoor scenes; the other half was shown pictures depicting urban scenes that lacked natural beauty. When they were retested, the "nature" group had recuperated nicely from stress. The "urban" group? They actually tested worse on certain measures of stress and anxiety, according to Dr. Ulrich.

Another study measured the physiological impact of watching a nature film. To get the subjects sufficiently stressed, Dr. Ulrich and a collaborator showed 120 volunteers a disturbing film about work accidents. After viewing the film, the volunteers watched one of six different videotapes depicting an outdoor environment. Two of the films were of nature and four were of unblighted urban scenes.

When the subjects were tested for such stress indicators as increased muscle tension, blood pressure and heart rate, the findings were consistent. "Those who saw nature tapes recovered much faster and more completely than those who saw the urban tapes," says Dr. Ulrich.

Another test showed that surgery patients recovered faster if they had bedside windows that looked out on nature, as opposed to windows that fronted a brick wall.

The Adventure of Rain

Is this enough to get you racing to the nearest babbling brook or towering oak every time stress rears its head? What's that—a trip to nature would be a major interruption of your day? Keep in mind that there are near-constant opportunities to experience nature.

"You can take advantage of those opportunities even if you only spend a few moments looking out the window or checking what's going on in the garden," says Stephen Kaplan, Ph.D., an environmental psychologist and psychology professor at the University of Michigan, Ann Arbor. He adds that people should not feel guilty about taking nature breaks. "Recognize that it's a way to enhance your effectiveness."

Traditionally, religious leaders turned to wilderness for divine inspiration. You can, too, and right in your own backyard. "Sunrises and sunsets are particularly compelling," says Nold. So get up in the predawn, step outside and experience the building crescendo of a new day. No sun today? Go out and stand in the rain, recommends Nold. "You will experience yourself in a new way, an experience that is renewing."

Dr. Kaplan says it is therapeutic to "make a great adventure out of a small thing." That's a lesson Nold learns from novices who return from jaunts alone in the wilderness as part of survival programs. He says they frequently tell stories about such experiences as intently studying an ant that crawled across their arm.

You, too, can discover the universe in a grain of sand.

Chapter 43

NUTRITION

When we're under stress, our bodies use up nutrients faster and less efficiently than they ordinarily do. Just when – for our bodies' sake – we should be dining on fish or whole wheat pasta, we're often up to our elbows in chocolate chip cookies and ice cream. Seeking comfort in special treats, we're sabotaging our bodies. We're also probably unsettling our digestion, which may already be in open rebellion against the stress we're under.

This then is a formula for a nutritional deficit – a poor diet plus poor digestion, combined with an increased demand for nutrients. And this stress spawns another. "Our stress responses often consume great amounts of energy, and as our energy is depleted we are less able to respond to stress," says Derrick Lonsdale, M.D., a preventive medicine physician in Westlake, Ohio.

What to do? The obvious answer for most people – one you learned at your mother's knee – is to eat three well-balanced meals a day. The advice, however, is easier said than done.

If you're too stressed to cope with menu planning, do yourself a good turn by trying to meet your body's greatest nutritional demands at times of high stress.

You may need more B vitamins. Many nutrition experts agree that the B vitamins – probably more than any other nutrients – take it on the chin when a body is under severe stress. "They are used up in the process of becoming exhausted, physically or mentally, and they have to be restored," says Charles Tkacz, M.D., medical director of the North Nassau Mental Health Center in Manhasset, New York.

The B vitamins play a complicated role. They are required for the body's process of turning food into fuel. They're needed to supply the brain with glucose, its energy source. With insufficient glucose, the brain begins to perform poorly, according to Dr. Tkacz.

In addition, several of the B vitamins are involved in the production of neurotransmitters, biochemicals that allow the brain cells to pass messages along their nerve pathways. Without sufficient vitamins B_6 and B_{12}, a person may experience depression, fatigue and confusion. Moreover, B vitamins enhance the body's immune mechanism and help protect us from responding to stress with illness, says Dr. Tkacz.

Foods high in the B vitamins include organ meats like liver and kidneys, whole grains, nuts, seeds and beans.

You may need more vitamin C. "Stress is a factor that steps up your vitamin C requirements," says Robert Haskell, M.D., a San Francisco physician who specializes in preventive medicine and nutritional support. "If anything helps you battle the effects of stress, it's vitamin C."

As Dr. Haskell explains, stress washes out our supply of vitamin C, so we must replenish it by eating foods high in vitamin C or taking a supplement. How much you take should vary with your size and weight, so Dr. Haskell suggests that each individual be sure to get an adequate amount for his or her needs. (Of course, don't take high dosages of vitamin C or any other nutrient without your doctor's approval and supervision.)

You may need more protein and calcium. Scientific studies show that under emotional stress, the body loses an excessive amount of nitrogen through the urine. This generally indicates protein in the body tissues is being used up, says Arline McDonald, Ph.D., a nutritionist at the Northwestern University Medical School Department of Community Health and Preventive Medicine. And protein is needed as a source of amino acids, which are necessary for growth and maintenance. These acids produce enzymes important in combating stress. B vitamins are "co-enzymes," helping the amino acids to do their work.

The answer, says Dr. McDonald, is simply to get more protein. But that doesn't mean you should throw a slab of sirloin onto your plate at each meal. During times of high stress, your stomach is not ready to handle more food. "Instead, eat a little protein at a time, distributing it over the day," says Dr. McDonald. She recommends chicken, fish, egg whites and plain old peanut butter sandwiches on whole wheat bread.

And drink milk, of course. Calcium, like nitrogen, is lost through the urine in times of high stress. To compensate, Dr. McDonald suggests you increase your intake of low-fat dairy products. Not only do they contain calcium, but they will also help supplement your protein needs, too.

You don't need fats. According to Dr. McDonald, they contain little nutrition but *lots* of calories.

You don't need caffeine. "It's a stimulant to the adrenal glands that will cause all of the cells in the body to work overtime," says Nan Kathryn Fuchs, Ph.D., a Santa Monica nutritionist. "It won't let the body rest and recuperate."

You don't need much sugar. Because sugar has only minuscule amounts of some minerals, a trace of B vitamins and no protein, it can't do much to satisfy your body's hunger for nutrition. But if a slice of apple pie can help you get through an occasional crisis, use it for solace. Just be sure you wash it down with a big glass of skim milk.

Chapter 44

ON-THE-JOB
STRESS

The 40 hours or more you spend each week at work represents a large chunk of your life. On-the-job frustration and conflict can reduce productivity. And if you think a bad work scene doesn't take a serious toll on your body and mind, pay attention.

Robert Collier Page, M.D., studied 100 employees who were placed in jobs that did not meet their level of intelligence or match their aptitudes, personality, behavioral characteristics and aspiration. After carefully examining the employees, this early student of workplace stress and one-time medical director of Standard Oil Company of New Jersey (now Exxon), learned that they suffered from sleeplessness, headaches, despondency, stiffness, backaches, fatigue and gastrointestinal symptoms. None of them were found to have a disease as such. Rather, their symptoms seemed to stem from their jobs. In his landmark 1963 book *Occupational Health and Mantalent Development,* Dr. Page writes: "If no one else happens to observe what is happening, the individual will continue to push himself blithely into the performance of tasks against which his entire inner being rebels. Eventually this inner being or subconscious will strike back in the only way it knows how, by producing a symptom of illness to warn the misassigned that it is time to stop, look and listen."

It gets worse, he writes. "The same habits of self-deception which he has acquired in order to stick to his job will enable him to shrug off the first minor symptoms of potential functional illness. . . . If by this time he is fairly well advanced into his middle years, this creeping loss of health will be progressive and, when he is finally forced to recognize his true predicament, irreversible."

An Abundance of Research

In the decades since that study, an abundance of research has linked job stress to illness. The link is so great that Paul J. Rosch, M.D., president of the American Institute of Stress, says, "Stress in the workplace may well be the number one health problem for the working adult population in the United States." Here's a sampling of stress-related illnesses.

- Working excessive hours and holding down more than one job has been associated with coronary heart disease.
- Monotonous work has been associated with job dissatisfaction, poor mental health, coronary heart disease, peptic ulcers and gastritis.
- The stress of conflicting job demands has been linked to depression and such physiological strains as increased heart rate and increased blood pressure.

What, exactly, makes working so stressful? For one thing, a lack of control. A study of nearly 1,500 workers found that nonparticipation in the decision-making process at work was related to low self-esteem, escapist drinking and overall poor health. These were the same symptoms of workers who faced an uncertain employment future.

For another thing, feeling angry. A team from the University of Pittsburgh's Department of Epidemiology compared those who frequently experience anger-producing job stress *and* suppress their anger, with others. What researchers found is that people who experience job stress and suppress their anger have a greater risk of high blood pressure than those who either experience similar levels of job stress or suppress their anger. The trouble comes from experiencing both stress *and* suppressed anger, according to Eric M. Cottington, Ph.D., an epidemiologist from Pittsburgh's Allegheny-Singer Research Institute, who headed the research team.

What is a worker to do about lack of control or on-the-job anger? One approach is to change the job so that it becomes less stressful. The other approach is to change the person's reaction to the job.

Changing the Job

"One option is to develop a strategy for changing the work environment. Calmly, rationally and with a well-devised plan, ask your boss for more guidance, more freedom, more money — whatever it is you need," suggests Dr. Cottington.

You can work to change the job with the help of a boss, co-workers, a labor union or other organization. This can mean changing the responsibilities or the hours. It also can mean organizing a lunch-hour volleyball game.

If you can't improve your workplace, maybe you can improve the way you view it. "An employee who feels he has control over what he is doing is a much happier and healthier employee," says Stewart G. Wolf, Jr., M.D., professor of medicine at Temple University, Philadelphia, and director of the Totts Gap Medical Research Laboratory in Bangor, Pennsylvania. You can reduce the stress of any job by seizing as much control over the situation as possible.

Let's go to work with Bobbi White, the office manager for a busy Pennsylvania car mechanic shop, to see how she manages to achieve a level of control over a tough situation. White often finds herself in an awkward place: between customers who are griping about getting their cars repaired and mechanics who sometimes cannot accommodate the onslaught of ill vehicles. "The favorite thing that customers do is to make their problems your problems. They call up and say, 'What do you mean you can't take me today? My inspection runs out,' " says White.

Her response? "I put it back squarely on their shoulders. I make them aware of the fact that they had three months in which to get their car inspected. I don't say it abruptly. But I tell them that they had the time to do it earlier and that I'd be happy to make an appointment for the first available time. They have to settle for it. I can't tell a mechanic to hurry up. You'd be rushing something that involves safety," she says. "I tend to get extremely bothered by people who yell at me. But I can't yell back. The worst I'll do is get abrupt."

"She's doing the right thing," says Albert Finestone, M.D., associate dean of continuing medical education at Temple. "If they delay until the last day for car inspection, she can dump the stress right back on them." White's real problem, however, is more complicated than handling disgruntled customers. She has to fit clients' car repairs into the mechanics' schedules – and she has no control over the number of cars needing to be fixed or the schedules.

"When you're placed in a situation where things are beyond your control, this creates an enormous amount of stress," says Dr. Finestone. "It's the same problem facing a waiter whose food is backed up in the kitchen trying to satisfy an impatient diner. I would suggest he recognize it's not his fault, go back to the customer and say, 'Look, the kitchen's backed up. I guarantee I'll be in there trying to rush the cook, but that's the situation.' Meanwhile, if you can't stand the heat, get out of the kitchen."

The Value of Peer Counseling

Sometimes it's helpful – or downright crucial – to talk about your job stress with co-workers. That's the lifesaving lesson learned by Ed Donovan of the Boston police.

Donovan had been a police officer in Boston for only five years when he reached his limit. He no longer could handle the day-to-day dealing with danger or take the responsibility of having to make major decisions in a split second that would affect him for the rest of his life. He couldn't live with the image that he was supposed to be Superman, that he was not supposed to have problems but was instead expected to solve others' problems. He couldn't face the daily descent into society's low depths. Few professionals are subject to as much stress as policemen are, and Donovan simply could not take it. So he overdrank; he became addicted to drugs. One day he stuck a gun in his mouth and tried to pull the trigger.

He found he couldn't take his own life.

Donovan didn't trust psychologists. He found the only people he could turn to were peers, the two cops who ran an alcoholism program for the Boston police. Eventually, their peer support helped Donovan learn to deal with the stress of his job. And as chronicled in his book *The Shattered Badge,* it led him to launch the Boston Police Department Stress Program, perhaps the most extensive stress-reduction operation serving law enforcement. Donovan is still its director.

Boston's 13-year-old stress program has helped thousands of area policemen deal with the particular stresses of being a cop, a profession whose members, Donovan says, are among those least likely to seek advice from mental health professionals. "How much more macho can you get than swaggering around with a gun?" he says. And because of Donovan's experience, the Boston program relies primarily on peer counseling; professionals are used only for backup.

"We can get a cop to open up better in front of three or four other cops than in a one-on-one situation with a psychologist," he says. The program includes training, education, counseling, group therapy and crisis intervention. And among some 200 police department stress programs in the United States, Boston's is the only one that operates autonomously from the police department's administration. That way, cops under pressure feel secure that their group therapy discussions — which often focus on problems emanating from above — won't reach the ears of their superiors.

The experience in Boston underscores three crucial points. First, there's nothing wrong with admitting you have difficulty coping with the stress of your job. This holds for all jobs, even those that are substantially less demanding than police work. Second, there's an abundance of relief to be gained by talking over your workplace woes with co-workers you can trust. And third, there are professional career counselors waiting in the wings if you feel your peers lack the skills to help or if you begin to threaten a relationship by overindulging in your miseries.

If you are not comfortable discussing your job-related stress with company personnel, try an outside professional. (For a list of certified career counselors in your community, write to the International Association of Counseling Services, 5999 Stevenson Avenue, Alexandria, VA 22304.)

The sad news is that even where good in-house help is available, some folks refuse to seek it. Last year five Boston police officers committed suicide. Ed Donovan says, "Four of those could have been prevented if they were referred to us."

The Dreaded Raise Discussion

"An enormous change can take place in one morning when a demanding boss comes by to say, 'You've done a great job. We couldn't get along without you,'" says Dr. Wolf. That kind of comment from a supervisor can make you feel that you're important, that you're somebody with a well-defined place who does things that are appreciated.

Unfortunately, few bosses are that thoughtful and appreciative. Many are downright hostile. And so, if you want to better your relations with your boss, *you'll* have to do the work. A better relationship can improve your work environment and even increase your odds of getting what you want. Take the dreaded raise discussion as an example.

"One of the biggest mistakes employees make when they finally decide to ask for a raise is that they don't relatively assess a few things," says Peter Wylie, Ph.D. "They don't consider the perceived value on the part of the boss—how dispensable they are. And they're also not good at putting themselves in the shoes of their boss."

Dr. Wylie is coauthor of *Problem Bosses: Who They Are and How to Deal with Them,* and he suggests that before you march in and make your little plea for a raise, you should do some homework.

Develop a well-worked-out rationale for why you deserve a raise. Be objective. The fact that your production increased over the past six months may reflect added support personnel more than your own performance. Therefore, objectively construct a case for a raise. Outline your argument on paper and back it up with a strong verbal presentation that you rehearse to persuasive perfection, suggests Dr. Wylie.

And even if you're a prime candidate for a raise, keep in mind that your boss may have a host of reasons why he must turn you down. There are good times and bad times to ask for raises. Obviously, when profits are down, budgets are tight. If that's the case, you probably won't get a good hearing from your boss, regardless of how worthy you are. And often your boss can't make the decision on his own. So you need to understand how the chain of command works, who your boss has to go to for approval and the degree to which your boss is weak in fighting for your case, says Dr. Wylie.

If your request is turned down, make certain you understand why. If the company has imposed a freeze on salary increases, find out when the freeze will be lifted and what your chances are for a raise at that time. If your boss informs you that your performance does not merit a salary raise, ask him what you need to do to get back on track. Tell him you appreciate getting feedback on your performance. Make it clear that you're serious about improving. If possible, offer to establish work goals that will lead to an eventual raise, then achieve them.

"The important function of an employee is not simply to be a passive recipient of what's handed down from above," says Dr. Wolf. "You've got to learn to react to the machinery. You have to learn diplomacy. You have to have a reasonable case. And you can't exaggerate. If you've got three things to say and one's shaky, your boss is going to focus on the shaky one and ignore the others," he says. "Don't say too much, and stick to the strong points."

A Job You Can't Handle

Say your employer promoted you into a coveted management job but you find yourself overwhelmed by the new responsibilities and are constantly unhappy. The advice from Beth Ann Wilson, a Philadelphia career counselor, is basic: "Be clear why the situation is not working."

Ask yourself whether the problem is that you don't like the job or that you just don't have the skills to do the job properly.

By taking a strong look at the situation, many people discover they simply lack appropriate job skills. If that's the case, go to your boss or personnel administrator and ask for training in how to manage or how to delegate. That's a strategy that gets you needed training while also demonstrating your maturity and desire to do a good job.

De-Stressing an Unrewarding Job

Many of us suffer in jobs that are unrewarding, and for one reason or another we cannot quit or shift jobs right now. How do you remove yourself from the stress of such a bad work scene? Career counselor Wilson provides a practical list of suggestions.

- Build up other things in your life. Volunteer to do something in the community that's rewarding to you and gives you satisfaction.
- Take a course in a hobby or to develop a new skill that can help you eventually land another job.
- Talk to people who work in similar jobs – a teller at another bank or a teacher at another school.

- Identify what you want to do next, career-wise or job-wise. Then focus a fixed amount of time each day on helping you get there. That time could be spent working, for example, on the United Way campaign to make yourself more visible to potential new employers in the community.
- Get out of the building, if only for ten minutes at lunchtime. A walk will help relieve stress.
- Figure out what is the source of your stress. Focus on whether or not it is your fault and, if so, if there's anything you can do about it. If you've determined you're not at fault, be very clear that it's not you that's contributing to the stress.
- Talk to someone about your situation who will help you develop an objective perspective. It doesn't have to be a professional; it could be someone at work whom you trust.

Maybe You'd Better Start Looking

The fear of job hunting, the fear of being unemployed and the fear that they'll wind up in an even worse situation keeps people trapped in miserable, stressful jobs. "People come in and tell me that at least they wake up in the morning and know exactly how miserable they'll be. There's some comfort in that familiarity," says Wilson.

Even people who quit a job to look for a new one have more control than those who stay, lose interest to the point that they cannot function well, and are eventually laid off or fired. There's little to be gained by staying in an unhappy job if you can devise a careful strategy for a job search. Be honest with yourself: Do you really need to stay?

Each Monday evening Beth Wilson runs a support group for people who are employed but are looking for new jobs. The point of the discreet group is to motivate its members, to provide group support and to make participants accountable for their week-to-week job seeking activities. If you don't think you can develop and stick to a job search on your own, check with a local career counselor about a job-seekers' support group in your community.

When There's Not Enough Stress

Finally, some people find it difficult to perform in laid-back workplaces. They flourish in antagonistic environments and thrive on anxiety. "These are people who get into organizations that are so supportive they can't stand it. So they might find themselves instigating things at work," says Wilson.

The problem is particularly relevant in companies that are following the current trend of giving an employee vast amounts of freedom to accomplish projects at the worker's own pace. The presumption is that employees will work harder and be happier if they are doing their own thing and are out from under constant supervision. But by merely giving an employee a project and saying "work on this for six months," an employer might be doing the worker a disservice.

"You're coming from an educational system that's structured and a back-ground that's structured. So when you go into an unstructured job where you're told to use your creativity, you're subject to a lot of stress," says Wilson. It may be great for some people, but it's torture for others.

In such a situation, Wilson suggests you try to structure your own workload so that you will impose some pressure on yourself. Set personal deadlines. If you're on a long-term project and don't feel comfortable about the lack of guidance or supervision, tell your boss you'd like to meet every two weeks for 15 minutes to discuss what you're doing.

If your workplace is too stress-free for your liking, you can compensate by structuring high-pressure after-work activities. Play a highly competitive sport. Volunteer to work on a rescue squad. Or you can seek out a job in a high-pressure industry or in a company whose corporate culture runs on stress. But it's important to look at what you need and what has worked for you in the past.

Chapter 45

OVEREATING

You're tense and harried. Suddenly, you crave food. What do you reach for? A cookie? A candy bar? Anything you can get your hands on?

Do you stop after a nibble or two? Or do you, like many people, go into a double-fisted feeding frenzy that leaves you feeling overstuffed and guilty?

Diagnosis: the "Eat, you'll feel better" syndrome. And you're only doing what you've been programmed to do, Pavlovian-style.

"It's no mystery why I eat when I'm upset," says one woman. "Whenever I skinned my knee as a child, my mom would give me a Band-Aid, a kiss and a Popsicle. And I still associate food with comfort."

Food, especially sweet, sugary foods like ice cream, cookies and candy, is hypothesized to have a calming or soothing effect as well. One theory, based on animal experiments, proposes that eating sweets prompts the body to secrete endorphins, natural opiate-like compounds in the brain that dull pain. (Not surprisingly, they therefore also have the potential to buffer stress.) Other evidence suggests that high-carbohydrate foods increase the production and release of serotonin, a nerve messenger that eases anxiety and tension.

Regardless of the mechanism at work, we almost seem destined to reach for the sweets under stress. "Studies show that stressed animals eat more sweets than do nonstressed animals," says Dean Krahn, M.D., director of the Eating Disorders Program at the University of Michigan Medical Center in Ann Arbor. "What's more, they go for exactly the kinds of comfort foods that people do. Rats *love* Oreos. And hardly anyone who eats under stress reaches for vegetables or other healthy food."

If one Oreo is good, does that mean the whole box is even better? No such luck. While seeking solace in food isn't nearly as deadly or dangerous as other stress-provoked habits such as smoking or tranquilizer abuse, "eating away your troubles" won't do anything to resolve what's causing the stress in the first place. What's more, habitual food overdoses show up as unwanted pounds, which translate into guilt — and more stress.

Even if you don't gain weight or feel guilty, "stress eating" can contribute to heart disease or nutritional problems, since many of the foods people like to eat under stress tend to be high in fat and sugar, according to Dr. Krahn.

What's Eating You?

Perhaps you eat under stress but don't realize it. Food wolfed down in a frenzy may disappear so fast you honestly don't remember having eaten it.

"I find it helps for people to keep a log of what they eat and when and where they eat it — like a diet diary," says Dr. Krahn. He also suggests diary-keepers note what they were thinking when the urge to eat hit ("The boss is a jerk") and how they felt ("I'm angry").

"After keeping a diary for a while, it occurs to them that eating doesn't do anything but make them feel guilty," says Dr. Krahn. "They still have a boss who's a jerk, and they might start to think they're not doing a good job. But if they think things through instead of trying to 'eat their troubles away,' they might conclude that they *are* doing a good job and otherwise deal with the issue."

Keeping track of stress-induced feeding frenzies is just the start. To avoid eating too much and too often under stress, Dr. Krahn also gives the following advice.

Eat regular, nutritious meals. Most people who eat under stress are people who restrict what they eat the rest of the time, according to Dr. Krahn. "Dieters — people who deprive themselves of food and get too few calories — set themselves up for bingeing under stress," he says.

Distract your attention. "Diverting activities are very useful," says Dr. Krahn. "Take a walk, play the piano, read a magazine, then ask yourself, 'Do I still feel like eating?' If you do, go ahead. But the urge for food, like the urge for sex, tends to come and go."

Expect relapses. "The biological urge to eat under stress is no different than the urge to urinate," says Dr. Krahn. "We can only control the urge up to a point. It's naive to think willpower has anything to do with it. Coupled with a wide availability of highly palatable foods never before seen in human history, we are almost predestined toward a certain amount of 'stress eating,'" he says. "It's not only okay but more realistic to give in to the urge occasionally, when it's most overwhelming."

Don't let yourself feel guilty. "That will only leave you feeling more guilty—and vulnerable to further relapses," says Dr. Krahn.

Some behavioral scientists speculate that another reason we eat under stress is for the oral gratification provided by chewing and sucking, a holdover from infancy. And animals do gnaw on nonnutritive objects under stress. But Dr. Krahn hesitates to suggest that people who eat under stress chew gum, suck on a straw or crunch ice cubes to satisfy their urge. "For one thing, chewing by itself seems to stimulate appetite," he says.

If you must nibble but don't want to gain weight, judicious snacking on crunchy, low-calorie foods such as air-popped popcorn, pretzels and bite-size shredded wheat cereal may supply what you need to calm you down.

Chapter 46

PERFECTIONISM

Are you a perfectionist? To find out, take the quiz below.

1. Do you believe that to be a worthwhile person you must be at the top of everything you try?
2. Do you overlook your accomplishments and concentrate on your failings?
3. Once you accomplish something, do you prefer to look at the next challenge instead of experiencing the rewards of your accomplishment?
4. Do you procrastinate at any task or project that will be judged by others?

Well, nobody's perfect.

Simple words of wisdom, true, but if you're among the folks who answered yes to the questions above, you probably won't find it so simple to incorporate that bit of wisdom into your life.

"Perfectionism is the world's greatest con game," writes David D. Burns, M.D., in his popular self-help book *Feeling Good.* "It promises riches and delivers misery." Like many con games, you don't know you're playing until someone points out the ways you're getting cheated.

In a study of more than 700 men and women, Dr. Burns discovered that perfectionists experience distress and dissatisfaction with their careers and personal lives. And he found no evidence that they were more successful than their nonperfectionist peers.

The Harder You Strive,
the More Disappointed You Get

Here's the con. For any one of a number of reasons, a perfectionist is convinced that total failure lies ahead unless everything is done *perfectly*. But perfection is an illusion. And the harder one strives for perfection, the worse the ensuing disappointment will be – because perfection is unobtainable.

The first step you should take to stop playing the game is to recognize your stress-inducing behavior.

Recognize that you're never satisfied with what you do. "Perfectionists can never rest on their laurels, never tell themselves they did a good job," says Asher Pacht, Ph.D., a professor of psychology at the University of Wisconsin.

Recognize that you're a procrastinator. People often procrastinate at tasks and projects because they're afraid of being judged on results that may be less than perfect.

Once you've identified your perfectionist behavior, systematically learn how to expect less from yourself. We're not suggesting you slouch off at everything, not work to the best of your ability or not set high standards for yourself. But don't judge yourself so harshly if you fail to meet your lofty goals.

Be selective. "Choose one or two things you really want to do well at, and concentrate your best efforts on those activities," recommends Don E. Hamachek, Ph.D., a professor of counseling and educational psychology at Michigan State University.

Give yourself permission to be imperfect. "It's important to recognize that 100 percent is unattainable, and that if you continue to shoot for that goal, you're likely to always feel under a lot of stress, depressed and anxious," says Dr. Pacht. "Settle for 90 percent and recognize that it's a pretty damned good accomplishment."

Choose at least one activity you can do without self-criticism. Dr. Hamachek runs three or four miles each day and is proud that he doesn't care how long it takes him to do it.

Change Your Thinking

Begin to identify those thought patterns that lead to built-up stress and cause postperformance judgments or depression. Perfectionists tend to indulge in several varieties of self-defeating thinking.

They may overgeneralize. ("I didn't get up to snuff. I'm really falling down and I'm no good.") They may engage in dichotomous thinking. ("I'm really good at some things and I'm a failure at others.") They may engage in selective thinking. ("Once I accomplish something, that accomplishment becomes insignificant.")

Why do perfectionists torture themselves so? Because, in an odd sort of way, it makes them feel good, too.

Become aware of the gains that *you* get out of being a perfectionist. Sometimes people are able to change their stressful self-dialogue when they realize they may be telling themselves, "I am a special person because I'm tough on myself," says John C. Barrow, Ed.D., a psychologist at Duke University's Counseling and Psychological Services.

Then develop new ways of thinking. If you're so anxious about the outcome of a task that you can't concentrate on it, put your mind on the task as opposed to the consequences.

Adopt what Dr. Barrow calls a "coping dialogue." His examples? "Here I go again. I'm already worrying about the future. Let me settle down and do my best." Or, "This task is important, but I have a lot to do in a limited amount of time. Hang on, there are only 24 hours in a day."

Learn Why You're Like That

Challenge the basic assumptions about yourself and what makes you feel like a worthwhile human being. A professional therapist may help you understand that your self-worth is based on gaining the approval of everyone who is important to you, says Dr. Pacht. Or that your self-worth is based on your ability to perform. Or that being perfect will not bring you love and a great sense of well-being.

It's easy to understand how people convince themselves otherwise. As San Francisco psychologist Debra White, Ph.D., says, "The obsession with being perfect infiltrates families and is passed on from one generation to the next. A child in a perfectionistic home soon learns that worth is defined by performance."

In such homes, simply "being" is not good enough, she says. "Standards for what is 'good' and 'bad' are set from the outside, not from within, and have clear demarcations: A letter grade of 'A' is acceptable, a high 'B' is failure. There is nothing in between. Spontaneous and creative expression becomes risky and is muffled out of fear of disapproval."

If your anxiety over being perfect is disrupting your life, taking a physical and psychological toll, remind yourself that nobody's perfect. Try to recognize the underlying causes of perfectionism and begin to accept yourself as you are.

Chapter 47

PERFORMANCE JITTERS

Here's an incredible fact: Among our top ten fears, the fear of death ranks number six. So what's number one? It might surprise you, but holding first place among our fears is the fear of speaking before a group. This, according to a market research study of 3,000 Americans.

Those who aren't petrified to speak or perform before an audience may go on to flourishing careers in politics, theater or television. The rest of us just suffer, avoiding and dreading that semiannual presentation before the budget committee or the toast we agreed to deliver at our friend's wedding. We may even go into a fit of madness if we host a party.

Doctors classify such performance anxiety as a form of social phobia, the fear of doing anything under scrutiny that can result in humiliation. Most of us are all too familiar with the symptoms: sweaty palms, shaking, voice tremors, rubbery legs. That's the "fight-or-flight" reaction, our body's natural response to fear. Inside our bodies, the adrenal gland shoots the hormone adrenaline (also called epinephrine) into the bloodstream. Blood pressure climbs, heartbeat increases, and blood vessels to the digestive tract narrow, while blood vessels to the trunk's muscles expand, according to Patricia Normand, M.D., instructor in psychiatry at Harvard and associate director of psychopharmacology at the Cambridge Hospital in Boston.

The Adrenaline Rush

For some folks, the shot of adrenaline produces a high. But for many, it's a tormenting discomfort. Yet whether your performance anxiety happens once a year or once a day, there are ways of overcoming it.

Say you get particularly nervous when you are about to deliver a toast before a wedding party. Obviously the best thing to do is be well rehearsed. So practice the toast, simulating it before a group if possible, advises Valerie Adami, an actress and instructor at Weist-Barron in New York City, a school that teaches acting for television commercials.

The same simple advice holds true if you are delivering a speech. The more nervous you ordinarily get, the more prepared you should be. "It's less stressful if you know what you're talking about," Adami says.

In either case, you should avoid things that make you nervous, such as caffeine or nicotine. Alcohol, too, can be detrimental. Initially it may calm you down, but often it later produces anxiety. And tranquilizers tend to slow down your motor skills.

Relaxation Techniques to the Rescue

The advice gets a great deal more complex if your performance anxiety is a constant affair. In that case, there are relaxation techniques to help you cope.

Systematic desensitization. This is a process in which you relax your muscles and then imagine yourself performing a series of situations, progressing from something simple like speaking to a few friends and leading up to a speech before a huge auditorium.

Flooding. This technique requires you to confront your fear directly and work through it. If you fear public speaking, you could deliver the dreaded speech before a therapy group. You learn that you can survive such a trial.

Modeling. This method requires you to watch other people (even if only on videotape) satisfactorily perform a public speech. By observing, you lose some of the fear of doing it yourself, says Dr. Normand.

If your stage fright is so bad that you structure your life to avoid even rare performances – you turn down a job promotion because the new position requires you to deliver an occasional speech – you may be a candidate for medical intervention. A medication such as propranolol may be prescribed, to be taken a few hours before your performance. It works by blocking the effects of the adrenaline your body produces. You won't sweat, you'll stop shaking and your heart palpitations will cease.

Telling Yourself You Can

Then there's the powerful force of positive thinking to get you to overcome your jitters. Positive thinking is a keystone in the decades-old advice preached by

Dale Carnegie to salesmen and others who flocked to his lectures and purchased his popular books *How to Win Friends and Influence People, How to Stop Worrying and Start Living* and *The Quick and Easy Way to Effective Speaking.* Carnegie's philosophy contends that almost anyone can speak in public if they have self-confidence and an idea that is boiling and stewing within them. What he taught those who crowded his classrooms, and what his instructors continue to teach, is that to develop self-confidence, you must do whatever it is you fear doing and get a record of successful experiences under your belt.

If you feel you would benefit from the instruction, the group support and the intensified practice of a Dale Carnegie course, why not sign up? The basic public speaking course runs 14 sessions and costs approximately $800. For information on courses in your area, check the yellow pages in your local telephone directory.

The Nervous Host

You can have performance anxiety about almost anything, but some people experience their worst anxiety when it comes to hosting a party. "The thing to do," says Dr. Normand, "is question why you are being so nervous about having a party. You might separate the worry about what people will think of *you* from what you are actually doing. This separation will help make you less nervous. Then you can realize that it's not the end of the world if not everyone thinks it's the best party ever given. Ask yourself why you're being such a perfectionist."

Facing, then getting over, such unrealistic expectations of yourself may free you from the grip of performance anxiety.

Chapter 48

POSITIVE THINKING

I think I can; therefore I can.

—Not René Descartes

You may have heard folks say an optimist sees a glass as half full and a pessimist sees it as half empty. "The real question is, What are the odds of filling it up?" says Michael F. Scheier, Ph.D., professor of psychology at Carnegie-Mellon University in Pittsburgh, Pennsylvania. "An optimist will say, 'Yes, we can fill that glass.' But the pessimist may say, 'What's the use? It's only going to evaporate or spill.'"

And if you think life is just one spilled glass of milk after another, chances are it will be. Studies by Dr. Scheier and Charles S. Carver, Ph.D., of the University of Miami, have discovered that a tendency to view events in either a positive or negative way can affect our actions—and the ultimate outcomes of stressful situations.

More than Just Another Happy Face

"Until recently, we assumed that a positive orientation—optimism—was simply an internal perception of circumstances," says Dr. Scheier. "But we're now finding that anticipating a favorable outcome leads an optimist to do things that actually determine the final outcome. Optimists *expect* things to turn out well, but they also do things that can change the course of events." (That's fitting: *optimism* comes from *ops*, the Latin word for "power.")

Since stress arises largely from our perception of events as being harmful or threatening, whether your perception is positive or negative is pivotal in determining how you cope with stress. Primed with positive expectations, optimists regard potentially stressful events – such as financial setback, failed love, career disappointment – as opportunities for change or growth, not as excuses for giving up. Obstacles become stepping stones, not stumbling blocks. And the positive attitude, it seems, can significantly affect how your body *and* soul react to stress.

How Optimists Master Stress

Exactly how do optimists transform positive thoughts into positive results? "By active coping," says Dr. Carver.

"Optimists do better in the face of stress, at least in part, because they choose and use specific coping strategies that increase their likelihood of success," says Dr. Scheier. Here's a rundown of some of those strategies.

Problem-focused coping. Optimists are planners, say Dr. Carver and Dr. Scheier. "Examine the situation and, to the degree that you *can* do something, try to resolve it," says Dr. Carver.

"Optimists take action sooner," says Dr. Scheier. Acting quickly often prevents a small stress from snowballing into a big, unstoppable stress.

"Break big problems down into smaller, more manageable problems," he says. "Optimists tend to formulate subgoals – intermediate steps that will help them to eventually reach their ultimate goal."

You can apply this "paint-by-number" approach to any overwhelming commitment or obligation. "Say you plan to write a book, for example," says Dr. Scheier. "The enormity of the project could be daunting – and paralyze you – unless you say something like, 'I can write two pages a day, so I can write a chapter a month,' and so forth."

Perseverance. Spurred by positive emotions – and past successes – optimists keep going when others might quit.

"Problems often have reverberations that you never expect, beyond the effects on your morale or your finances," says Dr. Carver. So a certain amount of tunnel vision also keeps optimists focused on their objective – and pointed toward active coping.

Positive reinterpretation. People who think positively tend to emerge from their trials thinking, I developed greater trust in my judgments of situations or people, I modified personal or career goals to more closely match my true interests, abilities or values, I gained confidence in my ability to handle other difficulties, or I discovered I could rely on others for help in getting through difficulties. Such thoughts suggest the person feels that stress enables them to change for the better or grow as a person in a new way, renews their faith or reveals some important truth about life – a kind of modern, personal *Aesop's Fables.*

"As a coping strategy, positive reinterpretation is important when something happens that you can't do much about – death of a loved one, for example, or an effort that failed," says Dr. Scheier. "There's a lot of confidence and satisfaction to be gained from surviving stress and being able to say, 'I handled that pretty well.' "

"Stress provides 'lessons' that make you more capable of dealing with events in the future," says Dr. Carver. "Optimists tend to see these lessons more readily than pessimists."

Somehow, finding a reason for your suffering makes it more endurable or less devastating. In conversations with Julius Segal, Ph.D., just after their liberation from Iran, American hostages described certain "benefits" of their experience. One said, "Sure, I lost 40 pounds, but I'm now down to my normal weight."

Call it rationalizing perhaps, but reinterpreting trouble in this way preserves your self-esteem, sense of control or mastery over stress, and restores your belief in the world as just, rational and predictable, according to Darlene Goodhart, Ph.D., of the Department of Psychology at the University of Illinois, Champaign.

Social support. Optimists believe others can help. They tend to talk to someone about how they feel under stress, or ask for – and follow – advice.

Acceptance or resignation. Optimists are realists. When reason tells them a situation is out of their hands, they accept it and refuse to dwell on their troubles.

"We don't want to imply that people should put on a happy face and go around being mindlessly cheerful all the time," says Dr. Carver. "Even optimists have occasional doubts or fail sometimes. By resignation, we mean the ability to say, 'I'm not going to pretend this isn't happening, but if I have to put up with it, I will.' "

What's more, optimists seem to instinctively know when to charge forward and when to back off. Dr. Scheier found that optimists leaned toward problem-focused coping in situations they perceived to be under their control. They relied on social support and acceptance or resignation when things were beyond their control. Positive reinterpretation, in turn, seemed to buffer stress in either type of situation.

Negative Thinking: A Self-Fulfilling Prophecy?

You can also identify an optimist by how he or she *doesn't* cope, says Dr. Carver. Optimists don't deny the problem exists, don't blame themselves and don't try to escape through fantasy (such as daydreaming about the perfect revenge or finding a million dollars).

Basically, pessimists tend to think any efforts to change themselves or the situation would be futile, so they don't try, minimizing their chances for success.

"A little bit of denial is good – it prevents us from overreacting," says Dr. Carver. "But I suspect that if a problem is real, the longer you put off dealing with it, the worse it will get."

Instead of focusing on the cause of their stress, pessimists become preoccupied with anger, hurt, frustration or other emotional distress that results. In short, they get upset and give up.

"Acknowledging and expressing your feelings is good – up to a point," says Dr. Carver. "But the more you lie around feeling sorry for yourself, the more you reinforce those negative feelings, until your negative expectations are eventually fulfilled."

Where do negative expectations come from? What makes a Gloomy Gus so glum? "Past experience," says Dr. Scheier. "Pessimists are the way they are because they've experienced trouble in the past and expect more of the same."

"Pessimism, like optimism, is cyclic," says Dr. Carver. "It perpetuates itself."

Can a Gloomy Gus learn to be a Sunny Sam? With a little work, yes. "When faced with a challenge, don't automatically think, 'I can't do it,' " says Dr. Scheier. "You must have had some past successes. Think back to similar situations and ask yourself, 'What worked before that might work now?' "

"Don't overreact to stress or overinterpret events," adds Dr. Carver.

Other negative thoughts to avoid include, If anything can go wrong, it will, Nothing ever goes my way, and Good things never happen to me.

Optimists Suffer Fewer Symptoms of Stress

Winners are healthier than whiners. Studies show that problem-focused coping, of which optimists are masters, is associated with less depression, while simply venting your emotions or refusing to acknowledge the stressful situation is linked with higher levels of depression and other reactions to stress. Optimists also suffer fewer of the physical signs of stress. In one study, Dr. Scheier and Dr. Carver tracked the progress of 141 college students during the final four weeks of a semester. They found that optimistic students reported fewer symptoms of stress – muscle soreness, fatigue, dizziness and coughs – than pessimistic students.

In a related study, the psychologists measured the effect of optimism versus pessimism on how well 54 people dealt with coronary artery bypass surgery – a major stress by anyone's standards. Compared with pessimists, optimists showed fewer signs of complications during the operation, and they recovered faster. The difference seemed to lie in how they expected things to turn out. "Prior to surgery, optimists were more likely to be making plans for themselves and setting goals for their recovery than were pessimists," say the researchers. "In contrast, optimists were much less likely to dwell on the negative aspects of their emotional experience, that is, feeling nervous or sad."

Still another study found that being able to accept physical disability – in this case, from serious injury – is a good indication of how well one will continue to fare psychologically under the stress.

Evidently, optimists tend to be healthier even when injury or illness is the cause of stress. The psychologists suspect they're more apt to follow a prescribed medical program, quit smoking or change other behavior that may cause illness. Optimists also seem less likely than pessimists to rely on alcohol or drugs as an easy escape from stress.

A Tool for Survival

These studies – and others like them – mesh with the widely held theory that "hardy" people have a sense of challenge, commitment and control in the face of stress, while helpless people tend to buckle under more easily.

"Hardiness has overtones of optimism," says Dr. Carver. "Also, there is some speculation that, culturally or societally, people tend to judge situations a bit more optimistically than is realistically accurate. And that's functional, because it keeps us moving forward."

You might say that, in a Darwinian sense, optimism is essential in order for us to survive both as individuals and as a species. Call it "survival of the most optimistic."

Chapter 49

PRAYER
AND RELIGION

Most chief executives are actively religious, according to a survey of leaders of the nation's top 100 corporations, published in *Forbes*. Sixty-five percent regularly attend church or synagogue. Many start their business day with prayer or devotional study.

"I think management is beginning to say, 'Look, I need help from somewhere else. I need some faith,' " comments one business analyst.

You don't have to be a highly stressed business executive to benefit from some form of spiritual belief, though. Anyone under stress can participate – with blessings not appreciated until recently.

"Prayer is essentially a form of meditation that induces relaxation, including decreased sympathetic nervous system activity," says Herbert Benson, M.D., "inventor" of the Relaxation Response, a well-known form of calming meditation (see chapter 50), and author of *Beyond the Relaxation Response: Harnessing the Healing Power of Your Personal Beliefs*. "But prayer has an edge over neutral forms of meditation – such as focusing on the word *one* – because it changes the ways you think about things," says Dr. Benson, who is associate professor of medicine at Harvard Medical School and director of the Division of Behavioral Medicine and Hypertension at Beth Israel Hospital in Boston.

Why Praying Works and Wishing Doesn't

Regular prayer works better than "foxhole" prayers – pleas made under duress, such as muttering, "Please, God, help me ace this job interview and I'll never let you down again."

"As a matter of fact, 'foxhole' prayers don't work at all," says Dr. Benson. "But the Faith Factor – a form of meditation, including prayer, that elicits the Relaxation Response, combined with a profound set of personal convictions – works to reduce stress in a number of ways. Prayer elicits relaxation and breaks up the chain of worrisome thought, the anxiety cycle that is so often associated with insomnia, digestive problems and other symptoms of stress. When rooted in religious belief, prayer also helps to put problems in perspective, further reducing overall anxiety. And by acknowledging that there's a bigger force at work in your life, it eliminates the stressful feeling that one is 'all alone out there.' "

Many people feel that their religious beliefs provide them with strength during times of loss or hardship – including the death of a loved one, illness or injury, financial problems (all major sources of stress, according to a widely used scale of stressful life events). Religious feelings and practices, especially those that teach forgiveness, patience and understanding, can also help people cope with internal stress such as blame, bitterness, discouragement, cynicism and hostility.

By establishing guidelines for what's right and wrong, religious convictions also help people make stressful decisions in their lives. "Religious teachings tie an individual into a larger system in which some of these decisions are made for them," says Dr. Benson. If, for example, your religion says "thou shalt not steal," you may find it easier to resist peer pressure to use the company phone for personal long distance calls.

In addition to serving as a source of spiritual strength, comfort and guidance, a belief system taps into the communal support and values common to people who share that belief – a proven factor in stress resistance.

Religion Is Powerful Medicine

Talking to one's God, then, may not change stressful circumstances, but it can change the way you *perceive* and *react* to stress, both determining factors in how well you weather stress. And anything that buffers stress can help decrease your chances of suffering from the many physical ailments associated with stress.

"People who pray regularly – and attend worship services regularly – have lower blood pressure," says Dr. Benson. They also suffer less irritability, fatigue, tension headaches and various other physical problems often triggered by stress and anxiety.

For years, doctors have observed that the vegetarian diet of Seventh-day Adventists lowers their risk of heart disease and cancer (both of which have stress as a component). Now doctors in Israel have found that religiousness itself, not just diet, may protect against heart attacks. They think that psychological and social factors could play a protective role.

"Orthodox religious Jews are generally characterized by the social cohesive-ness and strong social supports of their traditional culture," write the researchers in the *International Journal of Cardiology.* "It is also possible that strong belief in a supreme being and the role of prayer may in themselves be protective."

Breaking the Anxiety Cycle with Meditative Prayer

Dr. Benson says that people of any faith can tap into the Faith Factor and "re-duce overall stress and achieve greater inner peace and emotional balance." To combine meditation with your personal beliefs, he suggests the following technique.

Choose a word or brief phrase that reflects your basic belief system. It may be a familiar verse from the Bible or book of your faith, such as a brief phrase from the Twenty-third Psalm or the Lord's Prayer, the word *Shalom* (Hebrew for "peace") or another appropriate line or phrase.

"It's important to pick a word that has special meaning to you," says Dr. Benson. "This serves a dual function: It can activate your belief systems and the accompanying benefits by providing a greater calming effect on your mind than you might achieve with a neutral focus word; and it increases the likelihood of your use of the technique."

Choose a comfortable position. Try a cross-legged position or another comfortable sitting position, but not so comfortable that you fall asleep.

Close your eyes easily and naturally. Don't squint or squeeze your eyelids shut.

Relax your muscles. Start with your feet and relax each muscle group of your body. (Tighten your right foot. Hold for ten seconds, then release. Continue, tensing and releasing muscles in your left foot, your legs, your fists, your forearms, your shoulders, your back, your neck and your brow.)

Breathe slowly and naturally. Now, begin to repeat your focus phrase, silently.

Mentally "shrug off" worrisome thoughts or distractions. When a distressing thought or image enters your mind, simply say to yourself, "Oh, well" and return to your focus phrase.

Meditate for 10 to 20 minutes. You may peek at your watch or a clock from time to time, but don't use a timer.

Practice the technique twice a day, preferably before breakfast and before dinner. "It's interesting to note how many meditative prayers over the centuries have been taught to be utilized with some form of fasting," says Dr. Benson.

Chapter 50

RELAXATION RESPONSE

Whether we tip over the canoe, debut as Otello at the Metropolitan Opera or merely get trapped in a freeway backup, our body reacts roughly the same: with the fight-or-flight response to stress that we inherited from our primitive ancestors.

Our heart rate, blood pressure and breath rate leap. Our muscles tense. Our adrenal glands work overtime. This reaction is appropriate for the occasional tiger hunt, but we don't need it for most of life's everyday stressful challenges.

The stress reaction becomes part of our standard routine. As a result, it may usher in a host of stress-induced physical ailments, such as high blood pressure. There are emotional side effects, too. Our inability to cope with the stress may cause us anxiety. And then, of course, there is fatigue.

Wouldn't it be great to be able to invoke the complete opposite response, or to cut the fight-or-flight response off at the pass, unless we really need it?

The great news is that we can. In his famous book *The Relaxation Response,* Herbert Benson, M.D., introduced Americans to the flip side of the stress response. He dubbed the counterpart to fight-or-flight "the Relaxation Response." And it doesn't occur naturally. You have to summon it in regular sessions of serene solitude.

The Benson Method

The relaxation response is not new. It's been an integral benefit of centuries-old religious rituals. What Dr. Benson did was to study these rituals and devise a simplified way to achieve the same end: flicking the switch that turns off tension and turns on physical and mental peace. Here is Dr. Benson's method, which is a form of meditation.

1. Once or twice a day, sit comfortably in a quiet place and close your eyes.
2. Deeply relax all your muscles, beginning at your feet and working up to your face. Keep them relaxed.
3. Breathe naturally through your nose and become aware of your breathing. As you exhale, silently say to yourself the word *one* (or another word of your choosing).
4. Maintain a passive attitude. Don't worry about whether you're achieving a state of deep relaxation. Let relaxation come to you. When distracting thoughts enter your mind, try not to dwell on them. Instead, return to your word. Dr. Benson emphasizes that this passive attitude is perhaps the most important element in bringing on the Relaxation Response.
5. Continue for 10 to 20 minutes. You may open your eyes to check the time, but don't use an alarm clock. After you finish, sit quietly with your eyes closed for a few moments. Then open your eyes and sit still for a few more minutes before you stand up.

How It Helps

The many healthful benefits of the Relaxation Response continue for as long as you keep practicing the method. Dr. Benson and others have shown that it counteracts the stress response. It decreases blood pressure, lowers heart and respiration rate, decreases blood flow to the muscles and reduces body metabolism. It also increases alpha brain waves, the waves that are present when you're relaxed. And it decreases blood lactate levels (high levels of lactate are known to produce feelings of anxiety).

If you practice the Relaxation Response regularly, you'll probably sleep better and feel more energetic. If you have high blood pressure, it might drop to normal — without drugs. You may find that you don't fly off the handle or get anxious quite as easily. You'll probably calm down. "I've seen it make people more satisfied, content and peaceful," says Ronald Dushkin, M.D., a holistic physician with the Kripalu Center for Yoga and Health in Lenox, Massachusetts.

This doesn't mean regularly practicing the Relaxation Response will turn you into a wimp who is incapable of experiencing the fight-or-flight response when you really need it. But you'll probably be more calm in the face of those everyday stressors, the hassles that unnecessarily bring on the fight-or-flight response: the overcrowded subway, the shattered jar of jelly on the kitchen floor, the impending work deadline.

Is the Benson method better than other relaxation techniques? It depends on your preference, says Herbert Bloomfield, M.D., a psychiatrist at the North County Holistic Health Center in Del Mar, California.

"There are many techniques that allow us to unwind, and different methods work differently for different people," he says. "So the average person has to be an aware consumer and see what works for him. Some people need something with more of a mystical flavor, like transcendental meditation. Some people don't."

Keeping at It

Regardless of what technique you use, the key is to stick with it. "You'll experience more profound results over time," says Dr. Bloomfield. Some folks find it helps to incorporate the Relaxation Response into their daily lives if they use a calendar to keep track of the times they practice it. Make up your own calendar. Write the days of the week across the top of a sheet of paper, then write Week 1, Week 2, Week 3, etc., down the left side. Make a mark at the appropriate spot each time you practice the Relaxation Response.

If you feel you've got too hectic a schedule to fit in the two daily sessions of relaxation that Dr. Benson recommends, consider how some other busy people manage.

Dr. Benson writes about a homemaker who uses the Relaxation Response in the morning after her husband and kids have left the house and again in the late afternoon before her husband returns (she manages to keep her kids from disturbing her for 20 minutes). A businessman takes a Relaxation Response break for 10 or 15 minutes every morning behind his closed office door, while his secretary tells phone callers and visitors that he's "in conference." Others wake up 10 minutes early to practice the technique, do it on the subway, or find a quiet room at work and relax while others drink coffee.

Finally, while this ritual may help you cope with stress, you should take caution not to overdo it. People who meditate several hours a day for weeks at a time have been known to hallucinate. You shouldn't need more than two daily sessions of 10 to 20 minutes each.

And Dr. Benson cautions against using the Relaxation Response to "shield oneself or to withdraw from the pressures of the outside world, which are necessary for everyday functioning." It's a tool to be used wisely.

Chapter 51

RETIREMENT

Your Golden Years.

In theory, retirement does sound golden. You've got freedom, glorious freedom to do as you please. No alarm clocks, no bosses, no kids to raise. And for some folks, years in retirement – which can comprise as much as one-third of your life – are indeed the most enjoyable.

But for others, retirement is unrelenting stress. It is 50 extra hours of free time with nothing to do. It is a loss of self-esteem, an unexpected emptiness. It is guilt over being unproductive or guilt over not really wanting your grown-up son to move back home. It is insecurity about money and insecurity about health.

Even retirement humor emphasizes the dual nature, the mixed blessing of the situation. The nicely framed needlepoint maxim: "Retirement – twice as much husband, half as much money" hangs on the living room wall of Bernice Guy, a widow from Smith Island, Maryland. A friend gave it to her years ago, about the time her husband, Fred, a crabber, reached retirement age. (Like many people, he never could find happiness in retirement. Instead, he continued crabbing right up until the day before he died.)

"I married you for better or for worse, but not for lunch," is another humorous saying that describes a problem two otherwise happily married people suddenly have to face. Once, lunch may have provided a much-needed break from the day's work and an opportunity to socialize with friends or colleagues. After retirement, however, the simple meal can symbolize a couple's new struggle to make their marriage work. Must the wife forfeit her friends and daytime activities to make lunch for her husband every day now that he's going to be home?

Despite the inevitable stresses, some folks manage to thrive after retirement, while others are devastated by it. There are several factors that may determine how well an individual will handle retirement. "The more flexible a person is and the more options they have, the easier it will be to adjust to any change," says Robert Atchley, Ph.D., director of the Scripps Gerontology Center at Miami (Ohio) University. The most likely candidates for a successful transition, he says, are those in good health, those with enough money to enjoy a comfortable lifestyle and those who maintain a good attitude toward human development.

Retirement Planning

Other experts add a fourth group of likely candidates: those who plan. Several years ago a committee of the American Medical Association released well-publicized statistics to the news media that indicated that the average man dies within three years of retirement. Not pleasant news for those facing retirement. But further investigation revealed how erroneous – and irresponsible – the statistics were. They had been based on the facts that male life expectancy at birth was an average 68 years and that most men retire at age 65. In reality, average life expectancy for a man who reaches age 65 is about 14 years. That means you won't drop when you stop.

"It's not true that retirement has an adverse effect on health," says Thomas Wan, Ph.D., professor of health administration at the Medical College of Virginia and author of *Well-Being for the Elderly: Primary Prevention Strategy.* In fact, if you retire from a job because your health is poor, you may find your health *improving* in retirement. But if you have trouble coping with the stressful events that retirement often brings, you may experience a wide range of physical ailments as well as such psychological problems as depression and anxiety, according to Nan Lin, Ph.D., professor of sociology and public health science at State University of New York, Albany.

The way to counter retirement stress – and its possible health problems – is *planning.*

"Long-range planning is the key. You can start ten years in advance," says Dr. Wan. If you wonder why some people experience tremendous stress in retirement, consider that it's not uncommon for people to spend more time planning for a two-week vacation than they spend planning for the rest of their lives.

Part of the problem is that when you sit down to make retirement plans, you may be dealing with all sorts of nagging insecurities. You are forcing yourself to look into the future – into possible financial woes, into ill health and into your own mortality. These anxieties often lead to immobilization.

Many psychologists agree that you can start to shake these fears and anxieties by plowing ahead into retirement research: collecting data on retirement locales, working with a financial consultant, discussing your hopes (and fears) with friends and family.

Another way to decrease your retirement anxiety is to know what to expect. Many therapists suggest you take up new interests before you retire. Take a course to prepare yourself for a part-time job or craft that may enable you to supplement your income. Practice living on your retirement income. Openly discuss with your spouse the possibility of engaging in a few separate activities. Or, if you are one of the 30 percent of retirement-age people who live alone, spend some time investigating group housing alternatives – if you think you'd enjoy that option.

Such advice is prominent in *Planning Your Retirement,* a preretirement planning booklet published by the American Association of Retired Persons (AARP). For a free single copy, send a postcard to AARP, P.O. Box 2400, Long Beach, CA 90801. This 20-page booklet may do wonders for dispelling the negative myths and stereotypes about life in retirement.

Financing Your Retirement

What greater fear can there be than the fear of growing old in poverty? True, the Social Security Act of 1935 was a big step in helping people finance retirement But realistically, it is at best a supplement to savings, a pension or other income. The average monthly Social Security retirement benefit check amounts to only $688 for an individual retiree or $1032 for a retired couple. True, the advent of Medicare in 1965 enabled retirees to dispel fears that they could not afford medical treatment or hospital care. But in reality, Medicare covered on average only 74 percent of retirees' hospital care bills and 54 percent of doctors' bills, according to a study published in 1984 by *Consumer Reports*. Most retirees need supplemental insurance.

The average person will need about 75 percent of his or her preretirement income to maintain the same standard of living in retirement, according to Lewis J. Altfest, Ph.D., a financial adviser whose clients include many retirees. He says it varies widely, depending on such factors as whether the person lives in the high-cost cities of the Northeast or moves to the low-cost Sunbelt. Among the least expensive areas, he says, are areas of Florida and Arizona where businesses cater to older people, offering such benefits as early-bird dinner specials for senior citizens.

A complete understanding of your finances will influence virtually every retirement decision you make. Don't make decisions before you've taken a careful account of your financial situation. "People under stress often restrict themselves unnecessarily in the choice of activities and lifestyles in retirement, frequently because they fear that they will not have sufficient funds," writes Robert K. Kinzel in his book *Retirement: Creating Promise Out of Threat.* But examine your options. There may be more money than you think.

If you will receive a pension from your employer, you may have the option of taking it in a lump sum or getting it in the form of a monthly annuity for the rest of your life. Your decision is important, and it must be based on such factors as taxes and the availability of conservative investments. If you don't feel comfortable making the decision on your own, seek the help of a financial adviser, preferably one who operates on a fee-only basis. (Financial advisers who make their money on a commission basis may steer you in the direction of investments in which they earn commission.) You may need only a one-hour consultation with a financial adviser. The cost could be $100, but it may turn out to be well worth the expense.

And make yourself familiar with the intricacies of Social Security. Write for information that will tell you when to apply and what benefits you will receive. (Write to the Office of Public Inquiries, Social Securities Administration, 6401 Security Boulevard, Baltimore, MD 21235.) If you have no additional income and have no prospects of earning extra income with a part-time job, give some thought to sharing your home – or moving in with another retiree. Taking the steps to investigate such a move will probably help dispel some of your biggest fears of financial insecurity.

If you've constructed a savings cushion to help in retirement, make sure you know how much you can withdraw each month before the principal is depleted – or how much you can withdraw indefinitely through interest accumulations. If your nest egg is $10,000 invested at 7 percent compounded quarterly, you can withdraw $59 a month indefinitely or $116 for ten years, according to the AARP's *Planning Your Retirement.* Your banker should be able to help you with the calculations.

And learn what Medicare covers and what it doesn't cover. (Write to the Health Care Financing Administration, 6325 Security Boulevard, Baltimore, MD 21207.) Is the group health insurance your employer provides guaranteed to be convertible to an individual policy to bolster Medicare? If not, Dr. Altfest recommends you at least buy catastrophic insurance for large illnesses that could zap your savings. But he warns that too many retirees overinsure themselves to the point that they become insurance poor.

The earlier you start your financial planning for retirement, the better off you'll be. "People come to me two years from retirement and they have no funds," says Dr. Altfest. Ideally, preretirement planning should start ten years before retirement – five years at the very least. The first step, for those who have no funds stashed away, is to invest in a pension plan such as an Individual Retirement Account (IRA).

It may ease your mind to study two brochures published by AARP: "Money Matters" and "Take Charge of Your Money." To obtain them, free of charge, write to AARP Fulfillment, P.O. Box 2240, Long Beach, CA 90801. Above all, remember that unscrupulous individuals may be out to take your hard earned money. "I would caution people against giving anybody any money without knowing what they're going to get in return," says Katie Sloan, AARP's consumer adviser. "Have a contract. Understand the refund constraints. Older people very easily get sucked into financial scams. So you've got to know who you're dealing with."

The Second Career

Here are some seemingly contradictory facts: More Americans than ever are taking early retirement. Yet more Americans than ever over 65 are still in the work force. The explanation, of course, is that retirees are pursuing second careers in retirement, either on a full-time or part-time basis.

Among the many luxuries retirement affords is the possibility to explore a new career. Those who succeed in these second careers frequently are people who were deeply involved in an interest that easily carried over into retirement. But it's possible to pursue something totally new: the purchase of a small business, the training for a new skill that's sellable. Whatever the case, the transition from old job to new will be easiest if you lay the groundwork for a second career before you retire.

If you are the neighborhood Mr. Fix-It, helping your neighbors repair appliances, it may be wise to set up your basement business *before* leaving your job, so you can work out the kinks while you still have an income. If you're an accountant and plan to help friends and neighbors complete taxes, the transition may be smoothest if you drum up the clients before you leave your firm.

Just as the process of starting a business is fraught with problems for 35-year-olds, it can be disastrous for retirees, regardless of expertise, enthusiasm and energy level. One option available to retirees: Purchase a franchise of anything from a doughnut shop to a gift-wrapping business. The required investment is generally smaller than that needed to open and operate a comparable independent business. And you don't have to worry about how to run the business. The same franchisor who sells you the doughnuts or wrapping paper also teaches you the ropes and will give you management assistance if you need it.

But that's not such a good idea if you dislike having someone else give the orders – the same way your boss probably did before you retired. Also, franchisors quick to make a sale often underemphasize the amount of work involved in running one of their businesses. If you want to get a handle on the amount of time you'll have to put into the operation, talk to other franchisees of the same organization before buying your franchise.

And despite a relatively high rate of success among legitimate franchise operations, the industry still has a substantial sleaze factor. Unscrupulous franchisors love to separate retirees from their life savings. So before buying a franchise, check with the International Franchise Association (202-628-8000). In addition, carefully go over the franchise papers with a lawyer and talk with others who have franchises with the particular company.

Many community colleges offer free or reduced-tuition courses to retirees. This education can be a virtual gold mine for anyone interested in developing a skill or learning a craft that may lead to a second career. If you've got the interest, don't let your age discourage you. Continuing to work won't necessarily make you rich, but it can help you finance your retirement.

Barbara Newcombe is an Oakland, California, retiree who started a second career in retirement and is already looking forward to a third. Two years ago she left her job as the librarian for a major metropolitan newspaper in the Midwest (it was a career she had begun in her fifties) and moved to California to be closer to her children and grandchildren. She wanted to go into business for herself doing indexing for publishers. So she bought herself a computer, learned how to use it and began gathering customers for her service. Her volunteer work at the Center for Investigative Reporting may translate into a major source of income for her business.

Meanwhile, she anticipates the day when she can leave indexing behind to pursue a career in archives and genealogy, fields she enjoys. "I find it boring to stick to one thing," she says.

If you want to return to the work force in the same profession you left behind, there's an important thought to keep in mind as you hunt for work: You probably have a lot to offer a prospective employer. So don't approach a job interview as if the employer will be doing you a favor to hire you. Be confident. And if you don't get hired, look elsewhere — or think about what kind of career you'd like to pursue next. Heed the advice of retirement author Kinzel when he writes, "Be honest with yourself. If it is unlikely that you can continue to practice your vocation, it is better to acknowledge it now so that you can search properly for an alternative style of life."

When Retirement Shatters Your Self-Esteem

Retirement can be toughest for those who define themselves in terms of their work — or at least derive a great deal of their self-esteem from the job they left behind. Take the case of the executive or manager with considerable power, who suddenly finds that selecting the proper golf club is the biggest decision of the day. A big-shot businessman is now an average Joe. Former librarian Newcombe, who so successfully made the transition into a second career – and in a new community – remembers the early stress she experienced when "people were no longer calling me because I was the person listed as the head of a large department for a large organization. That position made a difference in how people regarded me. Suddenly I became almost a nonperson." Psychologists suggest you realize just how powerful the loss of prestige can be.

"The shock for many is not only great but also bewildering," writes Leland P. Bradford, who, with his wife, Martha, wrote *Retirement. Coping with Emotional Upheavals.* "Events are less under one's control, and the importance in others' eyes that power gives has evaporated. Must the person who has lost power continue to vie for it, or can the individual find power and importance within himself?"

Duke University psychology professor Martin Lakin, Ph.D., has worked extensively in this area of retirement and still considers that question "the $64,000 question." In his opinion, there are no easy answers for the person who placed a great value on work and career and now has neither. Most of the activities in senior citizens' centers are loathed by them. "They see it as child's play," he says.

"It's a matter of making the best of a bad situation in a society that values work," he adds. People who were specialists in highly technical fields are in a good position to regain some sense of importance through their value as consultants. At the very least they can maintain a connection to their preretirement life through professional organizations. Others, he says, should "try to find volunteer programs that have meaning for them. Some people find it satisfying to work with younger people in their area of expertise; others are satisfied working with Meals on Wheels." One bit of advice, he says, is to seek out others in the same situation – former colleagues, for instance – and talk over your dilemma. "Shared troubles are sometimes eased," he says.

Some people derive satisfaction from jobs that make them feel more knowledgeable than anyone else, says Sheila Miller, Ph.D., a professor at the Scripps Gerontology Center. She suggests such folks get involved in an organization or issue where, once again, they will know more than anyone else.

But those who want to beat the stress of suddenly being a nobody can take another approach: Learn to derive pleasure from other things in life, suggests Dr. Miller. It may not be easy, but it may be necessary in order to manage the stress of retirement. If you haven't yet retired, do a bit of self-analysis and try to determine your needs and activities that may satisfy them. Do you enjoy the physical nature of your job? Take up hiking and stick to a planned daily regimen. If you're already retired, there are a host of activities that may help you overcome your feelings of emptiness and uselessness – or the guilt you experience from being away from "work."

Meaningful Activities

Two mornings each week Robert Kennedy, 74, hikes up a steep block-and-a-half hill from his home in the Pittsburgh suburbs to Avalon Elementary School. And when he makes his way into a second-grade classroom, he is barraged with cheers of delight. Kennedy, a retired salesman, is a grandfather-in-the-classroom, sharing his knowledge, experience and friendship with a generation of youngsters.

He helps them with their vocabulary lessons or listens as they discuss the important issues in their lives. For Kennedy, it is a rewarding activity that he hopes to pursue "as long as I can make that hill." He misses the chance to nurture his own grandchildren – they live out of state – so the classroom volunteer program helps fill a void in his life.

As America's elderly population grows, an increasing number of programs are being formed that link retirees and youngsters. Although it is a relatively new phenomenon, the National Council on Aging knows of several thousand intergenerational activities. In western Pennsylvania alone, a program at the University of Pittsburgh named "Generations Together" brings retirees together with as many as 20,000 youngsters. Program director Sally Newman says a national study of retiree participants indicates they feel more satisfied with life and continue to grow mentally by volunteering in these meaningful activities.

But to chat with the retiree volunteers is to learn the true value of working with youngsters. Retired payroll accountant Mark Narr, 67, wanted "to give back something to the community," so he volunteered to work two afternoons a week at a school for youngsters who are disabled or retarded. He calls his volunteering "the most important thing I've ever done." Artist Ann Sawyer Berkley, 72, volunteers as a once-a-week artist-in-residence at the Pittsburgh High School for Creative and Performing Arts. Being around the students "makes me young," she says. She also gains pride from the fact that young black students view her as a role model.

And in Philadelphia, an improvisational acting troupe, "Full Circle," comprised of both retirees and adolescents, tours the region's senior centers and high schools. Its 18 members perform highly improvised scenes that deal with problems facing the young and old. Only one of the performers has had any previous acting experience, and none of them has had any professional training. It is just something they've always wanted to do.

If you'd like to do something meaningful in your retirement, there are more options than you can imagine.

Redefining Your Marriage

In addition to financial planning and finding a creative outlet, a third important facet of life is affected by retirement, and that is marriage. How well a couple weathers retirement may depend on the health of their relationship.

Redefining your relationship after retirement takes a lot of work, says Miriam Galper Cohen, a psychotherapist who has led preretirement workshops and has worked extensively with older people. Remember, you don't have to spend 24 hours a day together, seven days a week. Many retirement counselors say it's a good idea, sometimes even crucial, to pursue some separate interests. And if your home is big enough, stake out and maintain separate turf. It may be the garden for one spouse and a basement workshop for the other.

Do you feel guilty separating yourself from your spouse for some private time? In their book *Coping With Your Husband's Retirement,* authors Roslyn Friedman and Annette Nussbaum offer a script.

First, the "Don't" script ("Asking for Permission"):

YOU: Honey, do you mind if I meet my sister for lunch and the symphony tomorrow? She has an extra ticket.

HE: Well, I thought we'd do something. But if you'd rather be with her . . .

YOU: Oh, I'm sorry, I didn't realize . . . okay, I'll call and tell her to get someone else (guilty).

HE: No, go ahead. Do what you want.

YOU: No, I'll stay home (angry and frustrated) – or – Okay, I'll go (guilty, guilty, guilty).

Now the "Do" script ("Giving Yourself Permission"):

YOU: Honey, I have a date for lunch and the symphony with my sister tomorrow. I want you to know that I'll be gone most of the day.

HE: I thought we'd do something.

YOU: I'd love to do something with you. Why don't we plan a day together on Friday?

Authors Friedman and Nussbaum say they aren't suggesting that you aggressively demand time of your own but that you simply "recognize your need as being equal to his."

But, like many women who entered the work force late in life, you may be the one who is busily working while your husband retires. If that's the case, psychologists say it's important to recognize that his needs to play are equal to yours to work. They suggest you encourage him to find suitable outside interests that he can pursue alone or with friends.

The AARP's *Planning Your Retirement* preretirement booklet poses another scenario: You're both retired and you resent the fact that your husband spends five afternoons a week on the golf course. Possible solutions to consider? Don't hesitate to discuss your concerns with him. He may not be aware of how his golf is affecting his marriage. Or you can take up golf yourself and accompany him once or twice a week.

Communicate and compromise. "People ought to talk to one another about what their expectations are. It's good if they approach the process of developing mutual expectations with the spirit of give and take," says gerontologist Dr. Atchley.

Your relationship with your spouse may not be the only relationship that needs to be redefined in retirement. What about your connection with your kids? In retirement, you may not be able to afford to continue playing your role as party host to your children and grandchildren. And you may not want to be viewed as a convenient baby-sitter. In retirement, you may want to enjoy yourself by yourself — and hesitate to invite your grown-up son or daughter to move back home after living away for several years.

If that's the dilemma you're facing, Dr. Atchley suggests you be "real straight" with your son or daughter. "There are certain times when you have to grin and bear it. If somebody just got divorced and doesn't have a job, you've got to say, 'Come on home, we'll give you support for a while, but after six months we expect you to dust yourself off and have a new place.' That sort of understanding is good to have in the beginning," says Dr. Atchley. "They have to respect your agenda."

Making and Keeping Friends

Whether you are retired and married or retired and single, you can reduce stress by being part of a social network. A study headed by Carl I. Cohen of the Department of Psychiatry at State University of New York-Downstate Medical Center tracked 133 elderly New York residents and found that social networks reduce physical symptoms of stress by buffering the effect of increased levels of stress.

That's a fact to consider if you plan to move after retirement. Will your new home offer you access to people of similar interests? And if so, are you the type of person who can seek them out?

The importance of friendships can't be underplayed. In fact, a social network may be better than family in helping you weather the stress of retirement. "An older person with one good friend is better able to cope with the later years than a person with a dozen grandchildren but no peer-group friends," says sociologist Zena Blau in her book *Aging in a Changing Society*. And Dr. Atchley says that among retirees, a social network is a better magnet than a good climate.

If you can maintain old friendships or make new ones, you've got an antidote to the loneliness that sometimes overpowers retirees. If you're a shy person but would like to make friends, your solution may exist in the form of a social skills group. These are therapy groups designed to help you overcome shyness. Hundreds of them exist throughout the country. You can find out about them from the psychology department at any major university.

There are a surprising number of good retiree groups to join if you take the time to look. In Washington, D.C., a club called "The Fossils" has been bringing retired men together for 40 years. Some 400 men belong to the nonsectarian, nonpolitical, nonprofit organization whose only requirements are that members be retired and male. The group holds a monthly business meeting at a church in Chevy Chase, Maryland, at which the speaker could be a noted historian or a retired athlete. There are biannual luncheons and an abundance of groups within the organization: a camera group, a bridge group, an investment group. There's a duckpin bowling group that meets weekly; its members include a 92-year-old and a 96-year-old. In fact, one team accepts only those over 90!

Remember, the more time you spend with people of similar interests, the more friends you're likely to make. If you enjoy traveling to distant shores but you don't want to do it alone and have a limited budget, nothing beats a passenger-carrying freighter trip. The voyages can be as short as 30 days or last several months, and you're never totally certain of every place you'll visit. It depends on the cargo. You may wind up in Casablanca one day, Marseilles a few days later. You always have a place to sleep and eat onboard. You always have a group with which to tour the port of call. The trips are particularly popular among adventurous retirees. (For free information on freighter travel write to Pearl's Freighter Trips, 175 Great Neck Road, Suite 303, Great Neck, NY 11021, or phone 516-487-8351.)

For $25 a year, you and your spouse can join the National Senior Sports Association and participate in or become a spectator at special events in golf, tennis, and bowling. Write the organization at 10560 Main Street, Suite 205, Fairfax, VA 22030, or phone (703) 385-7540.

And then there's Elderhostel, a network of more than a thousand colleges, universities and other educational institutions that host week-long programs on campus for people who are 60 (you may bring a companion who is under 60 if you wish). Participants live like college students while they take noncredit courses in everything from Shakespearean literature or marine biology to cross-country skiing or human sexuality. Groups are limited to 40 participants, so there's ample opportunity to get to know fellow classmates. And a week-long program often includes field trips, concerts, plays and movies. For a catalog, write to Elderhostel, 80 Boylston Street, Suite 400, Boston, MA 02116.

Retired Philadelphians Larry and Sylvia Miner schedule two Elderhostel trips each year — one in the spring and one in the fall. They spend six weeks each winter in Florida and spend most of their summer days at a swimming and tennis club. And when Larry — who underwent heart bypass surgery several years ago — rattles off his regimen of activities, it's easy to believe him when he says, "The only stress in retirement is being too busy."

At age 65 he is an avid trader of old photography equipment and antique photographs; he plays tennis twice a week during the indoor season and more frequently during the warmer months. The couple belongs to two book discussion groups and a social group, and Larry is a member of a "semiamateur" therapy group named "Dynamics of Growing Old," where the issues of the aging are discussed and dealt with. He participates in a Pritikin support group, rides a stationary bicycle three times a week and does 25 minutes of stretching exercises each morning. He makes the rounds of flea markets, plays his guitar twice a week, lunches with friends and former colleagues from his years as a school administrator and plays computer games with his three young grandchildren every chance he gets.

All of this on top of the regular household routine. The retirement schedule has made the Miners so busy that they've decided to set aside a day each week to loaf by themselves.

Chapter 52

SMOKING

People smoke for many reasons. Stress relief is one of them.

"Nicotine [the active ingredient in cigarettes] releases opiate-like substances called endorphins, chemicals that give you a pleasant, mellow feeling and protect against stress," explains David B. Abrams, Ph.D., assistant professor of psychiatry and human behavior at Brown University and associate director of the Division of Behavioral Medicine at the Miriam Hospital in Providence, Rhode Island.

"Nicotine is a mood-altering substance that will help you cope with loneliness, anxiety and stress – it makes life more bearable. *And* it improves concentration and accuracy," adds Dr. Abrams. "I think that's why people in very high-pressure jobs – air traffic controllers, nurses, newspaper reporters – tend to smoke.

"In any situation that produces stress – that is, whenever you are strained beyond your limits in the face of a demand – nicotine and other chemicals in cigarette smoke can reduce fatigue and transform an unpleasant mood into a pleasant one," says Dr. Abrams.

Smoke and Stress: Double Trouble

But the instant stress relief afforded by cigarettes has a dark side. Every year, scientists add to the list of health problems fostered by smoking; it now includes prematurely aged skin and poor hearing along with the more serious problems like emphysema, lung cancer and heart disease. But the threat of bad health is rarely enough to prompt people to quit. In fact, just *thinking* about the damage caused by cigarettes can make you so edgy you need a light!

The problem is, cigarettes are the last thing an already stressed-out heart needs. A study at the University of Pittsburgh School of Medicine found that smoking and stress combined raised blood pressure and heart rates higher than either smoking or stress alone. The combined effects of stress and nicotine may well trigger heart disease in some smokers, say the researchers.

But here's the catch: Trying to quit smoking is stressful, too. It's breaking an *addiction.*

"Nicotine is one of the most addictive substances known," says Dr. Abrams. "In terms of its effects on brain chemistry, nicotine is similar to cocaine or heroin, but in much smaller doses.

"Plus, cigarettes are legal, relatively inexpensive compared to other addictive drugs, and convenient to use," says Dr. Abrams. "But a big reason nicotine is so addictive is that you can dose yourself so precisely. By either taking a tiny puff or inhaling deeply, by smoking frequently or infrequently, or buying low-nicotine or regular brands, you can tailor the dosage to maintain just the right blood levels that produce pleasurable effects. It's unlike cocaine or heroin, where one injection produces a tremendous rush followed later by a crash. And nicotine doesn't slow reaction time or interfere as much with performance, like alcohol does."

Smoking also is very habit-forming because it's associated with many other everyday habits. "Smoke even a pack a day or less," says Dr. Abrams, "and you end up smoking while you're on the phone, driving in your car, waiting to pick up your kids, watching television and so forth. In the course of a year, your brain has made thousands of connections between all those everyday situations and smoking.

"So like Pavlov's classic experiment with conditioned responses in dogs, smokers tend to light up whenever the phone rings, whenever they get into the car or have to wait, and so forth, to the point where their brain thinks something's wrong if they're on the phone without a cigarette in their hand."

How to Quit—For Good

What enables some people to kick the habit for good, while others pick it up again?

Dr. Abrams thinks one important key to kicking the habit once and for all is learning to cope with stress. He and some colleagues studied 44 smokers and ex-smokers to try to find out why some eventually resumed the habit after quitting.

"Social situations like parties, where others smoke, accounted for a lot of relapses," says Dr. Abrams. "But the people who seem most vulnerable – and most likely to smoke again – are those who don't know how to cope with stressful feelings like anxiety, anger, loneliness, boredom, depression and fatigue. In stressful situations, they feel they'll go nuts if they don't have a cigarette. If any cigarettes are available, they'll light one [or they'll seek one out]."

You can survive stressful situations without cigarettes, though. Here's how.

Stressed out? Sit it out. "The feeling that you can't go another minute without a cigarette – and the fear that that feeling will get worse is irrational," says Dr. Abrams. "Stress, depression, loneliness and fatigue come and go – and so does the need for a cigarette. If you wait a few minutes, you will feel better."

Talk yourself out of it. "As with an irrational fear – like agoraphobia or obsessive-compulsive behavior, for example – rational thoughts and phrases can get you through the misery," says Dr. Abrams. "Instead of saying, 'I can't possibly get through this without a cigarette,' say to yourself, 'Wait a minute. Slow down. Stop. I *can* survive without a cigarette.'

"We encourage people to confront situations without a cigarette," says Dr. Abrams. "The anxiety begins to wear off as the old patterns die away and your body adapts to the new situations."

Use your imagination. "Imagine yourself skiing over a snow-covered mountain," says Dr. Abrams. "Your craving for a cigarette is the mountain. Conquering that mountain is scary and thrilling, but you make it to the bottom and feel good. You say to yourself, 'I thought I was going to crash and fall, but I made it.' "

Pleasant imagery also acts as a distraction, taking your mind off cigarettes until the urge passes. "Activate a pleasant image the minute you begin to feel the urge to smoke – in the middle of a busy day, during a hassle with your kids, or after a desperate call from a friend, for example," says Dr. Abrams. "Think of this technique as a fire drill: Have a list of stressful situations that have given you the urge to smoke in the past. Then by identifying such high-risk situations ahead of time, you can use the imagery under pressure."

Reduce stress overload. "Set realistic goals and deadlines, don't take on more tasks than you can comfortably handle, and rearrange your day to allow for hobbies or exercise," says Dr. Abrams. "Good time management is common sense, especially for someone who wants to quit smoking."

"Keep Smoking While You Learn to Quit"

That's the motto of Smokenders, Inc., a nationwide program that combines social support, behavior modification and relaxation therapy. It's an approach that might be just the ticket for people who smoke under stress, because you don't have to give up cigarettes (at least not at first).

"Enrollees meet once a week for six weeks," explains Judith Brodsky, a former Smokenders group moderator. "Smokers are allowed to continue to smoke for the first four weeks, during which they gradually cut down by learning to deal with trigger situations and downshifting to low-nicotine brands. When the 'cut-off day' arrives, their bodies harbor approximately 85 to 90 percent less nicotine than when they started."

Here are a few of the techniques employed by Smokenders.

Deep breathing. "When you smoke under stress, you inhale differently than when you're relaxed," says Brodsky. "If you're watching television, for example, you might absentmindedly take a few light puffs. But if you're under tension, you'll take a good, hard pull and exhale slowly. And smoking in that manner does in fact cause a feeling of relaxation. So we teach smokers a deep breathing exercise that can achieve the same feeling of relaxation without the cigarette."

To practice deep breathing, stand up, bend forward from the waist and breathe deeply for 15 or 30 seconds, or however long it takes to fully expel air from your lungs, says Brodsky.

Take a break. When you feel overwhelmed – if you have 12 million gizmos to assemble or your "in" box looks like the Eiffel Tower – and you feel an urge to smoke, take a brisk walk for the length of time it would take to smoke a cigarette. Or get a cool drink from the water cooler. "Do something to repattern your behavior," says Brodsky.

Think about *why* you smoke. "Does smoking make you any better able to deal with your problems? Does it help you get caught up on your work? Probably not," says Brodsky. "Smoking is like thumb-sucking, but for adults. You associate smoking a cigarette with feeling better, so you reach for one under stress."

Free at Last

"The best quitting strategy is to use whatever technique is best for *you*," says Dr. Abrams. "We recommend that people experiment with different strategies – deep breathing, relaxation therapy, biofeedback or other ways to cope with anxiety and stress. If rational thinking doesn't work for one person, for example, thinking about a cool lake might. So there is no general prescription.

"Also, the only way to finally kick the habit is to accept the fact that for three to six months you will crave cigarettes very intensely," he says.

"After six months of talking on the phone without lighting up a cigarette, you will begin to unlearn the habit," says Dr. Abrams. "After six months to a year, a ringing phone – or other stimulus – will no longer trigger an urge for a cigarette."

Chapter 53

STRETCHING

Yawn.

Go ahead, do it.

Now pay attention to how you feel. Did you get a boost of energy from the oxygen you pulled into your lungs? Did your limbs become a little less tense than they were a moment ago? Did you loosen up your face – often the tensest part of your body?

Yawns are nature's way of forcing us to enjoy the de-stressing benefits of stretching. We can learn a lot from those yawns, like the fact that beneficial exercise doesn't have to be painful. If it hurts to stretch any more than it hurts to yawn, you must be doing something wrong, says Bob Anderson, author of the best-selling book *Stretching.*

Stretching allows us to bring the same great feeling of a yawn to any part of our body. It gives us something to do with the excess tension we store in our muscle tissues. That particular tension – the result of stress, the result of sitting still at the wheel or at sedentary jobs – can become chronic if we don't release it. The way Craig Daniels, Ph.D., former director of the Stress Research Center at the University of Hartford, West Hartford, Connecticut, explains it, our muscles get tired of being tensed and untensed. So they stay tensed. "It becomes a chronic state so the system doesn't have to keep responding," he says.

Some residual tension is released during sleep and some goes away on its own, but we still may have a lot of tension to get rid of. That's where stretching comes in.

"When you stretch, you get a limbering effect that minimizes any sort of injury," says Dr. Daniels. "As you get older, muscles lose their elasticity. When tensed, the muscles harden. By stretching, you make them looser, make them more elastic." It also forces you to use muscles that you ignore all day if you have a sedentary job.

Layne Longfellow, Ph.D., a psychologist who leads seminars in stress management, explains how stretching also tones up your mind. He says the mind and body are in a "continuous feedback loop." Stressors have a definite impact on the way you hold your body. Exposure to enough fear, for example, will cause your posture to contract. And your body in its contracted position is sending a "fear" message to your mind, says Dr. Longfellow.

You can use stretching to break the loop, to alter chronic tightened postures. "With stretching, your chronically contracted muscles will release, and you will release the psychological contractions that go with it," says Dr. Longfellow.

Learning from Kitty

A daily stretching ritual – or simply stretching whenever you feel tense – is simple, painless and effective. If you don't believe us, just ask the nearest four-legged creature. The delights of stretching have long been known by animals. You've seen your pet dog or cat stretch several times a day. You should do the same.

One of Anderson's favorite stretches is one you can do while sitting in gridlock, instead of fuming. It's called the Shoulder Shrug/Neck Stretch.

The Shoulder Shrug/Neck Stretch. This is great for tension in your neck, shoulders and upper body. Bring your shoulders up to your earlobes for three to four seconds. Then drop your shoulders down and think to yourself: "Shoulders hang, shoulders down." Let your shoulders relax for a few seconds. Do two or three repetitions.

That should help relieve the tension in your shoulders. Now you want to stretch your neck. To do that, tilt your head sideways to the right and visualize your left shoulder going down. Stretch it easily for five or six seconds. Now alternate sides (lean your head to the left and drop your right shoulder). Repeat for each side. This stretches both the neck and the top of the shoulder. "When you're stretching, you should feel that you're in control of the stretch," says Anderson.

Another Anderson favorite is an even simpler stretch, good for long airplane flights or weak moments at work.

Reach for the Sky. Interlace your fingers and raise your hands above your head, palms up. Push your arms upward and slightly back. Feel the stretch in your arms, shoulders and upper back. Hold the stretch for 10 to 15 seconds. Do not hold your breath – breathe normally.

Dr. Daniels offers an all-purpose stretch for the back that you can do while watching the evening news.

Getting a Leg Up. Lie on your back and bend your left knee. Take both hands and put them on your left leg, between the knee and ankle. Pull your left leg up so you are trying to touch your knee to your chest. Hold a few seconds (to start). Bring it back down. Repeat several times.

Do the same with your right leg. Then do the same with both legs together (for this version, make a loop around both legs with your hands).

Another stretch from Dr. Daniels works on the hamstring and calf muscles. It's a stretch that shouldn't be done in the home of neighbors you don't know very well.

Push Down the Wall. Stand about 36 inches away from a wall. Lean forward, placing your hands flat on the wall at shoulder level. Lean into the wall. Slowly walk backward – and keep your feet flat on the floor. You should feel your calf muscles stretch.

Chapter 54

TIME MANAGEMENT

Worrying about having too little time to do what you have to do or would like to do is stressful. But no one can create more time — each day has 24 hours, no more, no less. So the only solution is to better manage the time we do have.

"Pencil and paper are important tools to time management, and therefore to stress management as well," says Cliff Mangan, Ph.D., senior staff coordinator of counseling services, Temple University Counseling Center, Philadelphia. "By writing down how you spend your time and comparing it to what you'd like to do, you can better control time. Having a written agenda, you don't have to worry so much."

Here are some suggestions to use in order to manage this valuable resource.

Take a personal inventory of how you spend your time. "Keep a diary in the form of a compact, portable calendar for a week or two," says Dr. Mangan. Write down, in 15- or 30-minute increments, how much time you spend on various activities — eating, sleeping and getting dressed; cooking, grocery shopping and household chores; childcare, worship and other family activities; and reading, exercise, socializing and other leisure activities, plus various on-the-job tasks. (Don't wait until the end of the day to record your activities. You won't remember accurately.)

"A time-management calendar can be very revealing," says Dr. Mangan. "You may not realize how much time you spend chatting over coffee with co-workers, for example, until you log it on your calendar."

Spend some time thinking about your goals. "What do you want to do over the long run? Where do you want to be five or ten years from now?" asks Dr. Managan. "Fantasize about all your goals, major and minor. Then set intermediate goals. Then set specific, immediate goals that will help you achieve your long-term goals. Decide how to spend your daily time accordingly." Suppose you want to redecorate your house – the long-term goal. This month you plan to install hardwood flooring in the living room – your intermediate goal. Tomorrow you plan to buy the wood – your daily goal.

Write down what you expect to accomplish. And visualize the finished project. Picture the shiny oak boards. Imagine the smell of new lumber. Feel the wood's warm smoothness. "The more senses you employ in making your plans, the more attainable they seem and the more likely you are to execute them," says Dr. Mangan. "Committing plans to paper makes them less overwhelming and keeps you from worrying about when you'll get to them. Also, more 'urgent' demands are less likely to sidetrack you."

Make an agenda. "Take 15 or 20 minutes before you start the workday to decide what you're going to do, when you're going to do it – then do it," says Dr. Mangan.

"Planning time saves time," says R. Alec Mackenzie, author of *The Time Trap: How to Get More Done in Less Time.* He cites one study comparing two groups of projects in a company. One allowed a minimum amount of time for planning and the balance for execution. The second group of projects allowed considerably more time for planning, yet were executed more quickly and with better results, saving time and aggravation.

Set specific, realistic deadlines. Rather than making general, indefinite plans, such as telling yourself you would like to paint the bedroom someday, instead, say something like, "I'm going to pick out paint on Saturday and paint the bedroom by September 1" or some specific date.

"One of the problems with setting deadlines is unrealistic time estimates," says Mackenzie. "Poor projections lead to frustration and often to panic and crisis." The secret to getting things done on time is to make allowances for interruptions, distractions, errors and emergencies.

Review your calendar at the end of each month. "As you look over your daily records, think about what you've done to advance your goals," says Dr. Mangan. "Are you progressing? If not, you have all the data right in front of you to show what's stopping you."

Are You Wasting Time?

If your hourglass seems to empty far too quickly, look for stray fragments of wasted time.

Make a "hit list" of your ten biggest time gobblers. "Review your time-management calendar at the end of each day and ask yourself which activities moved you forward toward your goal and which didn't," says Dr. Mangan. A few common time wasters include meetings, interruptions (such as visitors and phone calls), paperwork, household chores, driving, errands, waiting and watching television. Then look for ways to eliminate or reduce those time wasters.

Block out interruptions. "Finishing a task in one session saves time because you need not reorient yourself to your work again and again," says Mackenzie. If you need large blocks of uninterrupted time, screen your phone calls (via secretary or answering machine), close your door and schedule meetings for late afternoon — or don't tell anyone where you're going to be.

Sometimes body language alone can discourage interruptions. "Sit facing away from your office door," says Dr. Mangan. "Otherwise, you'll be tempted to say 'hello' to everyone who walks by. If you work in an open office, don't glance up when people pass by. If you make it obvious that you're totally involved, totally committed to what you're working on, people will be less likely to interrupt.

"If others do interrupt, arrange to get back to them later," says Dr. Mangan. "Then write down on your calendar *when* you plan to talk to them. Put your words into action. Again, your calendar can help control how you spend your time."

Give yourself permission to say no. If your calendar is filled with work on school pageants, community bake sales and other commitments, you run the risk of breaking under the weight of time-consuming obligations. The trick is to jettison surplus obligations without feeling guilty.

Delegate. No book on stress management would be complete without mentioning the option of getting someone else to do what you don't have time for.

"Write down what you delegated, to whom, and when you expect it to be done," says Dr. Mangan. "Then you no longer have to do the job *or* worry about it."

The trade-off with delegating is that your delegate may not do the job *exactly* as you would. (For more on this vital time-management tool, see chapter 17.)

Take Time to Do Nothing

It's hard to go from trying to do two things at once to doing nothing at all. But everyone needs some "white space" on their calendar, to rest and reflect.

"I hesitate to tell people to *schedule* some 'down time,' " says Cliff Mangan, Ph.D., of Temple University's Counseling Center in Philadelphia. "But down time can be very uplifting. If you don't have time for yourself and yourself alone, to simply relax, you'll be tense, irritable and anxious, which is bound to affect others. So in that respect, I don't think it's selfish to be selfish."

Finding Lost Time

Here are still more rules and tools for chiseling hours off time spent on obligations and channeling it toward what matters the most.

Start the day prepared. Get your clothes (and your kids' clothes) ready the night before, for example. If clothes are color-coordinated, pressed and ready to report for duty when needed, you'll be less apt to waste precious time rummaging for a clean shirt or the right belt.

"Your brain is most receptive at two periods of the day – before you go to sleep and as soon as you wake up," says Dr. Mangan. "So make the most of the first and last 20 minutes you're awake. If you take these times to get organized, and perhaps read a brief inspirational message to set the mood, you'll be more efficient and effective throughout the day – and even sleep and dream more productively."

Schedule work that requires energy and initiative for your "peak" times. Energy levels tend to fluctuate in small peaks and valleys throughout the day. To harness natural bursts of energy, do difficult tasks at peak times and easier tasks during dips. After a heavy dinner, for example, you may feel too logy to paint the spare room or fix the leaky faucet in the bathroom. But you could do a routine chore like pairing socks. Conversely, if you're at your best at midmorning or an hour or two after dinner, these may be good times to exercise, organize a new project or tackle some other demanding task.

Set a five-minute limit to rehashing work hassles at the end of the day. "Continuing to think and talk about work problems – whether you're raising children or working in an office – only extends your workday into your scheduled personal time," says Dr. Mangan.

Stand up to sort your mail. Standing to sort your mail discourages you from lingering over bills, bank statements, junk mail, catalogs, flyers, magazines and memos when you could be working on more important tasks. Divide incoming paperwork into three piles: one stack for work you should do as soon as possible, one for semiurgent matters, and one to do whenever you get around to it. Discard the rest. Later, with urgent tasks complete, you can peruse magazines, catalogs or corporate reports at your leisure. (One time-management expert calls this the "art of wastebasketry.")

Shop by mail. With the profusion of mail-order catalogs, there's little you can't buy through the mail. What you don't like, you can send back – without wasting a lot of time circling the block for a parking space or hunting for a salesclerk.

Stock up. To further minimize time spent shopping, stock up on basics or items you use in quantity, like panty hose, all-occasion greeting cards, stamps, laundry detergent, canned goods, vacuum cleaner bags.

Buy Christmas or other presents *anytime*. Whenever you see something that would make a good gift for someone, buy it, even if the occasion is months away. By adding to your gift stash throughout the year, you can avoid crowded stores during the hectic holiday buying season, saving time and aggravation. (By shopping ahead of time, you also avoid selecting gifts by default, under a short deadline.)

Put things where they belong. For sheer exasperation, nothing beats wasting half an hour searching for misplaced car keys – or anything else you can't do without. Always put your keys in the same spot – on the dresser, by the door or in the side pocket of your purse, for example – to avoid wasting a lot of time hunting for them. The same goes for your watch, checkbook, wallet, car registration and other easily mislaid but essential items.

"All this is not as structured as it sounds, and the effort really pays off," says Dr. Mangan. "Paradoxically, the more you write down how long you spend on daily activities and seemingly structure your time, the more time you have for spontaneity and fun, and the less time you spend worrying or feeling guilty. Making conscious choices to restructure your time gives you more control and therefore reduces stress. You'll be more effective at what you do and have more time for fun."

Chapter 55

TRANQUILIZERS

Anxiety. Worry. Insomnia. Depression. They come and go like rain clouds over the emotional landscape. After a day or so, the sun will shine again. Every so often, though, extremely trying circumstances – a disabling illness, financial peril, an accident, the death of a loved one, a messy divorce – stir up an extended forecast of dark, stormy, emotional weather. You're depressed, exhausted, tense and preoccupied. And you need help *fast.*

At one time, phenobarbital and secobarbital, which are barbiturates, and meprobamate were standard issue for a bad case of "nerves." But barbiturates depress the central nervous system and have proved to be deadly for many – it's far too easy to overdose, especially when barbiturates are combined with alcohol (another central nervous system depressant). So prescribing barbiturates was like calling out the Seventh Fleet to settle a bar fight. Both barbiturates and meprobamate are also addictive – your body grows accustomed to their effects very quickly, until you can't manage without them.

Today, barbiturates and meprobamate are all but obsolete, having been replaced by so-called minor tranquilizers like diazepam (Valium) or flurazepam (Dalmane). You can even buy over-the-counter sleep aids like diphenhydramine hydrochloride (Sleep-eze 3) to help treat insomnia.

Sometimes anxiety is a symptom of depression, in which case antidepressant drugs like imipramine (Tofranil) or amitriptyline (Elavil) can help in as little as two weeks' time. A third class of drugs, mood stabilizers like lithium (Lithane and others), are prescribed principally for the dramatic mood swings typical of manic-depression. In contrast, "major" tranquilizers like chlorpromazine (Thorazine) are used primarily for psychoses and other serious disorders, which are beyond the scope of this book.

At times, these drugs are used in the treatment of anxiety and depression. However, they do not completely replace "talk therapy," a long-standing method of working out problems. Communication between doctor and patient is essential. And while there is no need to fear these drugs themselves, there is need to fear their potential for abuse.

While newer tranquilizers and other stress-management drugs are somewhat safer and less addictive than barbiturates, they are not a panacea for stress and, like all drugs, should be used with caution. Here's why.

Antianxiety Drugs and Sleep Aids

The close-knit family of drugs known as benzodiazepines accounts for 85 percent of all minor tranquilizers prescribed in the United States. Besides diazepam (Valium) and flurazepam (Dalmane), these include:

- Alprazolam (example: Xanax)
- Chlordiazepoxide (example: Librium)
- Clonazepam (example: Klonopin)
- Clorazepate dipotassium (example: Tranxene)
- Halazepam (example: Paxipam)
- Lorazepam (example: Ativan)
- Oxazepam (example: Serax)
- Prazepam (example: Centrax)
- Temazepam (example: Restoril)
- Triazolam (example: Halcion)

"These so-called minor tranquilizers are for pure anxiety without significant depression (with the exception of alprazolam)," says Jacob J. Katzow, M.D., associate clinical professor of psychiatry and behavioral science at George Washington University and director of the Washington, D.C., Clinic for Mood Disorders. If you get jittery before flying or speaking in public – or find yourself so worried and upset that you can barely get through the day – these drugs can help reduce stress. They can control anxiety's most unpleasant symptoms – insomnia, sweating, muscle tension, tension headaches, rapid heartbeat, vomiting and shaking.

In fact, the other benzodiazepines, like flurazepam (Dalmane), temazepam (Restoril) and triazolam (Halcion), leave you so relaxed that they're used specifically to treat insomnia. (Insomnia comes in three types – difficulty falling asleep, frequent awakening during the night and early-morning awakening – and can appear in any combination.) Other antianxiety drugs are a better choice if you want to relax but don't want to fall asleep.

Antianxiety drugs can also help pave the way for effective "talk therapy," if you need it. They can calm you down enough to enable you to talk over your troubles with a professional counselor.

"As for when to prescribe these drugs, how much to prescribe and how long they should be used, that's a matter of the physician's judgment," says Dr. Katzow. Much of that decision is based on how they work in your body.

How Tranquilizers and Sleeping Pills Work

Benzodiazepines like diazepam work by depressing the central nervous system, but to a far lesser degree than barbiturates. That difference makes benzodiazepines a safer pharmaceutical tool to help relieve anxiety. In fact, when these drugs first came out, doctors and patients alike were a bit overconfident. Now doctors are more aware that benzodiazepines can be somewhat risky: They can build up in your system, causing toxicity, and you can become physically or psychologically dependent on them. If they are taken with alcohol, you can go to sleep and never wake up. If you've ever been dependent on alcohol or other chemical means of stress relief, be forewarned: Benzodiazepines are potentially habit-forming.

What's more, dependency can sneak up on you. Anxiety and insomnia tend to be on-again, off-again problems, prompting frequent and sometimes long-term use of these drugs.

Such problems are avoidable, of course. The trick is to select the right drug for the right problem in the right amount for the shortest period of time, and to look for nondrug ways to handle stress or insomnia. You should ask your doctor if the drug prescribed is the safest, most effective drug for your problem.

The type of drug your doctor prescribes may be determined by how long it stays in your system. Some go to work quickly and wear off within hours. Others take more time to kick in, and the effects can linger for several hours. Triazolam and oxazepam, for example, have a short half-life – on the average, your body will use up half the dosage of triazolam in two to four hours and half the dosage of oxazepam in four to eight hours. When used for insomnia, they usually don't leave you with a "drug hangover" in the morning, making them reasonably good sleeping aids for elderly people who experience more than just an occasional sleep problem.

Sometimes, trial and error is the only way to find out which type of tranquilizer is best for you. "If two people take the same drug, one person may get drowsy and another might not," says psychiatrist Lynn Cunningham, M.D.

If short-acting drugs like triazolam don't work, your doctor may try intermediate agents like temazepam or lorazepam. Temazepam's half-life is approximately 10 to 15 hours and lorazepam's is about 12 hours. Unfortunately, they can leave you groggy the next day and are associated with memory loss – decided drawbacks.

Flurazepam is a long-acting drug: It's a powerful sleep inducer, but it has a half-life of 47 to 100 hours. If you need help falling asleep only once in a blue moon, that's of little concern, but with repeated use, the drug can build up in your system. That lingering effect is a special concern for older people, who metabolize drugs more slowly and may take longer to eliminate a drug than young adults do.

For that reason, short-acting benzodiazepines are preferred for older people with more than occasional sleep problems, according to R. Michael Allen, M.D., medical coordinator of adult services at Community Psychiatric Centers, Millwood Hospital, Arlington, Texas.

Diazepam, for example, has a half-life of 20 hours in a 20-year-old but a half-life of 90 hours in an 80-year-old. The difference results from the amount of time the liver takes to process the chemical, says Andrew M. Barclay, M.D., chairman of the Department of Family Practices at the University of Illinois College of Medicine, Peoria. Drugs and their dosages, however, should be dealt with on a case-by-case basis, experts warn.

These short-acting benzodiazepines like alprazolam (Xanax) and oxazepam (Serax) may also be appropriate for older people who experience occasional bouts of anxiety. But for persistent anxiety, intermediate-acting drugs like lorazepam (Ativan) may be the better choice simply because they last longer than short-acting triazolam (Halcion). Be aware, though, that your memory may suffer.

Long-acting agents such as diazepam (Valium) are reserved for people with chronic, general anxiety for whom other, nondrug methods haven't brought serenity.

Occasionally, someone taking benzodiazepines like alprazolam (Xanax) will experience what doctors call a paradoxical effect – they become anxious and agitated instead of calm. Should this happen, your doctor may switch you to another benzodiazepine like oxazepam (Serax).

Safety Strategies

"The antianxiety drugs are readily prescribed because they work – and they work fast," says Dr. Cunningham. To minimize any potential problems, doctors suggest these strategies.

Try the drug on a weekend at first, or whenever you don't have to drive. That way, if you become drowsy during the day or develop a "drug hangover," you'll face less risk. If side effects bother you, ask your doctor to change the dosage or switch to another prescription.

Watch for signs of dependency. If you find yourself needing more medicine (that is, more pills or higher doses) than your doctor prescribed, you may have grown physically dependent on the drug. If so, don't stop taking the pills cold turkey – you could become very sick. Completely deprived of your customary dose of sedation, you may feel tense and unable to sleep, or you may go into a full-blown withdrawal reaction, suffering shakiness, headache, nausea and vomiting. You could even experience more dangerous and frightening problems like seizures. To avoid withdrawal, the dose must be tapered off gradually.

Ask yourself if you can manage to cope without the drugs. If you can't, you may be psychologically addicted. "People who are psychologically dependent remember how they felt without the drug, so they're afraid to stop taking it," says Dr. Cunningham. "Also, many refills are called in to the pharmacist over the phone. So it's easy to ask for – and get – unlimited refills without stopping to consider if the drugs are giving relief or if there are other ways to control anxiety."

Be alert for signs of toxic buildup. Warning signs of a sudden overload of these drugs include poor muscular coordination, agitation and slurred speech. Chronic intoxication can lead to disorientation, and confusion may easily be misdiagnosed as senile dementia in older people – or just blamed on old age. Falls and fractures, too, are more common in older people who take benzodiazepines, says Dr. Barclay. Once again, tapering the dose gradually reduces toxicity.

How long you can use benzodiazepines varies. According to the *Physician's Desk Reference,* some should not be taken for more than four months. Some doctors feel that's unnecessarily restrictive – in some cases, anxiety may be severe enough to disrupt life for longer than four months, so doctors should decide on a case-by-case basis whether you need to continue or taper off.

Over-the-Counter Sleep Aids

Stroll through any drugstore or the health and beauty aids aisle of a supermarket and you'll undoubtedly run across do-it-yourself sleep aids like Nytol, Sleep-eze 3 and Sominex (all contain the active ingredient diphenhydramine hydrochloride) or Unisom (active ingredient, doxylamine succinate).

"Why go to a doctor for sleeping pills when you can buy them at the corner drugstore?" you might ask.

Well, it's a matter of using the right tool for the right job instead of improvising with what's easily available.

"Most drugs sold as over-the-counter sleep aids are antihistamines that just happen to make some people drowsy as a side effect," says Magdi Soliman, Ph.D., professor of neuropharmacology in the College of Pharmacy, Florida A & M University in Tallahassee.

Because these antihistamine-type sleep aids are less effective than benzodiazepines, you might have to take a higher dose in order to fall asleep, adds Dr. Soliman. And the more you take, the more likely you are to experience other, undesirable side effects — reduced alertness, foggy memory and confusion. (As with prescription sleep aids, the older you are, the more susceptible you are to drug-induced side effects.) And oddly enough, antihistamines actually make some people edgy or nervous. As a result, Dr. Soliman cautions that they — and prescription drugs, too — should be the last resort when treating insomnia.

Most important, though, artificially induced sleep is not of the same caliber as natural sleep. Antihistamines interfere with rapid-eye-movement (REM) sleep, which is associated with dreaming and considered to be the most restful stage of sleep, explains Dr. Soliman. You may "sleep" all night and still wake up feeling tired. Compounding matters, if you continue to rely on antihistamines, you may experience what doctors call "REM rebound." In other words, you'll eventually spend too much time in REM sleep and have nightmares.

According to studies, prescription sleep aids like flurazepam (Dalmane), temazepam (Restoril) and triazolam (Halcion) have the least effect on REM sleep and therefore the least potential for producing REM rebound. "So while prescription sleep aids are more potent, when prescribed correctly, they are better than over-the-counter preparations," says Dr. Soliman.

If you do try an over-the-counter sleep aid, proceed with care. The label is the closest you'll come to medical advice, so be sure to heed every word. Pay special attention to warnings against taking sleep aids with alcohol or other medicines that also depress the central nervous system.

Beta-Blockers for Anxiety Attacks

In addition to the standard antianxiety drugs, doctors can recommend drugs called beta-blockers, particularly propranolol (Inderal). These may be used to treat anxiety attacks like stage fright.

Beta-blockers block certain nerve impulses to the heart, in effect anesthetizing the heart. They are customarily used to reduce blood pressure, but they can also block a pounding heart, a trembling voice and other physical symptoms of anxiety associated with stage fright and other anxiety attacks. One advantage is that half-life is very short — only four hours — and the drug is completely eliminated from your system by the time the anxiety-causing situation passes.

Because beta-blockers lower your heart rate and blood pressure, they can change the way your body responds to exercise. If your doctor prescribes these drugs, ask if you need to change your activity level in any way.

Drugs for Deep Depression

Most people think of depression as sort of a blue funk—you lie around in your bathrobe all day, on the verge of tears, or just sit and rock for hours. But paralyzing sadness is just one face of depression. Anxiety and agitation may be symptoms of depression, too.

"The person who walks the floor nights wringing their hands may be depressed," says Dr. Cunningham. "We can treat that with benzodiazepines for the short term, to control the agitation, and antidepressants, which work more slowly, to lift the depression. It's a lot like treating pneumonia with cough medicine for the immediate symptoms and antibiotics for the underlying infection."

The arsenal of mood-lifting drugs at a doctor's disposal include:

- Tricyclic antidepressants like imipramine (example: Tofranil)
- Antidepressants with sedative effects like amitriptyline (example: Elavil)
- Combination antianxiety/antidepressant/sedatives like chlordiazepoxide and amitriptyline (example: Limbitrol)
- Monoamine oxidase (MAO) inhibitors like phenelzine sulfate (example: Nardil) for mixed anxiety and depression with phobic or hypochondriacal tendencies
- Mood stabilizers like lithium (example: Eskilith) for the manic phase of manic-depression

Deciding which drug, if any, is best isn't always easy.

"The most obvious, hard-to-dispute uses for antidepressants are for serious depression that lasts for months, where someone stays in the house, crying, and can hardly eat or sleep," says Dr. Katzow. "In these circumstances, it may be obvious to everyone, including the patient, that drugs are an appropriate way out."

According to Dr. Katzow, MAO inhibitors like phenelzine sulfate (Nardil) are often the best antidepressants when individuals aren't responding to other therapy. But they're complicated to use because you have to avoid a long list of foods, beverages and medications (including liver, pickled herring, all cheeses except cottage cheese and cream cheese, yogurt, beer, wine certain cold and allergy medicines, among many others). Eating any of these while taking an MAO inhibitor could produce a dangerous — and possibly fatal — rise in blood pressure.

So your doctor will most likely try a tricyclic antidepressant like imipramine (Tofranil) first, simply because this type is easier to use.

Mood-stabilizing drugs like lithium (Eskilith and others) are typically used for the extreme ups and downs – the manic highs and depressive lows – experienced with manic-depression. But when used in conjunction with antidepressants, they can help other forms of depression dramatically, adds Dr. Katzow.

When Are Medicines the Answer?

Someone who's suffering a major, short-term stressful event may benefit from a tranquilizer but not from an antidepressant. Also, for milder to moderate depression, extending for months or years, drugs may not be an appropriate treatment.

"Some psychiatrists say that relying on a drug is no better than relying on alcohol, that it sets a pattern, that it's an easy way out, that the correct approach is to work things out in therapy," says Dr. Katzow. "And because many of these drugs are addictive and have possible adverse reactions, it is better to learn to handle problems without recourse to drugs. But psychiatric medications are better than many people think they are."

Still, antidepressants, like antianxiety drugs, carry a long list of possible adverse reactions and cautions. So you have to weigh all the usual disadvantages of treating a problem with a chemical against the benefits. Complicating matters further, you may be depressed and not know it. Sometimes it takes a professional to pick up on the symptoms and determine if drugs or therapy – or both – are warranted.

"Most people fall somewhere in that middle range of the spectrum between easy-to-diagnose depression and more subtle problems," says Dr. Katzow. "And most psychiatrists prefer to try 'talk therapy' first and resort to drugs only if depression doesn't lift."

So, as much of a blessing as these drugs may be in providing relief, they should not be used without some effort to find out the true cause of your anxiety or depression. "Whether these drugs are prescribed by the family doctor, an internist or a psychiatrist, there is the danger of continuing to treat the symptoms but not the underlying disease or, in the case of stress, the cause of the problem," says Dr. Cunningham. "Nor should you assume that just because stressful things are going on in your life, stress is the cause of your depression."

A Lifetime Prescription?

Once you've been prescribed a mood-elevating drug, how long do you have to keep taking it?

"That depends," says Dr. Katzow. "For a short-term crisis you may need it for a short time only. If you have a predisposition toward tension or anxiety, you may need to use the drug off and on for the rest of your life."

"You have to weigh the benefits of a drug against the hazards," says David J. Greenblatt, M.D., chief of the Division of Pharmacology at Tufts-New England Medical Center, Boston. "But as a general rule, use medication in the smallest dose for the shortest possible time."

A Few More Words to the Wise

Here are some suggestions to further help your doctor decide what's best for you.

Discuss any medical conditions you have. Kidney or liver problems, for example, can affect drug metabolism. Also, if you have kidney or liver disease, it could be made worse.

Tell your doctor about any other medication you may be taking. Cimetidine (Tagamet) for example, slows metabolism of diazepam and other benzodiazepines and some antidepressants. Antihistamines (a common ingredient in some cold and allergy medicines) depress the central nervous system, adding to the effect of benzodiazepines.

Tell your doctor if you are pregnant (or planning a pregnancy) or nursing a baby. Some drugs can be passed on to a growing fetus or nursing infant, harming the baby.

Ask what side effects you can expect. Each of these drugs carries a long list of possible side effects, ranging from the mildly annoying (like fatigue) to the rare (like liver problems that turn your eyes and skin a bit yellow). Sometimes they go away, sometimes they don't, so contact your doctor.

Chapter 56

ULCERS

Kibby and Aphrodite, dolphins on display at the National Aquarium in Baltimore, Maryland, developed stomach ulcers. They were sent to a natural environment training center for dolphins in the Florida Keys for R and R, where their ulcers were treated with Maalox and Tagamet (standard medicine for ulcers in humans, their fellow mammals). The ulcers healed, only to recur when Kibby and Aphrodite returned to the aquarium. Apparently, swimming around and around in a concrete tank day after day while thousands of people stared at them through Plexiglas windows was stressful for the dolphins.

Dolphins share three things with people: Relatively few are susceptible to ulcers, reactions to stress may be connected to ulcers in some way, and once healed, ulcers will recur if the aggravating factors persist.

Ulcer, Ulcer, Who's Got the Ulcer?

Lots of people in the United States have ulcers. Are they all ambitious, hard-driving, "go-getter" executive types?

Forty or 50 years ago, doctors thought so. But subsequent research has since dispelled that myth: There is no "ulcer personality." And ulcers can and do affect anyone – white collars, blue collars, clerical collars, or – counting students, homemakers, retirees and the unemployed – no collars at all.

Enter myth number two: Stress causes ulcers. Animal studies showed that stomach ulcers in rats (personality unknown) can be brought about by psychological stress. But that idea was shelved when studies revealed that people with ulcers experienced no more stress in their lives than others. Consequently, research to find an ulcer treatment focuses primarily on physical factors, such as the secretion of gastric acid (digestive juices that break down protein) or a way to prevent the deterioration in the sticky, protective mucous lining of the digestive tract. These two forces can create a craterlike sore on the inner wall of the digestive tract. (Gastric ulcers occur in the stomach. Duodenal ulcers occur in the duodenum (pronounced *doo-oh-DEE-num*, the part of the small intestine nearest the stomach).

This hole in your stomach feels like – well, like a hole in your stomach.

"Classic ulcer symptoms are burning or gnawing [upper to mid abdominal] pain, which occurs one to three hours after meals and often awakens [you] at night, about two hours after retiring," says Grace Elta, M.D., in the journal *Modern Medicine.* "Pain [comes and goes] and is relieved by foods or antacids." Other symptoms include belching, bloating and intolerance of fatty foods, according to Dr. Elta. On the other hand, some ulcer patients feel no symptoms whatsoever.

Okay, now you've got it straight: Ulcers are a purely physical problem and doctors treat them as such. Well, that's *almost* the truth, because in the last few years doctors have found that the physical causes aren't as clear-cut as they thought: Ulcers occur in some people who secrete *less* acid than normal, but do not occur in others who secrete *more* acid than normal. Taking a look at psychological factors, they found that people with ulcers do not necessarily experience more potentially stressful events than others. What they did find, however, is that, as a group, people with ulcers differ from others in the way they *react* to events. Ulcer patients seem to experience more anxiety and fear than others when things threaten to disrupt their lives. And those emotions can fuel the fires at your core.

Despair and a Weak Stomach Lining

"Some, but not all, ulcer patients under stress experience an increase in acid production," says Charles T. Richardson, M.D., of the Dallas Veterans Administration Medical Center. "In those who develop ulcers, emotional distress may lead to a breakdown in the way the stomach and duodenum protect themselves against acid secretion. In other words, stress — or specifically, the physiological reaction to stressful events — may interfere with the defense mechanism in some way."

In an important study, published in the journal *Gastroenterology,* Mark Feldman, M.D., and others at the University of Texas Health Sciences Center and the Dallas Veterans Administration Medical Center examined various psychological and social factors in 49 men with ulcers, then compared them with men being treated for kidney stones or gallstones (which have no readily apparent psycho-logical component) and with healthy men. All experienced roughly the same number of potential stressors.

While all ulcer patients didn't fit one narrow stereotype, they did differ from the control group in a few significant ways. Most notably, ulcer patients were more likely than healthy people to view life events like a job change or relocation as negative. Many tended to be hypochondriacal (expressing overemphasis of bodily concern), overly pessimistic (expecting the worst, feeling threatened by low-risk situations) and overly dependent (tending to rely on people more than is healthy). They average lower scores than control groups on something psychologists call "ego strength," or the ability to bend, not break, under stress.

At the same time, the men with ulcers reported a higher average level of alienation than a control group, with slightly fewer friends and relatives whom they felt they could rely upon in times of crisis. And they were more anxious and depressed than men without ulcers.

Relax—Your Stomach Will Thank You

If a defeatist outlook can leave etchings on your stomach's wall, can a sunny outlook smooth them over?

Doctors are beginning to ask this question. Pamela Walker, Ph.D., a medical psychologist who worked on this study, states, "Some studies suggest that certain stress-management techniques, practiced in conjunction with medical treatment, may help people with ulcers make life easier on their sensitive stomachs."

Education. If you've read this far, you may already have taken one important step in preventing a repeat ulcer attack. "One early study suggests that intensive education of how stress affects people physically — specifically the gastrointestinal system — along with learning ways to change habitual thinking patterns that create worry, seemed to help. This education appeared to prevent ulcer recurrence in 29 out of 32 patients, which is unusual because ulcers tend to recur," says Dr. Walker.

Cognitive therapy. Also called self-talk, self-affirmation or cognitive restructuring, cognitive therapy may be another promising approach to consider for improving an ulcer sufferer's perception of stress. "Say you're given more responsibility at work," says Dr. Walker. "A negative reaction would be to automatically say, 'I can't handle it. What if I fail?' A healthier, positive reaction would be, 'Gee, that sounds like a real challenge, let's see what I can do.'

"Or say you have to move to a new city," continues Dr. Walker. "Rather than say, 'This is terrible, it's a whole new place, I won't know my way around, I'll be lonely because I don't make friends easily,' try to look forward to the move as an opportunity to discover exciting new places and meet interesting new people.

"Cognitive therapy may be a positive approach for ulcer patients because positive self-talk improves self-confidence, whereas negative self-talk tends to undermine one's ability to cope," says Dr. Walker.

"Also, negative thinking tends to be a self-fulfilling prophecy," she continues. "If you expect things to go wrong, your thoughts and actions may influence events in countless small ways to help determine the outcome. So if you think things will go wrong, you may be more likely to do things that lead to failure. You've got to break the cycle at some point, and cognitive therapy does the trick. It also gives the responsibility for control back to the individual, a basic principle of stress management."

Assertiveness training. "Dependent people often have trouble expressing anger appropriately. So they may either internalize it or communicate it to others indirectly," says Dr. Walker. This is counterproductive, because their behavior may end up alienating the very people who could help in a crisis – friends, family and co-workers. "Assertiveness training encourages people to express their feelings appropriately, ask for what they need and get along better with others, giving them better access to social support." (The importance of social support in stress management is discussed at length in chapter 25.)

Relaxation training. "Meditation or other relaxation techniques may be useful for people experiencing stress-related symptoms, because relaxation is the opposite of the stress response," says Dr. Walker. She adds that ulcer patients who practice relaxation or any other stress-management technique should continue to seek appropriate medical treatment.

Dr. Walker, Dr. Feldman and Dr. Richardson emphasize that there are many unknowns in the link between stress and ulcers. Studies such as theirs have not proven stress to be a cause of ulcers, although researchers continually seek to better understand that relationship. They also are investigating the developing area of stress management to find uses of its techniques to help people who are suffering from ulcers, as well as other stress-related illnesses.

Chapter 57

UNEMPLOYMENT

Lose your job, and you lose much more than a regular paycheck.

"It's like bowling," says Barrie Greiff, M.D., an occupational psychiatrist in Boston and visiting professor of occupational psychiatry at Harvard Business School. "Your job is the kingpin. Knock that over, and everything else falls with it."

"Everything" includes friendships with co-workers (a major component of social life), a big chunk of your identity ("And what do *you* do for a living?") and a reason to get out of bed in the morning (it's amazing how much you miss that alarm clock when it doesn't ring anymore). And not least of all, your job gives you something to talk about – even if all you do is gripe about the incompetents in the next department.

"Talking about where you work is one of the most common pastimes in America," remark Robert Levering, Milton Moskowitz and Michael Katz in their well-known book *The 100 Best Companies to Work For in America.*

"Most of all, though, losing your job tells you that someone or something else is in control," says Jeanne Curran, Ph.D., professor of sociology at California State University-Dominguez Hills at Carson, California. "And it's lack of control that makes job loss so stressful, especially for people who feel that as long as they work hard and try their best, they can control their fortune."

Some people feel *better* after losing their job, usually because it frees them from on-the-job stress. One man who worked for a major steelmaker and survived wave after wave of massive personnel cutbacks for years experienced great relief when his number finally – and inevitably – came up. But he's one of a small minority. Most people are upset after they're "terminated," as employers like to say. And getting the gate seems to be stressful even if you didn't like your job.

"For many, losing their job is like being raped: Their sense of control over life has been violated," says Dr. Curran. "The people who break down are the ones who thought they were in control."

So while it's financial insecurity that worries jobless workers the most, money is not all that matters. And stress tends to increase the longer you sit on the bench, leveling off at about six months.

Why They Called It "The Great Depression"

Lose your job and you're apt to feel anxious, depressed – or just plain apathetic. Perhaps you find it hard to concentrate or make decisions. You may also find yourself drinking, smoking or eating more than usual or acting a bit surly toward your spouse and kids. Sex becomes a chore – or a memory. Parties leave you feeling like an outcast. Movies are out – you hate to spend the money. You dread Christmas.

If you feel really down, don't be alarmed. In effect, you're mourning the loss of your job, and that's normal. In fact, family therapists are struck by how similar a family's response to unemployment is to bereavement over loss of a loved one, another major stress in life. One study of plant closings, for example, found that workers experienced a classic grief reaction to losing their jobs, including a spate of various physical complaints, just as they might after the death of a loved one.

"The first stage is shock: Nobody believes that it is going to happen to him," says Richard Smith, assistant editor of the *British Medical Journal,* in a series of articles on the health of those who are unemployed. "The next phase is one of denial and optimism, the 'holiday feelings,' but within a few weeks this gives way to anxiety and distress. In this stage, [people] seek work with great energy, but repeated failures drive them to resignation and adjustment. But this is not a healthy adjustment; rather, time drags, the day is empty and [his or her] personality and relationships are corroded."

Losing Your Job
Can Be Hazardous to Your Health

Job loss leaves many people more susceptible to colds or other infections, because unemployment, like other major stresses, lowers immunity, according to research.

The physical aftershocks of unemployment are not to be taken lightly. If you have borderline high blood pressure, for example, unemployment could also nudge blood pressure into the hazardous zone. Rising cholesterol levels can increase your risk of heart attack. All this when your paid medical coverage is about to expire! Talk about adding insult to injury.

Middle-aged workers – who often have heavy commitments like college tuition and other large debts to pay, or are too young to retire – suffer more than younger or older workers, according to one source.

"No one handles the loss of a job smoothly – *no one*," says Dr. Curran. "But the people who suffer the most are the ones who don't show their distress or ask for help," she adds. "Outwardly, they may look cool, but underneath they're scared to death – and they may pay for it later with a heart attack or ulcers."

So take a deep breath and start "resetting your pins," one by one.

Your immediate instinct after losing your job will probably be to tell your family. But wait: First, take some time to process the news yourself and prepare for their reaction.

"There's no point in hiding the fact that you're now out of work," says Dr. Curran. "But telling them is never an easy or pleasant chore. And you can automatically transfer your anger at yourself or your company to them. So the best thing to do is vent your feelings *before* breaking the news, away from home.

"Go to a bowling alley and knock down pins. Rail at a sympathetic friend. Do *something* to recognize and deal with your anger on your own, before you tell your spouse," says Dr. Curran.

"Then, couched in words that say, 'I feel bad and I need your help,' break the news. But don't be surprised if you look for support and get anger instead," says Dr. Curran. "The full effect of the shock wave will hit them the same way it hit you, and if they don't handle the news too well, you have to allow them to feel and act devastated without taking it personally," she says. "The spouse is bound to hurt, and you both need protection. But if you don't recognize that need, you may end up whimpering to each other like a couple of two-year-olds trying to say, 'Take care of me!' "

Swamped with Anxiety? Send an S.O.S.

Panic or despair is hard to hide. But if you're entertaining suicidal thoughts, try to resist blurting them out to your spouse. "Call your minister or rabbi, call a counselor, call a crisis hotline, so you can enlist these people to help you with your spouse," says Dr. Curran. Your husband or wife has too much at stake to be able to help you work through your despair the way a trained professional can. "*I'm* a trained professional, and I've called hotlines myself for personal problems," adds Dr. Curran.

"Job loss is a terrible blow, and it can strain a marriage at a time you need each other more than ever," says Dr. Curran. "Both spouses need time to adjust, and sometimes counseling can help."

"Group counseling may be helpful for people who avoid social gatherings out of embarrassment, but still need someone to talk to," says Margaret W. Linn, Ph.D., director of social research at the Veterans Administration Center in Miami, Florida, and professor of psychiatry at the University of Miami School of Medicine. "If interpersonal or emotional problems contributed to job loss, full-fledged counseling may be in order.

Spouses of Job Hunters
Feel Stress, Too

If your husband or wife loses their job, you may feel as angry, upset and scared as they do. How do you cope with *your* feelings without making your spouse feel even more depressed and humiliated?

"The spouse of the unemployed may not suffer the loss of self-esteem that the out-of-work partner does," says Margaret W. Linn, Ph.D., director of social research at the Veterans Administration Center in Miami, Florida, and professor of psychiatry at the University of Miami School of Medicine, who has studied the effects of unemployment on mental and physical health. "But the situation is equally stressful in other ways."

"Everyone sympathizes with the jobless spouse," says Jeanne Curran, Ph.D., professor of sociology at California State University-Dominguez Hills, Carson, California. "But the partner of the unemployed spouse is under stress, too.

"Say a man and wife both work and she loses her job," says Dr. Curran. "The husband of an out-of-work woman gets little sympathy, even if she earned as much or more than he did, because people still assume he is the main provider.

"If the wife does not work at a paying job outside the home and her husband suddenly loses his job, she will feel stressed by the fact that she's thrust into the supportive role, which can endanger the relationship," says Dr. Curran. "Her husband, in turn, may feel hostile toward her in her new role, which wasn't in the marriage bargain."

Sometimes the spouse of someone who's unemployed can find help in applying the old adage "misery loves company."

"Talking to husbands or wives of other unemployed workers can also be helpful to an anxious spouse," says Dr. Linn. "Spouses need to vent their feelings with sympathetic listeners who are going through the same thing. They also need to get out and recharge their batteries at times.

"By all means, though, don't avoid talking to your husband or wife about unemployment," says Dr. Linn. "The unemployed spouse needs to feel understood. And so do you."

"Talking about your feelings can help you get over the difficulties and raise your self-concept, especially if you need help convincing yourself that you're not to blame for losing your job," says Dr. Linn.

A study conducted by Dr. Linn and others on the effects of unemployment found that men who had a supportive family and other social contacts to rely on weathered the emotional and physical effects of unemployment better than those who did not. Evidently, feeling that others care and are at least willing, if not able, to help plays a critical role in salvaging your professional life as well as your pride and self-esteem.

A Cure for the Out-of-Work Blues

Keeping in mind that social support is the key to surviving unemployment with your self-esteem intact – and to landing a new and possibly *better* job – here are some tactics for success.

Get out of bed in the morning. This seems to be simple enough advice. Yet Dr. Linn's study found that those who lost their jobs spent nearly five times as many days in bed during the first six months as men who continued to work.

Look for a job elsewhere within your company. Surprising as it may seem, getting booted out of one department doesn't necessarily mean no one else will want you. They may even welcome you. One advantage here is that you can hang on to valued friendships in the workplace – and your place on the company softball team.

Or, consider applying for a job at a competing company or one with which your former company had a business relationship, such as a supplier or producer of essential goods.

Line up allies. "Make a checklist of people who can help you," says Dr. Curran. "Include friends and colleagues outside of work who can support you objectively, without feeling the guilt of having survived a job that you didn't. Ministers and rabbis, too, are often good at helping people regain their sense of control over their lives."

Dr. Linn says that keeping in touch with people you used to work with and feel close to can help in some cases. "Retirees do it all the time," she says. "Who knows? They may end up helping you locate another job."

Cast your net wide. Include relatives, friends, schools, professional societies and employment counselors on your list of contacts, says Dr. Greiff.

"Look to people in your church or synagogue, or on community service committees, in the Kiwanis club – any organization – not to ask them to hire you but to find out what they know," says Dr. Curran.

In researching their book *The 100 Best Companies to Work For in America,* authors Levering, Moskowitz and Katz asked all sorts of people for leads: executive recruiters, management consultants, market researchers, public relations counselors, business school teachers, newspaper reporters, magazine editors, radio and TV news staffers and others in close contact with the job market. There's no reason why you can't tap into the same network to track down job openings. (Many job openings never appear in the help-wanted ads.)

Make looking for work a job in itself. One of the ironies of unemployment is that even though you have oodles of free time, you can't seem to get nearly as much done as when you were employed. That's because the unemployed lose what psychologists call "traction."

"[When you're employed] the structure of your work pulls you along," explains Richard Smith. "Something that you quickly achieve when you are busy and working can somehow fill your day when you have nothing in particular to do."

Job hunting with zeal serves two purposes: It increases your chances of landing a job and keeps time from hanging heavy on your hands.

"Pursue work with a sense of purpose: Work at it every day, between nine and five, like any other commitment," says Dr. Curran.

Log all your applications and job inquiries on a calendar. And let the kids help. "This helps you keep a quantitative record of your efforts, but more important, it keeps the kids from getting scared, because they see that their parents are doing something," says Dr. Curran. "Otherwise, they'll sense that you feel powerless, and they'll feel powerless – and scared." Making the job quest a family project also helps prevent family members from feeling alone and anxious about the future.

Consider volunteer work. "This has several benefits," says Dr. Curran. "It gets you out of the house every day. It looks good on your resumé. And it tells prospective employers that you're not depressed. And any useful, meaningful work helps restore your sense of control."

Maintaining Morale over the Long Haul

Statistics say that the average period of unemployment is 19 weeks. But jobless workers have little use for statistics. (As the saying goes, "When everybody else loses their job, it's a recession. When *I* lose my job, it's a depression.") If weeks drag into months and you still haven't found a job, it's easy to get discouraged. It's also okay to feel a little frayed around the edges.

"You can't expect to cope well all the time," says Dr. Curran. Still, you want to sustain hope. Otherwise, depression and poor health may interfere with your efforts (or desire) to find new work, completing the cycle of joblessness and despair.

Step up your exercise program. Unemployment is a great opportunity to get serious about an exercise program. Exercise reduces stress, counteracts insomnia and other physical complaints associated with the out-of-work blues *and* helps you look good for job interviews. So take up the exercise you always put off for lack of time.

"Recent studies have shown that unemployment lowers immunity," says Dr. Linn. "Activities like exercise, which have a positive effect on the immune system, would certainly be a good way to feel better and maintain resistance to certain kinds of illness."

Keep in touch with your old friends — but look for opportunities to make new ones. "Fraternizing with members of your bowling team, church or a community group can fill the gap often left by friendships made on the job," says Dr. Linn.

Treat yourself — you deserve it. Some people are reluctant to spend money on movie tickets when the mortgage is due, school is about to start and the tires are bald. "But if you can possibly allow for some form of leisure and recreation in your budget, you should," says Dr. Linn. Sports (like jogging) and hobbies (like sewing or carpentry) are excellent because they give you a sense of accomplishment.

Stay current in your field. Keep up on technical matters and continue your association with professional groups.

Think positive. "If you were good enough to get your last job, you're good enough to get another one," says Dr. Greiff.

The Hidden Benefits of Losing Your Job

"It may sound corny, but the up side of all this is that you may very well end up with a better job than you had before," says Dr. Greiff. "I don't necessarily mean better in terms of money, position or other tangible benefits, but better in terms of finding a job that fits you better, so to speak."

Some management styles, for example, may suit you more than others. If you found it stressful to work for a rigid taskmaster, a new job may provide an opportunity to work for a coach, not a controller.

One man took up painting after he lost his job and said it had become more important to him than his job had ever been. Another was equally passionate about gardening. And one survey of young unemployed parents found that in 14 cases the fathers were grateful to have more time to be with their children.

"Losing your job may give you an opportunity to reevaluate your standards and expectations of where, how and if you want to work — a luxury few people ever have," says Dr. Greiff.

Chapter 58

VACATIONS

And on the seventh day God ended his work which
he had made; and he rested on the seventh day from all his
work which he had made.

—Genesis 2:2

All creatures great and small experience stress. As such, vacations from
stress have been a God-given right — and necessity — from Day One.

"It is a person's birthright to have some moments alone, to play, to relax, to
rest," say Stephen A. Shapiro, Ph.D., and Alan J. Tuckman, M.D., in their book
Time Off: A Psychological Guide to Vacations.

Given the number of ailments linked to stress, regularly spaced vacations are
downright therapeutic.

"Many physicians believe that vacations often play an important role in
relieving work-related tension," says Geoffrey Godbey, Ph.D., professor of recreation and parks at Pennsylvania State University, in his book *Leisure in Your Life.*
Apparently, the more R and R you get on vacation, the bigger the spillover into
daily life. A study of 128 full-time workers before and after their regularly scheduled vacation showed that overall, people who enjoyed their vacations generally
felt more satisfied with their jobs and life in general afterward.

Why You Can't Afford *Not* to Take a Vacation

Most people need little coaxing to trade in their time card for a get-away ticket. Yet one out of six people who are entitled to paid vacation don't take one, according to one source. Some think they can't afford a vacation, because they assume that a vacation by definition has to cost a lot and take you somewhere exotic. (It doesn't.) Couples with small children often assume that going off by themselves is simply out of the question. (It isn't.) And many, many people feel guilty about "wasting" their time or money on a vacation. (They shouldn't.) So instead, many well-deserving souls spend their time off washing the car, painting the house, cutting the grass or cleaning out the attic, basement or garage.

Few reasons for not taking a vacation are good enough, though. "Much stress is rooted in feelings of lack of control of the elements of your life," explains Dr. Tuckman. "On the job, your boss has all the control. Or maybe things are *out* of control. Or your home life is controlled by certain demands — the kids, the bills, household repairs. By taking a vacation, you are arranging and controlling your time for one segment of your life. And, when you return from vacation, you can carry some of that control and the feelings of mastery produced back to your daily life."

Five Signs That Say, "You Need a Vacation"

Do you feel irritable lately? Are you tired even when you first get up in the morning? Are you making more mistakes than usual? Do you think about work and nothing else? Or do you find yourself daydreaming about being somewhere else?

If so, you may not only need a vacation — you may be long overdue for some time off.

"If you're feeling anxious, irritable and overwhelmed, by all means take a vacation, even if you can get away for a long weekend only," says Dr. Tuckman. "But don't habitually wait until you're overloaded with stress before taking vacations. Because if you start your vacation with a high level of tension, that will contaminate your vacation experience and you won't get the full benefit. Similarly, if you want to get full relaxation value out of your vacation, try to resolve marital difficulties or other conflicts *before* you leave. Otherwise, you'll take the baggage of unresolved conflicts along with you on vacation."

Sun, Surf and Stress Management

The problem with most vacations is that even if you leave your worries behind when you go, they're waiting for you when you return. Suppose, however, you came back from vacation not only rested and relaxed but with the tools to help you *stay* that way? William R. Newman, Ph.D., psychologist and director of Stress Management Vacations International, organizes planned vacations that provide ample time for fun and sightseeing but also manage to work in time to learn muscle relaxation, deep breathing and other methods of tension control that you can take back home with you.

The trips vary from season to season and include fitness vacations where you can hike, canoe, play tennis, snorkel or enjoy other activities. You can sail in the Caribbean or ski in New England or the West.

For more information on vacations that teach you how to ease tension, at home and away, contact Stress Management Vacations International, Inc., 189 Washington Street, Gloucester, MA 01930; phone, (617) 283-6969.

Recipe for Relaxation according to Taste

If your idea of the ideal vacation is jetting off to an isolated beach and spending hours lying in a hammock with a cold drink in your hand, you're not alone. In reality, though, few people live out that fantasy — mainly because doing nothing isn't what it's cracked up to be.

"Not many people can remain in a state of continuous relaxation for long without some kind of planned activity to reduce the 'weight' of just doing nothing," say Dr. Shapiro and Dr. Tuckman.

"Although the *idea* of a holiday 'just to relax' is perhaps the easiest of all to come up with and is, in many ways, the most appealing, it is at the same time a most difficult idea to sustain."

So for many people, the best way to "rest" is to do something different and interesting, especially if their daily routine is, well, too routine. Learning a foreign language. Rambling through the Amish countryside in search of handmade quilts. Carving wooden decoys. Hiking in Vermont. Prowling through flea markets shopping for Art Deco bric-a-brac.

One important caveat, though: If your vacation begins to resemble your work week, watch out! If you overschedule your activities, your vacation will demand the same kind of energy and determination as did the responsibilities you left behind.

Case in point: One couple took up scuba diving and, in their initial zeal for the sport, signed up for a full complement of diving on their first couple of trips to the Caribbean. They found, however, that reporting to the dive boat promptly every morning, noon and sometimes night began to feel like a job. On their next vacation, they planned to dive less and schedule some afternoons and at least one whole day for nondiving fun.

Soon, though, the couple loaded up their "free time" scrambling over Mayan

---

One If by Land, Two If by Sea

Suppose your spouse's idea of an idyllic vacation is piling the kids into the station wagon and driving down to the shore for a jam-packed week of sightseeing, shopping, golf and waiting in line for hours to see Shamu, the killer whale. But you fantasize about back-to-nature treks in the wilderness, sitting around a campfire listening to crickets chirp or shooting the rapids on the Zambezi River. How do you negotiate how and where you spend your hard-earned vacations?

Alan J. Tuckman, M.D., who is well-versed in vacation psychology, offers these tips:

- Discuss your needs. Don't give in without expressing an interest in where to go, what to do. Otherwise, your companions will assume you have no objection.
- Explore new options. Don't get into a rut of spending your vacation at the same place year after year.
- Consider spending time by yourselves, either alone or together. Kids don't need vacations as much as adults do. If you have children, there's nothing wrong with farming them out to a trusted baby-sitter so you can get away. Or take a baby-sitter along on vacation so you can enjoy each other undistracted.
- Split the time. Do something you like for part of the trip and something the others like for the rest.
- Be willing to compromise. "It may be impossible to fulfill everyone's vacation needs every year," says Dr. Tuckman. "But don't be rigid in your plans. Improvise."

ruins, photographing elusive flamingos or exploring rain forests and volcanoes. Once again, they returned from their vacation feeling like they needed a vacation. Clearly, something had to change if these two were ever going to get any stress-reducing benefits from their vacations. So they stretched their next vacation from one week to ten days. That gave them time to "do it all" and still "do nothing."

"A time of recuperation should be an important part of a well-planned [vacation]," say Dr. Shapiro and Dr. Tuckman. "In between the sightseeing, the scuba diving, the dining out, there should be some moments set aside for unwinding and absorbing."

It's a matter of balance: The key to true relaxation is rest and recreation in porportions suited to your temperament and needs. Balancing R and R is especially important for people who feel guilty "wasting" time on vacation or who feel out of sorts away from a highly structured routine.

"A vacation is supposed to reduce stress. Don't defeat the purpose by letting guilt or lack of structure generate stress," says Dr. Tuckman. He suggests that people who have trouble downshifting into the vacation mode do some task—read a book, run, write letters—part of the time so they then feel free to "play" or do nothing the rest of the time.

Four Steps to Really Getting Away from It All

Unwinding requires more effort than meets the eye, if you're not used to loafing. Dr. Shapiro and Dr. Tuckman have analyzed the vacation process and conclude that you can't expect to feel instantly relaxed the minute you go off-duty. Rather, "vacating" our normal routine and the tension and worry that often come with it is a step-by-step process. To shed tension—and return refreshed—you have to do the following things.

Stop running—physically, mentally and emotionally. "Learn to let go," says Dr. Tuckman. "The first day on vacation, you're only partly disengaged—you're partly on vacation and partly back home. It takes a day or two to decompress. To put it another way, you can't expect to go from 80 miles per hour to a dead stop."

Resolve feelings of guilt about "wasting time." "This is the barrier between most people and real relaxation," say Dr. Shapiro and Dr. Tuckman in their book.

"Tell yourself, 'It's okay not to work,'" Dr. Tuckman says. "Convince yourself that not only do you deserve it, you *need* it. Otherwise, you can't go on to the next phase."

Learn to tolerate fantasy and play. "Many people find that vacations are an excellent opportunity to play with their kids, get to know them away from the routine of your job, their schoolwork," points out Dr. Tuckman.

Savor the serenity. "Just as sports and games are recreation for the body, so relaxation and the aimless play of the senses are recreation for the mind."

An occasional long weekend may turn your tension meter down a notch or two, but in order to truly relax, you may have to take off for a week or longer. "For a vacation to be of most benefit, it must be extended for at least a week," say the authors. "The first two or three days are devoted to the unwinding process, the gradual letting go of the routines of daily living. Not until the third or fourth day is there a real separation and an unhindered participation in the new environment."

The Right and the Wrong Reasons for Taking a Vacation

"But I love my job!" some will say. "Why should I tear myself away?"

"Nobody can be continually creative — no matter how much you love your job — without breaks," says Dr. Shapiro. "When people say that they feel stable and healthy without vacations, I want to interview their spouses and co-workers, too. Do *they* agree? Are these nonvacationers as sharp, appreciative and interesting? We're often very poor witnesses about ourselves," adds Dr. Shapiro. (If you and your family disagree over how to spend your vacations, see the box on page 248.)

One last bit of advice before we bid you bon voyage: A vacation is not a substitute for dealing with the underlying causes of stress in your life. "Refusing to face the problem and going off on a vacation merely ensures its continuation," say Dr. Tuckman and Dr. Shapiro in their book.

"And by all means, don't wait until stress reaches a critical level to take a vacation, even if it means taking 'minivacations' on the weekends — or taking a long walk one Saturday," says Dr. Tuckman. As medicine against stress, a vacation works better as a preventive than as an antidote.

"Vacationing in this taut world is not a luxury; it is a necessity," conclude Dr. Shapiro and Dr. Tuckman.

Chapter 59

WORKAHOLISM

Let's start with the basics: There's nothing inherently wrong with workaholics. That's the conclusion of an in-depth, landmark study on the subject by Marilyn Machlowitz, Ph.D., a New York industrial psychologist and author who professes to be a workaholic herself.

Dr. Machlowitz's book *Workaholics, Living with Them, Working with Them* blasted workaholism's bad reputation. People who are addicted to work, she suggests, often are surprisingly happy. True, a workaholic may be working all the time. But he or she also may get an abundance of pleasure from the job – more pleasure than from tennis or opera or family life.

"People whose life is their work are doing that because they like what they're doing," says Richard G. Lonsdorf, M.D., a psychiatrist and professor of law at the University of Pennsylvania in Philadelphia. Dr. Lonsdorf sees many patients who are in the legal profession – a vocation noted for its long hours. "Although there are some compulsive people who are compulsive about anything, It's true that workaholics often are very healthy people," he says. "And you usually don't find workaholics in jobs that don't interest them."

"It's the *inflexible* addiction to work that's unhealthy," says Robert Rosen, Ph.D., director of the Institute on Organizational Health at the Washington Business Group on Health. "If you're avoiding something or if the need for manipulation and power becomes the overriding fuel for the commitment to work, you're placing yourself at risk of affecting your health."

But that's not always the standard profile. "Some workaholics are just enthusiastic about their work and could do it 24 hours a day, seven days a week, without resentment or bitterness," says Maurice Prout, Ph.D., director of cognitive behavior therapy at Hahnemann University in Philadelphia.

The problems arise when you mix these curious animals with nonworkaholics. It's easy to understand how people who don't get such a tremendous satisfaction out of long hours on the job can resent those who do. And there are other problems. Working for someone who lives to work can make your life miserable if you aren't so inclined. It's also easy to be angered at a loved one who is married to work and treats you with somewhat less regard. The spouse, lover, parent or child who is bent on reforming a workaholic is bound to meet with frustration. And then there's the overstressed existence of 40-hour-week types whose co-workers (read: competitors) are workaholics.

To Reform or Not to Reform

Fears that workaholics shorten their lives through stress may be unfounded, according to Dr. Machlowitz. It depends on the individual's response to stress. Some people flourish in stressful jobs, particularly if they feel they can exert some control over events, if they feel deeply involved in the activities of their lives and if they anticipate changes as exciting challenges. Others may be virtually incapacitated by the same level of stress, regardless of the potential psychic rewards. It's important to understand which type you are, and, as much as possible, to live within the structure dictated by your own personal needs.

But that doesn't mean workaholics are destined to live out their years alienating family, friends and co-workers, missing out on the marvelous non-work-related joys of life. If you are a workaholic and want to end the resentment that may be building up around you, or if you want to gain value from things other than work, there are steps you can take.

First, pay attention to the words of Dr. Lonsdorf when he says, "It's an enormously egotistical thing to be a workaholic. It says to people around you that what you're doing is more important than they are." He adds that when workaholics understand the impact of these words, they often work to modify their values.

Get to know what's at the root of your workaholism, even if it takes a therapist to help you do it. It could be a compulsion. "Often workaholism is an escape from something else — difficulties in interpersonal relationships, an inability to achieve intimacy," says David Sirota, Ph.D., a New York industrial psychologist. "Or it could be their own particular compulsion to see themselves as working all the time," he says. That may be understandable, adds Dr. Prout, because "culturally, we're rewarded for the concept of working hard early on. If you didn't get a good grade, a teacher may have boosted it for effort." Or it could be that your entire self-esteem is connected to making more money than others.

Then there's the matter of corporate culture. At many companies, long hours are a fact of life. Many psychologists suggest you take some responsibility for your own long hours. Ask yourself, are they really necessary?

Often workaholics have convinced themselves that their long hours are required, but that's not always the case. Unless you work for an organization that is understaffed, you should not have to put in the 60-hour work week that is standard among workaholics. Chances are that you are squandering at least 10 of those hours on trivialities or on make-work projects. Often, workaholics who are pressed to examine their activities will determine that they waste time for one reason or another.

But if you're dismayed at the prospect of spending those ten extra hours at play, don't fret. "You don't have to do what other people define as play. If you do that, you'll just wind up with the desire to go back to work. Instead, you have to define what form your play is going to take," says Dr. Prout.

So your "play" time could mean volunteering to "work" with a nonprofit organization or charity. Or your "play" time could mean "working" on your house. It's your time, your decision. Channel your work addiction into something constructive.

When the Family Loses

But if your workaholism is frustrating your family — and if you want that to change — it won't make sense to exchange your hours at work for hours at the Red Cross or hours spent papering the den. Your family needs you, and giving them the time they deserve may require a systematic approach.

Start by scheduling regular time to be with your spouse. "Do something every Thursday night. Hire a baby-sitter and go someplace, even if it's just a ride around the block," says Dr. Lonsdorf. He suggests you force yourself not to work. Buy tickets for 13 baseball games and attend them all with your kids. Get involved in activities that used to give you pleasure — or try new activities. If you develop an interest in hiking through the woods with your spouse, try not to become obsessed with the identification of every item of flora and fauna if it makes your partner feel as if you're still at work.

If overtime forces you to miss your child's performance in the fourth-grade pageant, you should explain to the youngster that you cannot make it to the event and ask what he or she would enjoy doing together in its place. "The only way you can diffuse a child's resentment is to give him or her more time, not only so-called quality time but also 'down time' — time when you do nothing but talk," says Dr. Prout. And remember that there's nothing wrong with writing into your calendar: "Saturday afternoon: play in sandbox with Johnny."

That brings us to the old joke about married couples who are so busy that they have to "pencil" an episode of sex into their crowded calendars. Dr. Lonsdorf thinks that's not such a silly scheme if it ensures the couple will take time away from work to enjoy time together. "The notion that sex has to be spontaneous to be good is baloney," he says.

And keep things in perspective. "Decide if you want your family to feel they're last on your list," writes Dr. Machlowitz. "You really are more indispensable to those at home than you are to those at work. Your parents will appreciate your presence at their golden anniversary party more than your colleagues will miss you at a company dinner." And it's not just the big events that count. She continues, "Showing up to watch your child's basketball team practice counts more than merely making it to the championship game." Above all, adds Dr. Rosen, open a dialogue with family members so that they feel comfortable telling you if their needs are not being met.

Living with a Workaholic

If you're on the other side of the equation, a workaholic's resentful loved one, you've got a decision to make. Do you want to remain in a relationship with a person who may or may not want to reform?

There *is* some point to trying to change a loved one, says Dr. Lonsdorf. "It's legitimate for a wife or husband to say, 'I married you because I wanted to share your time and interests and you're not doing it.' " But even when workaholics express an interest in changing, they may not. Don't believe a workaholic spouse who says he or she will cut down on hours after reaching some goal such as an anticipated promotion or the attainment of a particular salary level. The new position may bring more responsibilities – even more overtime. The new salary level may only set the stage for a subsequent salary goal. And how do you know your loved one really wants to end his or her devotion to work?

Let's first assume you opt to live with your workaholic. Keep in mind that your life together will demand an abundance of compromises. You can try to interest your spouse in old activities that gave you both pleasure at a time before work became so important – if any such activities existed. Or you can try to engage your spouse in new activities with scheduled-in "play" time. But if your workaholic isn't interested in changing, you don't have to let your spouse's enthusiasm about work rob you of the opportunity to enjoy life on your own. "You may have to develop activities on your own so you can grow and mature," says Dr. Prout.

In any event, try to make the time you do spend together as enjoyable as possible. Work to minimize the stress of everyday household hassles. Don't get into the habit of resenting a workaholic who won't help around the house. Instead, and if you can afford it, pay someone to help with the household chores. Don't spend your precious time together doing things you don't enjoy doing.

Anticipate some readjustment problems if you get your workaholic to reform. You and your family may have adapted to your status as second fiddle, and you may be angry or alienated. Now you must deal with a change in your relationship to the workaholic. Expect your workaholic to be irritable. After all, you're taking him or her away from something that's rewarding and important. Your workaholic may even become depressed. "There's a chance that the workaholic may resent the changes. There's the possibility that they'll be sad because their needs aren't being met," says Dr. Rosen. Often, professional help in the form of individual or family therapy is the best answer.

When You Work for a Workaholic

In the annals of business, there are legends about the heads of major corporations who relinquish corner offices with sweeping views in favor of an office with a window from which they can see the company parking lot – and keep track of the comings and goings of employees.

That's a great environment for workaholics. But if you're not one, and your organization worships overtime hounds, you're probably in for some trouble. "If your boss is a workaholic, he or she may say, 'I'm the boss and everybody's working for me,' " says Dr. Prout. "It could be the kiss of death for someone who's not in there seven days a week."

"You probably can't change a workaholic boss," says Dr. Machlowitz. But you probably can put up with one if you know it is only for a specified period of time. Some people accept a job with a workaholic boss only long enough to gain experience to move on. This strategy is wise only if you have some assurance that the job (and its long hours) will make way for something that better suits your personality. In general, you probably won't survive over the long run. Square pegs don't fit into round holes. "I would never advise people to conform to a pattern of a boss if in fact you're not that way and the job doesn't require it," says Dr. Sirota.

One obvious strategy is to try to discuss the problem with your boss. "If working long hours of overtime is not the way you choose to lead your life, tell your boss. Put it on the table. In my experience, often it works – say, 90 percent of the time. The difficulties are when it's not discussed," says Dr. Sirota. But he adds one caveat: The individual must be producing top-notch work to achieve a positive response.

There are ways of helping protect yourself from getting in the employ of a workaholic in the first place. "Past work experience is the best indicator of future work experience," says Dr. Machlowitz. "So in the interview, ask your potential boss about part-time jobs he had in college. Try to determine if he is a person who just does the minimum or who may be a workaholic." Ask others at the organization if long hours are required.

If You're the Workaholic

Just as it can be catastrophic if you're a nine-to-fiver in the employ of someone who is wedded to work, it can be a terrible mismatch if you're a workaholic and your boss isn't. You'd think that any employer would be thrilled to have someone so dedicated to a job. But that's not always the case. Many bosses, particularly those in large, competitive organizations, feel threatened by a workaholic subordinate. They may convince themselves that the workaholic is after their job. "If you're a workaholic and your boss isn't, it can be very threatening to your boss. You've got to be sensitive about that," says Dr. Rosen.

Dr. Prout advises against telling your boss that you merely enjoy working endless overtime and that you're not after his or her job. "The boss won't necessarily believe you," he says. Instead, he suggests you find another place to spend your extra energy. Volunteer at a nonprofit organization. Work with your family at home. Or find a job in an organization that appreciates your drive and capacity for work. But if you need to stay in the mismatched job, Dr. Rosen suggests you stay late only if you're very conscious not to threaten the boss.

The Co-Worker Trap

Pressure from peers, as well as from bosses, lengthens the workday. Dr. Sirota tells of one transportation company in which employees feel compelled to come in on Saturdays, even though there is nothing to do. So they chat and go to lunch. It's all part of a game of one-upmanship that people play. The winners are those who stay at work the latest.

Actually, the winners are those who don't succumb to such pressure. To exit yourself from the game, be comfortable with the fact that you are not a workaholic and don't have your self-esteem based on the number of hours you put in — regardless of what others do. "You have to be comfortable with who you are, with your values, your interests and your goals in life," says Dr. Rosen. "It's very easy to be swayed by what other people do and think." He says you should ask yourself, "Am I going to let other people's workaholism affect my sense of self?"

Chapter 60

WORRY

Worrying is like a rocking chair – it will give you something to do but it won't get you anywhere.

Baseball may be the nation's favorite sport, but worry seems to be our true national pastime. If we live in California, we worry about earthquakes and freeway backups. If we live in New York, we worry that the IRT express at 14th Street will be stalled in the station again. In between, we worry about our kids' tonsils and our own chances of breast cancer. We worry about money and friends – about not having enough of either.

In his research on worrying, Pennsylvania State University psychology professor Thomas D. Borkovec, Ph.D., estimates that 15 percent of the population are chronic worriers, those who have spent more than eight hours a day during the last six months worrying. Nonworriers – those who report worrying less than an hour and a half a day and who do not consider worry to be a problem – comprise 30 percent of the population. The majority of folks are moderate worriers and fit between these two extreme groups. They worry between 10 percent and 50 percent of each day and may or may not be troubled by their worrying, according to Dr. Borkovec.

That's a lot of agonizing.

Worries reflect your attempts to mentally cope with your concerns and fears. You can view it as the thinking part of anxiety. While you await the results of your son's college board exams or your own blood test, you experience a sinking feeling in your stomach. Your muscles tighten. And ruminations have taken over your mind, replacing all the unimportant thoughts.

Making Worry Work for You

Worrying can be useful if it helps make you more vigilant or if it helps you take steps to prevent something negative from happening, says Roxane L. Silver, a professor of psychology at Canada's University of Waterloo. So worrying is not a stressful waste of energy if it gets you to quit smoking, have a breast examination or replace your brakes.

And worrying can help prepare you for a dreaded event or outcome. In *Through the Looking Glass,* the Red Queen advised Alice to do her worrying in advance. That way, said the queen, when the real trouble came along, she would be ready to deal with it calmly. That's roughly what one retired psychology professor reasoned. In *The Work of Worrying,* Irving Janis wrote that worrying lets you rehearse negative possibilities and allows you to prepare for the experience. You'll cope better because you worried.

Some psychologists suggest that instead of worrying in the abstract, you plot out how you'll cope if you do, in fact, fail. Instead of just sobbing over the possibility of not qualifying for a mortgage, for example, you can put your energy into developing alternative housing plans. Planning helps you to take some control. And James W. Pennebaker, Ph.D., a professor of psychology at Southern Methodist University who has conducted studies on worriers, recommends you don't get angry with yourself because you're worrying. Don't beat yourself up for having negative thoughts, he says, although he admits that's not always easy.

When Your Worry Troubles You

There comes a point, however, when worrying becomes counterproductive — not to mention stressful. It's fruitless to worry when there is no way to prevent your worries from becoming reality, or when the worrying is so pervasive that you are immobilized.

How do you stop these troublesome thoughts? Don't try to simply set them aside, says Daniel M. Wegner, Ph.D., a psychology professor at Trinity University in San Antonio, Texas. In extensive research, Dr. Wegner learned that if you make a point of trying to forget a random thought — much less a worry — it'll return again and again. "In trying repeatedly to avoid a thought, the person processes the thought frequently. As you try to get rid of it, it'll keep coming back," he says. Unconsciously, you're rehearsing the thought and making it more accessible to your conscious mind.

"It's the impulse to set it aside that may create the problem," says Dr. Wegner. Instead, he recommends you *express* your worries. Think them through very carefully and discuss them with friends.

Dr. Pennebaker instructs worriers to write out their concerns. In his research he asked participants to spend a regular part of four or five consecutive days writing about their most upsetting traumas. He found that the writing had a positive impact on their health. It increased the immune functions and, over time, reduced blood pressure.

Psychologically, writing about your worries is likely to help you assimilate them. The writing forces you to organize your thoughts and fears. Dr. Pennebaker says writing for 20 minutes a day is probably sufficient. And don't expect instant results. It may take days or weeks for your worries to ease.

Besides the writing, he suggests you talk about your concerns with someone you trust. And find a creative outlet to take your mind off your woes. Draw, or play a musical instrument, or dance.

The Worry Period

But if you find that strategy doesn't work, you may get some relief by trying a little trick suggested by Dr. Borkovec. Schedule a worry session into your day. Dr. Borkovec reasons that because you are free to worry at nearly any time or place, worrying becomes associated with many situations. So to reduce its frequency, you can limit the conditions in which you allow yourself to worry. Eventually, you will learn to associate it only with limited circumstances. His self-control strategy involves five steps.

1. Establish a half-hour worry period to occur at the same time and place each day. "It may just be a trick," says Dr. Borkovec, "but if you know you have a special time during which you will worry, you may be able to postpone it for that time. If you simply try to postpone it forever, the worries might keep cropping back up."
2. Monitor your worries during the day, identifying as soon as possible the beginning of any episode. "Most worriers don't know they've been worrying until they're well into it. But the earlier you pick up on it, the easier it is to change," says Dr. Borkovec.
3. Once you notice yourself worrying, make the decision to postpone it. Let go of the worries until your worry period.
4. Dislodge the worrisome thoughts by focusing your attention on the task at hand. If you're driving, focus on the environment – the billboards, the cars, the beauty of the landscape. Or try to concentrate on skillful driving.
5. Use your prescheduled "worry period" to work intensely on your woes.

You can do one of two things: You can worry, or you can problem-solve. Problem solving might involve sitting down with a pencil and pen, listing your worries on one side of a sheet of paper and on the other side listing possible solutions that would reduce the source of your worry. If you're worried about taxes, your solution might be to schedule time to work on them (or a list of conceivable sources of money to pay them).

As part of problem solving, force yourself to take a look at the bottom line on your worry. Ask yourself, "What's the worst thing that can happen?" "Is it survivable?" "What's the probability of that happening based on past evidence?"

If you're worried about the possibility that you won't make any friends in a new town you're about to move to, look to your past experience to get your mind back on track. Remind yourself that you've done okay before and that there's little reason to worry about meeting people in the future. If there *is* reason to worry, if you don't have a strong record of making friends easily, you can spend your worry period figuring out a strategy for making friends — drawing up a list of groups to join or activities to explore.

Dr. Borkovec suggests you determine which worry period activity — worrying or problem solving — is best for you. Neither is better than the other, he says.

To study the effects of his worry-postponing strategy, Dr. Borkovec tracked a group of chronic worriers who followed his advice during a four-week period and kept careful note of the hours they worried. By taking regular worry breaks, they reduced their overall worry time by an average of 35 percent.

INDEX

Rodale Press, Inc., publishes PREVENTION, America's leading health magazine.
For information on how to order your subscription,
write to PREVENTION, Emmaus, PA 18098.